"The author's acknowledged fallibility inspired this book, and the many faults of this reader were ample reason for the Holy Spirit's sanctifying use of it in me. Larkins' humility, Scriptural dependence, clear prose, and cogent observations are masterfully interwoven to help the reader graciously mature in Christ on this side of heaven. Take up and read, for we're not just saved by Christ but in him as well!"

—PAUL GORMAN, ruling elder, Presbyterian Church in America

"*Christian Character* is a well-written, biblically instructional book with practical lessons for both individual and group study. This study provides real-life examples of how the kingdom of God should work its way into our lives and skillfully guides readers into a deeper understanding of self-control. Ernest Larkins challenges us to be more like Christ."

—DANNY MAYS, health information management consultant

"Having sat under Ernie's teaching in a men's Bible study, I was eager to see how his gifts would be exercised in writing. I am not disappointed! This is a fine example of careful thought and study combined with humble reverence for God's Word and the application of it to our everyday relationships with God and each other. I will be buying copies for all our grandchildren!"

—BILL LEUZINGER, associate pastor of counseling and shepherding,
Christ Community Church

"I found Ernest Larkins' book, *Christian Character*, to be a delightful and encouraging read. With patience and clarity, the reader is walked through many aspects and perspectives of how the life of the Christian should reflect the life of his Savior. I am thankful for Larkins' work and happy to recommend to others."

—KEN FARMER, elder, Presbyterian Church in America

D1196033

Christian Character

Christian Character

Why It Matters, What It Looks Like, and How to Improve It

Ernest R. Larkins

RESOURCE *Publications* · Eugene, Oregon

CHRISTIAN CHARACTER
Why It Matters, What It Looks Like, and How to Improve It

Resource Publications
An Imprint of Wipf and Stock Publishers
199 W. 8th Ave., Suite 3
Eugene, OR 97401

www.wipfandstock.com

PAPERBACK ISBN: 978-1-6667-3752-3
HARDCOVER ISBN: 978-1-6667-9705-3
EBOOK ISBN: 978-1-6667-9706-0

To enhance a verse's contextual readability, the author sometimes added bracketed information or substituted it for the actual language. Also, the author sometimes italicized words for emphasis. The intent, in all cases, was to enhance readability in the context or bring clarity to the biblical text, not change the meaning of the infallible Word.

Initial ideas for using some activities and Bible passages came from Jim and Jeanie Carden's *Christian Character Curriculum*. Used by permission of Children's Ministry International.

The excerpt in the "Thankfulness" lesson came from "Broken Things" by Dr. Bob Jones, Jr. Used by permission of Bob Jones University.

Dedication

God uses various means of grace to sanctify his people, making them more and more holy day by day. In addition to his Word, the sacraments, and prayer, the Lord often uses less-ordinary means. Through family, I've learned many valuable lessons. Prominent among them are how to live less selfishly and trust God more completely. In appreciation, I dedicate this work to my wife Nancy, Joshua and his wife Katie, Esther and her husband Cody, and Hannah.

To these six, I offer some gentle admonishments and heartfelt encouragement. Pray for the Holy Spirit's grace, wisdom, and strength to cultivate your Christian character, following God's moral law. Love the Lord supremely and love one another as fellow sojourners. Seek daily to be more like your divine Messenger, Mediator, and Master. With this overall focus, treat everyone you meet with due respect as an image bearer of God. Always seek to understand and repent of your personal wrong, and always forgive others who personally wrong you, even if they don't ask or deserve it. Avoid and flee the sinful allurements of this temporal, deceptive world. Resist temptations the devil, society with its earthly concerns and priorities, and your own sinful nature incessantly thrust before you. Yet know that even the most stalwart believers stumble and sometimes fall. When those darkened times come, return with a broken and contrite heart in godly repentance and sincere faith to the God of steadfast love, great faithfulness, abundant mercy, boundless grace, and perfect goodness. Indeed, make the gifts of repentance and faith your daily companions and practice.

To my wife, thanks for your companionship through forty-one years of marriage, many of them spent childrearing. To my three adult offspring, thanks for being my kids and forgive me the times I have failed or disappointed you. To their spouses, thanks for being part of and a blessing to our family. I love you all.

Contents

Dedication v

Preface ix

Acknowledgments xi

Introduction xiii

Attentiveness 1

Availability 9

Caution 16

Compassion 25

Contentment 32

Courage 43

Decisiveness 53

Deference 64

Diligence 71

Discernment 79

Endurance 87

Fairness 96

Faith 104

Forgiveness 113

Generosity 123

Gentleness 132

Humility 141

Joyfulness 150

Patience 157

Purity 165

Repentance 176

Respectfulness 187

Responsibility 199

Thankfulness 208

Truthfulness 218

Watchfulness 233

APPENDIX A: Definitions of Christian Character Traits 241

APPENDIX B: Review Answers 243

APPENDIX C: Similar Traits 272

APPENDIX D: Teaching and Learning Guide 278

Bibliography 295

Name Index 299

Scripture Index 303

Subject Index 311

Preface

During my twenty-six-year academic career, I sometimes received teaching assignments for which I felt ill-equipped. Students may have assumed I possessed expertise in my subject matter that far exceeded their own. But the truth is, at times, I knew little more than them. My lack of expertise, however, often proved to be precisely the thing that led to their better comprehension. It was, indeed, such lack that motivated me to spend long hours preparing well, resolving perceived inconsistencies, grasping complex relationships, reducing the complex to simple terms, and discerning the best pedagogy. If I had begun with a superb grasp, I may have given my preparation short shrift, making me less effective as a teacher. This might seem an unexpected paradox between professorial knowledge and classroom learning, but it often proved true in my courses.

I hope the same odd relationship holds in this present project. Not being a flawless model of Christian character did not dissuade me from writing a book on the subject. Indeed, my past failures and present weaknesses spurred me to learn more about what Scripture teaches and communicate that clearly to a larger audience of whom, if you're reading this, you have become a welcome part.

And so, here is my perspective. I am one earthly pilgrim sharing with fellow sojourners what the Word has taught me concerning Christian character—specifically, why it matters, what it looks like, and how to improve it. Like the vagrant finding warm sustenance on a wintry night, I desire others who hunger and thirst for righteousness to sit awhile and enjoy one or more spiritual meals with me around this modest text. Just as the Lord blessed me when preparing the manuscript, I pray the Holy Spirit will use each lesson to encourage and strengthen many believers in their daily walks, helping them become more Christ-like to the glory of God.

Before diving into the lessons, please see the "Introduction" and "Teaching and Learning Guide." Bringing focus to your classroom instruction, small group discussion, or independent study, the "Introduction" cautions about two dangers when contemplating this topic: (a) ignoring God's moral law, which involves disobedience, and (b) trying to become moral without gospel power, which involves legalism. The "Guide," which appears in Appendix D, addresses several topics that may benefit, whether exploring the text as teacher, student, bookworm, or casual reader. Among other things, it explains how to combine lessons for specific emphases (e.g., to concentrate on the Beatitudes, romantic relationships, or decision-making) and how to obtain and use the free PowerPoint slides.

And now, believing short prefaces are more likely to be read, I end.

—Ernest R. Larkins

Acknowledgments

In the 1980s, Children's Ministry International (CMI) first published a children's series by Jim and Jeanie Carden entitled *Christian Character Curriculum*. As a starting point, the authors adopted, with permission, character qualities and definitions from the Institute for Basic Youth Conflicts. Then, they developed teaching notes through Bible stories, activities, and other enhancements. In the 1990s, Tom Waldecker and Brad Winsted revised the series.

In 2018, the author of this present effort, volunteering as a part-time editor, arranged with CMI to revise *Christian Character Curriculum* again. From the beginning, I had no thoughts about publishing a book. However, as the task progressed, it became clear that little remained of the prior publication in the more recent endeavor, the latter taking a life of its own. Though a new work, I feel a great debt to the earlier effort from which I first identified many key verses, Bible characters, and activity ideas.

I'm especially grateful to George Uterhardt at CMI for giving me the opportunity to begin this project as well as his steadfast friendship and encouragement along the way. I thank Marlys Roos and others at the PCA Discipleship Ministries, who, in wisdom and kindness, alerted me to a central theological point that required rethinking and rewriting, dramatically improving the final product. I appreciate insights from Michael and Carolyn Riggs of Lamp & Quill International, which provided direction for the text and tightened its focus. I thank the church leaders who have particularly influenced me through their faithful teaching, wise counsel, and imitable lives, among them A.J. Babel, Fred Brugger, Tom Champness, Charles DeBusk, Ken Farmer, Paul Gorman, Rich Hastings, John Hunt, Alan Johnson, Alan Larson, Wayne Leininger, Bill Leuzinger, Bob Morris, Jim Powell, Scott Willet, and Bill Wilson. Above all, I thank the only living and true God for his soul work in me; I often felt keenly aware of his presence and guidance in writing this book. May it be used for his glory and his alone.

Introduction

The premier, fundamental statement of moral law appears in the Bible as the Ten Commandments (Exod 20:3–17). The so-called first tablet contains Commandments One through Four and states mankind's vertical duties to God. These include worshiping only the living and true God, worshiping him in the right way, respecting his person and works, and keeping his Sabbath Day holy. The second tablet contains Commandments Five through Ten and explains mankind's horizontal duties to other people. Specifically, God demands respect for authority while forbidding murder, adultery, theft, deceit, and covetousness. Jesus summarizes the Ten Commandments like this: "You shall love the Lord your God with all your heart and with all your soul and with all your mind. This is the great and first commandment. And a second is like it: You shall love your neighbor as yourself" (Matt 22:37–39). In essence, Jesus pares the Ten Commandments down to two summary edicts, which correspond to the two tablets.

Though the Ten Commandments and Jesus' summary state the moral law in broad terms, the Bible provides many expressions, interpretations, or clarifications of the moral law. Consider, for instance, this Old Testament verse: "Guard your steps when you go to the house of God. To draw near to listen is better than to offer the sacrifice of fools, for they do not know that they are doing evil" (Eccl 5:1). This moral law demands attentiveness in worship, elaborating on Commandment Four about keeping the Sabbath holy and Jesus' first and greatest commandment to love God with the entire heart, soul, and mind. As another example, ponder this New Testament text: "You have heard that it was said to those of old, 'You shall not murder; and whoever murders will be liable to judgment.' But I say to you that everyone who is angry with his brother will be liable to judgment" (Matt 5:21–22). This moral law clarifies the meaning of Commandment Six, saying it also forbids hatred. And, certainly, this prohibition against hatred is consistent with Jesus' teaching that the moral law requires people to love others just like they do themselves.

Christian character traits reflect Scripture's moral law. Some traits relate, at least partly, to the first tablet or Jesus' greatest command to love God, notably attentiveness, faith, and thankfulness. But most traits pertain more directly to the other tablet and Jesus' second command about loving people. Indeed, love for God and mankind undergirds all Christian character traits, "bind[ing] everything together in perfect harmony" (Col 3:14), just as it does the entire moral law. For that reason, this text does not devote a separate lesson to love. Rather, every lesson rests on the foundation of love, the preeminent character trait.

In short, Christian character traits represent habitual, distinguishing, and loving behaviors, thoughts, and attitudes based on things God's moral law says to do or not do. The moral law requires certain actions, thoughts, and perspectives that, if developed through the Holy Spirit's power, result in good Christian character. Put simply, keeping the moral law produces good character traits or morals. Individuals with strong Christian character are those who, consistent with Jesus' teaching, love God supremely and love other people as much as they love themselves. Indeed, God's moral law is so closely intertwined with Christian character traits that one cannot be discussed apart from the other.

Yet, many religious people question the moral law's continued relevance. Some ask, "Does God really expect me to follow his commands and, thus, develop good character traits?" He does—real danger arises from dismissing God's moral law and treating Christian character development as optional.

Other religious people strive to become moral on their own terms, not pursuing morality from an overtly biblical perspective. Does it matter how they seek morality so long as they become good, respectable, tolerant, and responsible people? Yes, it matters quite a bit—real danger exists in trying to become moral while ignoring the only power that enables true morality.

In simple terms, two distinct dangers exist: (a) embracing the good news of the gospel while downplaying the moral law and (b) seeking a morality apart from the gospel's power. The former involves disobedience; the latter leads to legalism. The following sections address these two spiritual dangers.

Danger of Dismissing Moral Law

Some people do not think God's moral law applies today. This misguided notion is somewhat understandable in view of the constant, distorted, or even ungodly messages received through the entertainment industry, social media, the educational system, liberal pulpits, the corporate world, and, indeed, society in general. To combat the resulting dearth in true moral standards, many organizations devise and adopt secular "core values," which are weak, inadequate substitutes for Scripture's moral law. In contrast to such attempts, this book confronts readers with a clear message about what God requires and the Bible teaches.

From a theological perspective, the belief or practice that views God's moral law as irrelevant is sometimes called antinomianism, meaning without, against, or opposed to law. The phenomenon is not easily pigeonholed but exists among congregants across denominational divides, though often conflicting with official creeds and doctrine. Many professing Christians with antinomian tendencies or perspectives, as the saying goes, live like the devil. Misleading themselves and others through self-righteousness and hypocrisy, they change "the grace of our God into a license for immorality" (Jude 4, NIV). So, it's important to examine the presumed biblical support for this belief or practice.

A common antinomian support text is: "For sin will have no dominion over you, since you are not under law but under grace" (Rom 6:14). But when interpreting Scripture, context matters. This verse explains that sin no longer masters or controls the behavior of believers as it did before God's grace saved them. However, the verse does not mean the saints, after conversion, need no longer contend with personal sin and, thus, can ignore law. In the two preceding verses, the apostle says, "*Let not* sin therefore reign in your mortal body, to make you obey its passions. *Do not present* your members to sin as instruments for unrighteousness" (Rom 6:12–13). Why would such commands or admonitions be necessary if the moral law no longer applies to believers? Indeed, the New Testament exhorts Christians to depart from all kinds of lawlessness again and again.

Consider a second proof text often cited to argue against the law's relevance: "Now that faith has come, we are no longer under the supervision of the law" (Gal 3:25, NIV). The context deals with the doctrine of justification under which God declares his people righteous. Earlier in the chapter, the apostle explains that justification comes through faith in

Christ, not by law keeping. Indeed, anyone trying to become righteous through "human effort" (Gal 3:3, NIV), "works of the law" (Gal 3:10), or "supervision of the law" (Gal 3:25, NIV) are cursed since they cannot acquire righteousness that way. Here's the point: the chapter deals with justification, not sanctification. Though Gal 3:25 says justification is through faith in Jesus rather than through keeping the law, it does not focus on the relationship between sanctification and law keeping. Thus, the verse does not nullify the moral law for purposes of sanctification. Whereas God declares the elect righteous in justification, crediting Christ's righteousness to them, God progressively makes the elect more and more righteous during their earthly lives through sanctification, which involves following the moral law. In a nutshell, the moral law points to the gospel for justification; but then the gospel points back to the moral law for sanctification. As before, context matters.

Terminology also matters. In the Bible, the word "law" refers to different things in different places. When the New Testament alludes to Old Testament law, it's not always a reference to moral law. Though involving some overlap, God gave three types of law in the Old Testament—civil, ceremonial, and moral.

Civil law involved judicial decrees applicable principally to the Israelite community's unique social, economic, or political situation as God's people. For instance, one civil command prohibited plowing fields with an ox and donkey yoked together (Deut 22:10). Such civil laws have outlived their purposes and expired.[1] The Lord never intended them as inviolable directives for all communities, societies, or nations.

Ceremonial law specified rituals for offering sacrifices, foreshadowing a coming Savior. Christ abolished these laws when he freely offered the ultimate sacrifice for sin—himself—and became the elect's great high priest and mediator. In effect, Jesus became both priest and sacrifice, eliminating the need for all ceremonial laws. "He [Jesus] entered once for all into the holy places, not by means of the blood of goats and calves but by means of his own blood, . . . having been offered once to bear the sins of many" (Heb 9:12, 28). Thus, some New Testament allusions to the law ceasing refer to ceremonial rather than moral laws. Here's one example: "A former commandment [the Levitical priesthood under Aaron] is set aside because of its weakness and uselessness (for the [ceremonial] law made nothing perfect)" (Heb 7:18–19).

---

1. Westminster Assembly, *Confession*, chapter XIX (4).

In contrast to the civil law, which expired, and the ceremonial law, which Christ abolished, the moral law continues to express God's perfect character and his standard for mankind. Jesus explained this continuation:

> Do not think that I have come to abolish the Law or the Prophets; I have not come to abolish them but to fulfill them. For truly, I say to you, until heaven and earth pass away, not an iota, not a dot, will pass from the Law until all is accomplished. Therefore whoever relaxes one of the least of these commandments and teaches others to do the same will be called least in the kingdom of heaven, but whoever does them and teaches them will be called great in the kingdom of heaven (Matt 5:17–19).

Likewise, the apostle Paul understood the moral law's continued validity. "The law is holy, and the commandment is holy and righteous and good. . . . I delight in the law of God, in my inner being" (Rom 7:12, 22). "Keeping the commandments of God [counts]" (1 Cor 7:19). The apostle Peter also admonished believers to obey God's moral law and, thus, live godly lives. "As obedient children, do not be conformed to the passions of your former ignorance [before your effectual calling and new birth], but as he who called you is holy, you also be holy in all your conduct, since it is written: 'You shall be holy, for I am holy'" (1 Pet 1:14–16).

Summarizing to this point, the danger of dismissing the moral requirements of God's law arises from (a) misconstruing the context of New Testament passages, (b) misunderstanding the meaning of the term "law," and (c) overlooking clear statements from Jesus and the apostles that the moral law still applies. Thus, rejecting the antinomian view—namely, that Christians are free from the moral law—begs the following question: If the moral law is still valid, for what purpose? John Calvin identified three uses of the moral law, which are discussed next.[2]

The first use of moral law is pedagogical, applying primarily to unbelievers. Representing God's perfect righteousness, the law acts as a mirror into which sinners gaze to see, in contrast to God's perfection, their own personal weakness, wickedness, hopelessness, and condemnation. Like a schoolmaster, the law teaches and warns sinners about their unrighteousness, removing all excuses for sin. Yet, the moral law can never justify since nobody can keep it perfectly. "By works of the law no human being will be justified in his sight, since through the law comes knowledge of

2. Calvin, *Institutes*, 295-96.

sin" (Rom 3:20). Instead of seeking righteousness through law keeping, unregenerate sinners must depend on God's grace for forgiveness and righteousness; they must repent and trust Jesus for salvation and eternal life. "So the law was put in charge to lead us to Christ that we might be justified by faith" (Rom 3:24, NIV).

The moral law's second purpose is a civic one. Through restraining evil via the threat of punishment and protecting innocent parties from oppression, it provides the basis for just secular law. Secular law based on God's moral law leads to a more stable and peaceful society, curbing or bridling wicked behavior, tumult, and even anarchy.

Functioning as a rule of life, the moral law also has a didactic purpose for believers that promotes thankful and zealous obedience. Whereas the first use of moral law confronts unbelievers with their sin and guilt, this third use reveals to believers what glorifies God and, thus, how to live. This use can be expressed in various ways. For instance, the moral law instructs saints to love God with their whole hearts, souls, and minds and other people as themselves. The moral law teaches the justified to become more like Jesus, increase in holiness, walk in righteousness, conform to Christ's image, and grow in grace or sanctification. The moral law presents believers with God's will for their lives and then encourages them to follow it. However expressed, this third use of the moral law is its principal purpose and application.

To conclude, the moral law is not some weak, dust-covered relic left over from Old Testament times; it continues to be relevant and essential today. For believers, the moral law becomes their spiritual lamp, teaching them how to please the Lord and providing evidence of their redemption. Two passages—one from the Old Testament and one from the New—echo these points. "The end of the matter; all has been heard. Fear God and keep his commandments [moral law], for this is the whole duty of man. For God will bring every deed into judgment, with every secret thing, whether good or evil" (Eccl 12:13–14). "We know that we have come to know him [Jesus Christ], if we keep his commandments [moral law]. Whoever says 'I know him' but does not keep his commandments is a liar, and the truth is not in him, but whoever keeps his word, in him truly the love of God is perfected. By this we may know that we are in him: whoever says he abides in him ought to walk in the same way in which [Jesus] walked" (1 John 2:3–6).

Returning to the original question: "Does God really expect me to follow his commands and, thus, develop good character traits?" Scripture confirms that he does. In short, Christian character matters because God says it does.

Danger of Ignoring Gospel Power

As mentioned, conforming a person's actions, thoughts, and attitudes to God's moral law develops Christian character, which is the subject of this text. However, anyone wanting to book passage on this voyage should be careful not to board the merely moralistic vessel, slipped of its gospel moorings. Just as those dismissing the moral law displease God, so great danger also lurks in predominantly legalistic pursuits of morality stripped of biblical truth and power. Such bearings erroneously rely on individual exertion rather than God's grace. Consider one such belief system—"moralistic therapeutic deism" (MTD)—that, like antinomianism, often subsists among congregants across denominations, despite conflicting with official tenets.[3] Of course, MTD flourishes among the unchurched also. Though originally identified through surveying American teens, MTD describes much of today's society. As an unofficial but widespread pseudo religion, it rests on several core beliefs about personal morality, expected feelings and outcomes proceeding from such morality, and God's role in the whole matter.

The moralistic dimension of this belief system involves being good; it posits that God desires each person to be nice and treat others equitably.[4] Contrast this supposition with the two tablets of the Ten Commandments, stating mankind's duties to God and duties to others. Contrast it with Jesus' summary of the law as loving God with the entire heart, soul, and mind while loving others as yourself. Contrast it with the Bible's call to a life of repentance, faith in Jesus Christ, and obedience to Scripture's moral law. How does MTD compare with God's Word? Well, for starters, it omits obligations to God entirely, ignoring the first tablet and what Jesus called "the great and first commandment." MTD's being-good moralism also disregards fundamental Bible truths such as (a) the misery and guilt of sin, (b) our inability to save ourselves, (c) Christ's sacrificial, substitutionary atonement, and (d) salvation through faith alone in Jesus alone. Indeed, according to MTD, people only need be good to enter heaven, where goodness depends on what a conglomerate of major

3. Smith and Denton, *Soul Searching*, 162–63.
4. Smith and Denton, *Soul Searching*, 163.

religions supposedly teach. Notwithstanding a vague reference to various creeds and an assumed unifying cohesiveness, an individual's self-assessment and society's cultural norms, no doubt, enter the mix when defining MTD's brand of goodness.

The therapeutic component teaches personal goodness will lead to happiness and a sense of well-being in this life and the next.[5] Its self-centered focus encourages adherents to please parents, teachers, friends, co-workers, bosses, and others. These various individuals, in turn, will like and respect the MTD adherents, contributing to the latter's happiness and feelings of self-worth. Though "man's chief end is to glorify God, and to enjoy him forever,"[6] MTD attaches no importance to pleasing or extolling God. Consider Scripture's recurring themes of praise, worship, and glory. "Ascribe to the LORD the glory due his name; worship the LORD in the splendor of holiness" (Ps 29:2). "Bless the LORD, O my soul, and all that is within me, bless his holy name!" (Ps 103:1). In contrast, MTD exalts personal well-being but assigns little value to glorifying God or keeping his law. As to MTD's assumption that all good people enter heaven, salvation has never been through anything mankind can do but only through God's gift of eternal life to those who believe. "For by grace you have been saved through faith. And this is not your own doing; it is the gift of God, not a result of works, so that no one may boast" (Eph 2:8–9). It's not the so-called good people who go to heaven but justified people, those whom God has redeemed and declared righteous. "The righteousness of God through faith in Jesus Christ [has been manifested] for all who believe. . . . [They] are justified by his grace as a [free] gift, through the redemption that is in Christ Jesus" (Rom 3:22, 24). In effect, MTD preaches a false gospel of self-fulfillment (Gal 1:6–7) rather than the gospel of Christ. Only the latter empowers individuals to become moral, bringing true therapeutic relief for sin and misery.

Traditional deism says God exists, created all things in the beginning, and then did nothing more to interact with people or intervene in their lives. As the great clockmaker, God wound up the universe and then let it run. He performed no miracles, answered no prayers, and did not reveal himself except through creation. In short, he didn't bother people and certainly was not going to judge or punish them. Departing from this strict, traditional view, MTD's third prong reflects more of a quasi-deistic

5. Smith and Denton, *Soul Searching*, 163–64.
6. Westminster Assembly, *Shorter Catechism*, Q&A #1.

notion in which God shows some minimal interest in and care about mankind, intervening occasionally when good people need him.[7] This modified deism, no doubt, provides some therapeutic-like benefits. But the God of glory bears little resemblance to the god of deism. The true and living God reveals himself time and time again throughout the Old and New Testaments, interacts with individuals through outward circumstances as well as deep within human hearts, provides a Redeemer to save his people from sin and misery, sustains and directs his creation, hears and answers prayers of faith, shows steadfast love and great faithfulness every day, expects obedience from his people, and enables the saints to follow his moral law. Instead of the passive, distant god of MTD, the God of Scripture is active and personal. Indeed, through grace and great power, the Holy Spirit constantly works in the believer's soul to develop and improve Christian character.

In summary, morals stripped of any solid foundational underpinnings are a wretched substitute for God's moral law and Christian character from a consistently gospel perspective. The underpinnings are essential. Moralism without the foundation of biblical truth and power eventually reveals itself to be but a weak, temporal guide that waxes and wanes or even disintegrates completely over time. Life's goal must not be simply to try hard to become or feel good or, if already good, to become or feel better. Many religions and philosophies—all false—teach self-improvement, self-actualization, self-empowerment, self-satisfaction, self-esteem, self-motivation, self-confidence, or similar self-delusions. The goal, however, lacks power beyond the individual's oscillating desire and fickle will. Mere moralism eventually leads to spiritual ruin. Later in life, moralists who never experience salvation through faith in Jesus are left with only an outward, self-centered morality, lacking power for this life and hope for the life to come. Some moralists smugly embrace their self-attained, self-approved goodness, clinging self-righteously to empty rituals, practices, and appearances. Other moralists abandon the church after failing over and over to be good through their own efforts and, as a result, feeling spiritually crushed. Disillusioned, some even turn to false teachers who promise easier paths to happiness, good feelings, and paradise.

Rather than settling for mere moralism, learn and teach what God desires and how the beautiful gospel of Christ, through all the means of

---

7. Smith and Denton, *Soul Searching*, 164–65.

grace such as the Word and prayer, empowers believers to glorify the Almighty. Never forget the Father adopts all who trust in Jesus to be his very own dear children and declares them righteous. Never forget Christ atoned for sinners at Calvary and, as the great high priest, mediates for his people before heaven's throne of grace. Never forget the Holy Spirit dwells within every believer to teach, guide, and comfort. Never forget the triune God promises steadfast love, great faithfulness, abundant mercy, sufficient strength, light for the journey, perseverance to the end, and eternal life. This is the good news of the gospel that motivates the elect, out of grateful hearts for undeserved favor, to improve.

Cultivating Christian character involves the Holy Spirit (as first cause) working in the elect, empowering them to change (the second cause). It's the grace and strength of the only living and true God that enables them to become more like Jesus, increase in holiness, walk in righteousness, conform to Christ's image, grow in grace and sanctification, and keep the moral law. "For it is God who works in you [first cause], to will and to work for his good pleasure" (Phil 2:13). The Holy Spirit enables each saint to understand the moral law and obey God's commands: "Work out your own salvation [second cause] with fear and trembling" (Phil 2:12). As you teach or study the lessons in this text, pray earnestly for such results and return often to the gospel well of God's truth, grace, and power.

On two final notes, a "Teaching and Learning Guide" appears in Appendix D. Whether teaching this book or reading it for self-study, the guide can help you maintain focus, choose lessons around a theme, schedule coverage, and understand each section's purpose. It also explains how to use the free PowerPoint slides as an optional teaching or learning tool (available at elark4.wixsite.com/character with password "allgrace"). Then, if you find this book helpful, would you consider leaving an online review so others might benefit too? If uncertain how to proceed, use this search request to find easy-to-follow instructions: "How do I write a book review on amazon.com and goodreads.com?" Thank you for supporting this work.

Attentiveness

Engage in one or more of these introductory activities:

1. Nature Study—Take a walk outdoors, preferably in a forested area. As animals make noises, look for the creatures or identify them solely by their sounds. Many critters emit different calls in different situations (e.g., one call when content and another when distressed). Alternatively, locate online audios of commonly-seen animals—such as gray squirrels, chipmunks, coyotes, pileated woodpeckers, and red-tailed hawks—and listen carefully to their various calls. Then, play them through again to see if you can identify each creature solely by the sound it makes. Even more challenging, try to discern the meaning behind each call.

2. Thimblerig—Using three inverted, opaque cups and one round object such as a marble or small ball, line up the three cups and place the object under one cup.[1] Move the cups around with both hands for several seconds, while others focus on the cup covering the object. When the cups stop, ask someone to identify the cup under which the object rests. After several rounds, go online and watch the video featuring Pop Haydn. How attentive is everyone when the master moves the cups?

These activities show how important ears and eyes are in identifying or tracking things. Without hearing and sight, it would be hard to identify animals or keep up with the round object. Yet, these physical gifts can be used for so much more important things like paying close attention to God's truth and other people. Indeed, being attentive is essential for showing respect, the topic of a later lesson. What is this Christian character trait of attentiveness? Here's one way to define it:

1. The initial idea of using a shell game to illustrate the character trait of attentiveness came from Carden and Carden, *Christian Character Curriculum* 1, 3.

Attentiveness entails listening and observing to learn truth or show concern and respect.

God desires his children to put their ears and eyes to good use. From a biblical perspective, what does this character trait of attentiveness look like, and how can Christians improve it? This lesson addresses these points under the headings of "God's Word to Mankind," "God's Work in Believers," and "God's Grace for Change."

God's Word to Mankind

Key Verses

"The hearing ear and the seeing eye, the LORD has made them both" (Prov 20:12). It's obvious that most ears hear, and most eyes see. Likewise, it's clear to anyone who believes the Genesis account of creation that the Lord made ears and eyes. But why single out ears and eyes from all the things God made? One reason might be that these two organs are particularly well-suited to learning truth and interacting lovingly and respectfully with people, and God wants his people to use their ears and eyes for these good purposes. Referring to truth, Jesus said, "He who has ears to hear, let him hear" (Matt 11:15).

"We must pay much closer attention to what we have heard, lest we drift away from it" (Heb 2:1). Old Testament prophets, the Lord Jesus, and many of those who heard Jesus (especially the apostles) spoke words of truth about a "great salvation" (Heb 1:1–2, 2:3). The phrase, "what we have heard," refers to such truth. The verse suggests people sometimes hear God's Word taught or preached with their minds and spirits only partially engaged and, as a result, drift into error. Conversely, those paying careful attention when someone teaches or preaches the truth may avoid such errors and their consequences.

Bible Characters

Listening Lord (Mark 10:13–16)

Moving from one city to another, Jesus constantly taught and healed many people. The physical and mental drain must have wearied him at times. Yet, he always paid attention to those with physical, mental, or spiritual needs.

In this account, the disciples tried to shield Jesus from the littlest of society. The parents and guardians wanted Jesus to touch and bless their children, but the disciples stood in the way and even rebuked them. But the rebuking ones themselves experienced rebuke. Indignant, Jesus insisted the small children be allowed access. Unlike many in that day's society, he did not see children as nuisances or less important. Gathering them into his arms and blessing them, Jesus must have listened intently to their simple words as he gazed directly and deeply into their wondering eyes. He lovingly paid attention to them.

Miffed Martha (Luke 10:38–42)

Jesus and his disciples came to visit the Bethany sisters, Mary and Martha. Martha immediately set about preparing food and drink for her visitors. In contrast, Mary plopped down at Jesus' feet and began listening. After a while, Martha could contain herself no longer. She complained to Jesus that her sister had left her to do all the work and even implied Jesus wasn't paying attention to the unfairness of her burden.

But Jesus had been paying very close attention and noticed three facts. First, Martha was "anxious and troubled about many things." This seemingly gentle rebuke pointed out her inattentive mindset. Indeed, people who are constantly worried, upset, anxious, or troubled find it difficult to calm down and pay attention. Second, Jesus said "one thing is necessary." Perhaps this meant Martha was making unnecessary or excessive preparations while leaving the most important thing—listening to Jesus—undone. Third, Mary's choice was better than, what may have been, Martha's unnecessary, fretful preparations. In effect, Jesus may have been inviting Martha to leave her less-important pursuits and pay attention to his good and true instruction like her sister. As a final note, it's essential to see that Jesus showed loving concern for Martha when he gently explained the truth about her inattentive mindset.

Review Questions

1. What is the Christian character trait of attentiveness?

2. What words are missing from this verse? "The _____ ear and the seeing ___, the ____ has made them both" (Prov 20:12).

3. What words are missing from this verse? "We must pay more careful _____, therefore, to what we have _____, so that we do not _____ away" (Heb 2:1).

4. When Jesus said, "He who has ears to hear, let him hear" (Matt 11:15), what did he want people to hear?

5. Who wanted Jesus to pay attention to little children, and who did not?

6. How did Jesus treat the little children?

7. When Jesus and his disciples visited Mary and Martha, what did each sister do at first?

8. What was Martha's complaint?

9. In the narrative about Mary and Martha, who paid attention?

10. In the narrative about Mary and Martha, who did not pay attention?

God's Work in Believers

Lots of things make paying attention difficult. Information today flits unrelentingly past at breakneck speed. The ubiquitous presence of smartphones and other electronic devices make near-continuous demands on time and focus. Ringtones intrude uninvited into the quiet stillness and sanctity of libraries, churches, and favorite fishing holes. Emails, text messages, push notifications, web feeds, consumer surveys, targeted ads, and social media carpet bomb everyman's consciousness every day as institutions, businesses, and organizations clamor for notice. In short, society places huge demands on an individual's wherewithal for paying attention, and the demands for most people's attention exceed its supply. Once society at large chows down on its ravenous share, precious little attention remains for other things. Residual time and capacity are increasingly scarce commodities in what some have dubbed the attention economy.

Have society's demands in this digital information age left you few resources for learning God's truth, showing sincere concern for others, or showing proper respect for authority? Like the people in ancient Israel, perhaps you "keep on hearing, but do not understand; keep on seeing, but do not perceive" (Isa 6:9). If so, maybe the first step in developing the Christian character trait of attentiveness is to limit existing demands on your attention. How to do that should be a matter of prayer and, of course, will vary among individuals. For some, it might mean canceling web feeds, restricting Facebook usage, or forgoing the internet on the Lord's Day. The point would be to cut back on society's demands for your notice so you can pay closer attention to God's truth; the needs of family, friends, and others; and those whom God has placed in authority. Pray for the grace to make such changes.

Nowhere is attentiveness more important than when God speaks. Don't just read Scripture; meditate on it with your eyes fixed on the holy page and your mind (or spiritual ears) tuned to the Holy Spirit. When listening to God's Word, give full attention, shutting out all competing or intrusive thoughts. Whether reading the Scriptures, listening to a Bible lesson, or hearing a sermon, focus entirely on what God says. Adopt the pinpoint attentiveness of young Samuel: "Speak [LORD], for your servant hears" (1 Sam 3:10). Like Mary, forget everything else in life when in the presence of Jesus. This takes practice, patience, but, above all, God's help. Pray beforehand for attentiveness and repent afterwards if it eludes you.

Being attentive to others emulates Jesus in his compassion for those with physical, mental, or spiritual needs. Remember how the Savior bid little children to approach; taking them into his arms, he blessed them. Remember that the Christ corrected Martha for her inattention to things that matter most. In each instance, no doubt, the Lord showed a pure and perfect attentiveness to those near him that mere humans cannot match but, nonetheless, should seek to imitate. How do you think Jesus did this? Don't you think he must have used his ears and eyes to let each child, as well as Martha, know how important they were and how much he cared for things concerning them? Consider that for a moment. How can you use your ears and eyes to communicate loving concern for others? Here are some ideas. When talking with someone, even if you'd rather be elsewhere, focus intently on that person, giving them your undivided attention and valuing them as someone made in God's image. Look them in the eye often during the conversation and resist all temptations to think about other matters, glance elsewhere at more interesting things, or answer your smartphone. Indeed, even checking text messages shows inattention and unconcern. Listen intently to the other person, strive to feel their concern or understand their need, and respond in compassion. That's showing godly attentiveness. Ask God to bring about such changes in your life.

Finally, pay careful attention to parents, guardians, teachers, employers, police, and anyone else God has placed in authority. For example, when a parent or guardian speaks to you, stop what you are doing (e.g., remove the earbuds), look straight into their eyes, and respond respectfully. When teachers explain an assignment, listen carefully (just like with parents or guardians) and, perhaps, take notes to assure your complete understanding. When an employer requires you to complete a task, ask questions if it's unclear what you are to do or how you are to do it. Pray for the Holy Spirit's help in becoming more attentive to authority figures in your life.

God's Grace for Change

Before examining your heart, considering how you might improve, and seeking divine help, ponder one last point—God always pays attention to you; not one concern or need falls on deaf ears. "My eyes will be open and my ears attentive to the prayer that is made in this place" (2 Chr 7:15). Let this brief reminder about and appreciation for God's undeserved grace prepare and motivate you to develop more of this lesson's character trait in yourself.

Then, complete the "Heart Assessment, Reflection, and Petition" (HARP) chart, assessing your own attentiveness. Reflect on times the Holy Spirit enabled or empowered you to pay careful attention to God's truth or show concern or respect for others as well as times God and others paid attention to you. Consider whether the Spirit might be revealing a need for you to improve. If you want God to increase your attentiveness, put that desire in writing. This is a very important exercise that can help you respond to God's direction for your life. Plan to pray over your completed chart once or twice this next week.

Finally, talk to the Lord, using the words that follow or incorporating the thoughts into your own prayer: "Great Father, how merciful that you fixed your attention on my sinful and lost condition, sending Jesus to bear my sin and save me. In contrast, I often am inattentive to your will.

Forgive me for not listening carefully to your words and not listening caringly to others. Cause me to learn your truth, show concern for people with whom you bring me into contact, and give my full attention to those you have placed in authority over me. Teach me to be like Mary, who sat at Jesus' feet and listened with rapt attention. In so doing, may I grow in grace and please you. I pray in Christ's name. Amen."

Remember, the Lord's help is vital to cultivating Christian character. Only his power can enable you to change. When you fail to show the character trait of attentiveness, confess it before God and ask for his forgiveness and help.

HARP Chart for Attentiveness

Definition: Attentiveness entails listening and observing to learn truth or show concern and respect.

Key verses: "The hearing ear and the seeing eye, the LORD has made them both" (Prov 20:12). "We must pay much closer attention to what we have heard, lest we drift away from it" (Heb 2:1).

Bible characters: The listening Lord Jesus paid careful attention to little children. Mary listened intently to Jesus, while Martha's miffed mind-set seemed preoccupied with unnecessary or excess preparations.

How often do you show attentiveness in your life: 5 = nearly always, 4 = most of the time, 3 = about half the time, 2 = less than half the time, or 1 = hardly ever? Your response is ____.
In what ways, if any, has the Holy Spirit enabled you to show attentiveness?
In what ways, if any, have God and others been attentive to you?
In what ways, if any, has the Holy Spirit revealed to you a need to be more attentive?
What petition related to attentiveness, if any, would you like to bring before the throne of grace?

Availability

Engage in one or more of these introductory activities:

1. Nature Study—Learn about opossums[1] and share your findings through online photos or short video clips. Opossums are marsupials, widespread in North and South America. The mother opossum gives birth to litters of four to twenty babies called joeys and then makes herself continuously available to them for up to four months. At birth, the joeys are blind, deaf, and the size of honeybees. They crawl the four inches from the womb to the mother's fur-lined pouch. Mom nurses them there for two to three months. When bigger, they crawl out of the pouch and cling to the mother's back during her forages for food. As they continue growing, less and less free space remains on mom's crowded back; some joeys fall off and begin living independently. Those continuing to cling leave on their own when around four months old.

2. Task Ask—Coordinate a group or individual activity such as making brownies, putting together puzzles, shelling beans, or drawing sketches. The specific assignment is not as important as it is that everyone be engaged. Once or twice, soon after the activity begins, interrupt the group to see if someone can help do something. For example, say, "Pardon me, Susie, but I wonder if you can assist in watering these plants," or "Excuse me, can someone move this desk?" Later, explain how those agreeing or volunteering to help made themselves available even though it interrupted what they were doing at the time. Explain in such a way that it doesn't reflect negatively on any who did not help or volunteer.

---

1. The initial idea of associating opossums' behavior with the character trait of availability came from Carden and Carden, *Christian Character Curriculum* 3, 59.

Making yourself available to help others requires sacrifice, and the timing may disrupt plans. Being ready and willing to help others according to their schedule can be inconvenient at times. So, what is this Christian character trait of availability? Here's one way to define it:

> Availability means reserving time to serve God and others while keeping plans, schedules, and priorities reasonably flexible to meet unexpected needs as they arise.

God desires his children to make themselves available for accomplishing his will, which often means making themselves available to people. From a biblical perspective, what does this character trait of availability look like, and how can Christians improve it? This lesson addresses these points under the headings of "God's Word to Mankind," "God's Work in Believers," and "God's Grace for Change."

God's Word to Mankind

Key Verses

"I appeal to you therefore, brothers, by the mercies of God, to present your bodies as a living sacrifice, holy and acceptable to God, which is your spiritual worship" (Rom 12:1). The apostle Paul urges believers to consider the great mercy they received through the gospel. Far from a license to sin, this mercy, instead, motivates them to offer their entire beings as living sacrifices. God wants the saints to live holy lives that exalt his name, making every day available as a spiritual act of worship. Desire to live sacrificially, offering personal plans, schedules, and priorities in holy service to the Lord and others. This availability is the reasonable and sensible response to God's great salvation and mercy through Christ.

"Let each of you look not only to his own interests, but also to the interests of others" (Phil 2:4). Sacrificial living always involves looking "to the interests of others." What are their difficulties? What are their physical, mental, and spiritual needs? Being available to others invariably means looking beyond and setting aside your "own interests." It always entails sacrifice and always glorifies God.

Bible Characters

Ready Representative (Isa 6:1–8)

In the year Uzziah, Judah's king, died, God appeared to his prophet in a startling vision. Isaiah beheld the great King of kings inside the temple, sitting on his throne arrayed in majesty, grandeur, splendor, and Shekinah glory. Six-winged seraphs hovered above, covering their faces and feet in sacred veneration and bursting forth in praise and worship, "Holy, holy, holy is the LORD of hosts; the whole earth is full of his glory!" Their voices reverberated throughout the temple, which then filled with smoke. Overwhelmed at this display, Isaiah feared death since he stood as a sinner in God's holy presence. But a seraph reassured Isaiah that God had removed his guilt and atoned for his sin.

Then, God asked, "Whom shall I send, and who will go for us?" Isaiah promptly set aside all other plans and answered, "Here am I! Send me." After God's great mercy to him, Isaiah desired nothing more than to become a living sacrifice. He was available to carry God's message to the Judean people.

Selfless Servant (Phil 2:19–23)

During Paul's second missionary journey, he met a young man at Lystra named Timothy, whom all the believers commended (Acts 16:1). Perceiving his good character, Paul asked this man to travel with him. And, so, began the long friendship between the great apostle and his young protégé, aide, companion, and brother in Christ. Timothy also accompanied Paul during his third missionary journey (Acts 20:4). A selfless servant, Timothy went where Paul directed and came when Paul asked. Later, Timothy even pastored the church at Ephesus (1 Tim 1:3).

What does this short history say about Timothy? He made himself available for God's work. Always ready, always willing, Timothy served God and the saints across modern-day Turkey and Greece. Any plans, goals, or ambitions he might have had growing up in Lystra had long been set aside for God's glory and the good of others.

In the current passage, Timothy had been ministering to Paul's needs during the latter's imprisonment in Rome. But Paul sends him to the Philippian believers, knowing their need and confident Timothy would be "genuinely concerned for [their] welfare." Indeed, through years of close contact, Paul had found "no one like him." Paul knew Timothy would put the Philippians' concerns and cares above his own. Always available, Timothy had a servant's heart.

Review Questions

1. What is the Christian character trait of availability?

2. What words are missing from this verse? "I _____ to you therefore, brothers, by the _____ of God, to present your bodies as a _____ _____, holy and _____ to God, which is your spiritual _____" (Rom 12:1).

3. What words are missing from this verse? "Let each of you look ___ ____ to his own interests, but also to the _____ of _____" (Phil 2:4).

4. When did Isaiah have the vision of God sitting on his throne?

5. What things caused Isaiah to fear?

6. What did the seraph say to calm Isaiah?

7. How did Isaiah show his availability to serve God and his Judean countrymen?

8. When and where did the apostle Paul first meet Timothy?

9. How did Timothy show the Christian character trait of availability?

10. Why did Paul think it a good idea to dispatch Timothy to the Philippian church?

God's Work in Believers

Availability is all about time and what you do with it. Everyone gets 24 hours a day, and much of that must be devoted to necessary things like eating, sleeping, attending school, doing chores, and working a job. Of course, even necessary things can absorb too much time; spending three hours over breakfast or sleeping 14 hours is unnecessary for most people. But what do you do with the rest of your time, time over which you have some freedom? How much of that "free" time is devoted to serving God and others, and how much of it goes towards your own desires and ambitions? Certainly, most individuals need some personal or down time, and there's nothing inherently wrong with recreation, hobbies, or even vegging out. However, if your plans, schedules, and priorities leave little or no time to serve God or others, there's good news—you now have an opportunity, through God's help, to develop the Christian character trait of availability. But that opportunity requires reallocation of your discretionary time.

First, are you available to God? Do you worship, commune with, and serve God? Are you attending worship services on Sunday, reading your Bible regularly, praying daily, and seeking to do his will? Sincere devotion to God, making time available for him, should be your top priority in life. Like Isaiah, eagerly volunteer for God's work. "For we are his workmanship, created in Christ Jesus for good works, which God prepared beforehand, that we should walk in them" (Eph 2:10). Set aside some portion of your discretionary time to focus entirely on God and do his bidding. Ask the Holy Spirit to help you make the time available.

Of course, part of serving God involves making yourself available to serve people. Are you available to meet the physical, mental, or spiritual needs of others? Are you ready to set aside your own plans and scheduled events when another person needs immediate help? Are you willing to spend quality time with other people even when no crisis exists? Look first to those near at hand. Are you neglecting to spend time with family? Do you often withdraw from them, making yourself unavailable? What about friends? Are you available when they need you most? Do you love hanging out with them but avoid their company when they become difficult or inconvenient (e.g., see Luke 11:7–8)? Again, reassess your plans, schedules, and priorities to see whether you should devote more discretionary time to family, friends, and others. Imitate selfless Timothy who exemplified what it means to be a "living sacrifice." And don't forget the example of Jesus: "Whoever would be great among you must be your servant, and whoever would be first among you must be your slave, even as the Son of Man came not to be served but to serve, and to give his life as a ransom for many" (Matt 20:26–28). Pray for a servant's heart that is always available.

God's Grace for Change

Before examining your heart, considering how you might improve, and seeking divine help, ponder one last point—God constantly makes himself available to you. He "will never leave you nor forsake you" (Heb 13:5). Let this brief reminder about and appreciation for God's undeserved grace prepare and motivate you to develop more of this lesson's character trait in yourself.

Then, complete the "Heart Assessment, Reflection, and Petition" (HARP) chart, assessing your own availability. Reflect on times the Holy Spirit enabled or empowered you to be available for God or others as well as times God and others made themselves available for you. Consider whether the Spirit might be revealing a need for you to become more available. If you want God to increase your availability, put that desire in writing. This is a very important exercise that can help you respond to God's direction for your life. Plan to pray over your completed chart once or twice this next week.

Finally, talk to the Lord, using the words that follow or incorporating the thoughts into your own prayer: "O Lord, how excellent are your mercies and great your favor. To those who call on you in faith, you always hear, you always answer, you are always available. But frail, cold-hearted, and self-centered, I often leave little time for you or others. Grant me true and godly repentance for spending so much time on myself and forgive. Starting now, cause me to consider ways to serve you as well as others and make changes in my life that will please and glorify you. I can only make such changes through the power you provide. How thankful I am that you hear and answer such requests. In the name of Jesus who made himself available to undeserving sinners like me, amen."

Remember, the Lord's help is vital to cultivating Christian character. Only his power can enable you to change. When you fail to show the character trait of availability, confess it before God and ask for his forgiveness and help.

HARP Chart for Availability

Definition: Availability means reserving time to serve God and others while keeping plans, schedules, and priorities reasonably flexible to meet unexpected needs as they arise.

Key verses: "I appeal to you therefore, brothers, by the mercies of God, to present your bodies as a living sacrifice, holy and acceptable to God, which is your spiritual worship" (Rom 12:1). "Let each of you look not only to his own interests, but also to the interests of others" (Phil 2:4).

Bible characters: Overwhelmed at God's holiness and thankful for God's forgiveness, Isaiah was a ready representative to carry God's message to the Judean people. Knowing him to be a selfless servant, Paul sent Timothy to help the Philippian church.

How often do you show availability in your life: 5 = nearly always, 4 = most of the time, 3 = about half the time, 2 = less than half the time, or 1 = hardly ever? Your response is _____.
In what ways, if any, has the Holy Spirit enabled you to be available to God or others?
In what ways, if any, have God and others made themselves available for you?
In what ways, if any, has the Holy Spirit revealed to you a need to be more available?
What petition related to availability, if any, would you like to bring before the throne of grace?

Caution

Engage in one or more of these introductory activities:

1. Perilous Pantomime—As in charades,[1] act out new or dangerous situations without speaking. Possible circumstances might include crossing a busy highway, defusing a bomb, parachuting from a plane, wading a flooded creek, climbing a mountain, or attending a new school. For each event, show either caution, carelessness, or both. Others attempt to guess the hazardous situation. Whoever guesses correctly gets to pantomime the next peril with the stipulation that no one can act out a second scenario until everyone has had a turn.

2. Trickling Tidbits—This interactive discussion encourages groups to think about what information they don't have and be cautious about passing judgment until they possess all relevant facts. Begin with a simple statement and ask for a conclusion. For example, you might start like this: "Tim kicked Christie's dog. What do you think about Tim?" You might even say this in a disapproving tone. Some, perhaps most or all, might conclude that Tim is mean and needs to be held accountable. But then, after the class reaches a negative conclusion, trickle out an additional fact to make Tim look innocent or, at least, less guilty. You might say, "Tim kicked the dog because it bit him on the knee. What do you think about Tim now?" After everyone starts thinking more positively about him, trickle out another fact that makes Tim look bad again. For instance, "The dog bit Tim on his knee because he trespassed on Christie's property after dark." Later, you might add, "Tim trespassed because a car accident with injuries occurred in front of Christie's house, and Tim knew Christie was a doctor." The idea is to impress people with the importance

---

1. The initial idea of using charades to illustrate the character trait of caution came from Carden and Carden, *Christian Character Curriculum* 1, 49.

of not reaching conclusions until they know all the facts and even encouraging them to think about what facts they still need to know. In other words, teach them to be cautious in making judgments. Congratulate those who catch on quickly and, rather than blurting out a conclusion, say something like, "Well, that depends. We don't know why Tim was trespassing, do we? That might be relevant."

These activities illustrate why it's important to exercise caution each day. A later lesson about watchfulness focuses on spiritual dangers from Satan and false teachers. In contrast, this lesson deals with potentially injurious circumstances, individuals, and judgments that more directly imperil body and mind. Here's the definition of this lesson's Christian character trait:

> Caution involves due care in dealing with new or dangerous situations, trusting people of uncertain character or motives, and drawing conclusions from incomplete or unverified facts.

God desires his children to exercise due care in their daily lives. From a biblical perspective, what does this character trait of caution look like, and how can Christians improve it? This lesson addresses these points under the headings of "God's Word to Mankind," "God's Work in Believers," and "God's Grace for Change."

God's Word to Mankind

Key Verses

"Desire without knowledge is not good, and whoever makes haste with his feet misses his way" (Prov 19:2). Zeal or enthusiasm in a worthy endeavor generally is a good thing, especially in contrast to apathy or indifference. But "desire without knowledge" is "not good." Indeed, some people let emotions dictate their actions rather than, before forging ahead, taking time to understand new situations. Those prone to over-hastiness often miss the right or safe path. When time permits, careful planning and thought trumps careless haste. Life presents many new and dangerous situations requiring caution.

"Whoever hates disguises himself with his lips and harbors deceit in his heart; when he speaks graciously, believe him not, for there are seven abominations in his heart" (Prov 26:24–25). Unfortunately, some people

who appear friendly and caring turn out to be scoundrels. Malicious people can be smooth talkers, expressing concern and inviting trust, while harboring deceit deep within their hearts. What's inside them cannot be seen or heard; it can only be learned or experienced over time. Thus, it's okay and, indeed, appropriate to exercise due caution around people of unknown character or motives even if they outwardly appear to be very nice.

"Every charge must be established by the evidence of two or three witnesses" (2 Cor 13:1). Experience often shows the wisdom of delaying conclusions until all relevant information is known and reasonably verified. This is especially true when reaching the wrong conclusion can damage someone's reputation. Establishing facts through the "evidence of two or three witnesses" is one (but not the only) way to value truth, reduce the chance of reaching wrong conclusions, and develop the character trait of caution.

Bible Characters

Negligent Nephew (Gen 13:1–13)

When Abraham left Haran to sojourn in Canaan and later fled to Egypt to escape famine, Lot (his nephew) went with him. But, after returning to Canaan, quarreling arose between Abraham's herdsmen and Lot's because their proximity could not support all their livestock. To maintain peace, Abraham suggested they separate and offered Lot first choice of the available land. This decision proved to be a turning point in Lot's life.

How did Lot choose? Does Scripture say he asked God for guidance? It does not; perhaps he did, but the Bible does not mention his prayer. Did Lot talk it over with his godly uncle to decide what would be best for everyone concerned? Perhaps he did, but the Bible doesn't say. The only thing Scripture says is that Abraham gave Lot a choice and then Lot "lifted up his eyes and saw" the lush, well-watered plains along the Jordan River and "chose for himself" that land. One might easily get the impression that Lot decided what would make him prosperous while ignoring the dangers involved. Having made his choice, however, he headed towards the Jordan River and pitched his tents near Sodom. Lot moved his family and possessions to an unfamiliar area near people who were "wicked, great sinners against the LORD." He moved far away from his uncle whom God had so carefully guided and abundantly blessed. In short, Lot's incaution led him to a very dangerous place.

Afterwards, distress filled much of Lot's life. Foreign invaders captured and whisked him away to the far north towards Mesopotamia, requiring Abraham to pursue the marauders and carry out a daring nighttime rescue (Gen 14). Afterwards, Lot relocated his family. No longer content to live near Sodom, he moved into the degenerate city itself, a city God purposed to destroy (Gen 19:1). Lot and his two daughters barely escaped Sodom as God obliterated the city with burning sulfur (Gen 19:15–26). Yet, Sodom's wicked influence continued to dog Lot. Dwelling in a mountain cave, his family transgressed God's law through sexual immorality (Gen 19:30–38). Perhaps Lot would have avoided these tragedies if he had only been more cautious about the choice Abraham placed before him.

Wayward Warrior (Judg 16:1–31)

God blessed Samson, a Nazirite, with tremendous physical strength. For twenty years, he led (or judged) Israel while punishing its enemies, the Philistines. But, among Old Testament personages, Samson was one of the most impulsive and rash.

Against his parents' advice, he sought to marry a Philistine woman. During the wedding festival, Samson wagered thirty Philistine men they could not solve a riddle he propounded about something sweet to eat coming out of a strong eater. At first, they were stumped, but then the Philistines threatened the bride-to-be to turn informant, who, in turn, coaxed the answer from her intended. So, Samson told her about the honey he ate from a lion's carcass, and she, in turn, told the thirty men. Solving the riddle, the Philistines won the wager, angering Samson (Judg 14). Many would have learned from this experience and been more cautious the next time. But Samson continued careless and unwary around pagan women.

He later fell in love with another Philistine named Delilah. At this time, the Philistines sought to capture Samson, but they feared his great strength. So, they urged Delilah to learn how Samson might be subdued. Repeatedly, Delilah asked Samson from where his great power came. Samson seemed unaware that she would betray him. Eventually, he succumbed to her persistent wiles, revealing that his long hair made him strong. Of course, God was the actual source of his strength, but Samson's disclosure, relating to his Nazirite vows, displeased God. The wayward warrior's incaution led to his capture and death.

Review Questions

1. What is the Christian character trait of caution?

2. What words are missing from this verse? "_____ without _____ is not good, and whoever makes _____ with his feet misses his way" (Prov 19:2).

3. What words are missing from these verses? "Whoever hates _____ himself with his ____ and harbors _____ in his heart; when he _____ graciously, believe him not, for there are seven _____ in his heart" (Prov 26:24–25).

4. "His speech was smooth as butter, yet war was in his heart; his words were softer than oil, yet they were drawn swords" (Ps 55:21). What does this verse teach about the Christian character trait of caution?

5. What words are missing from this verse? "Every charge must be established by the _____ of two or three _____" (2 Cor 13:1).

6. "The one who states his case first seems right, until the other comes and examines him" (Prov 18:17). What does this verse teach about the Christian character trait of caution?

7. When Abraham offered Lot first choice of where to live and graze his herd, what did Lot do?

8. What about Lot's decision appears incautious?

9. What apparent consequences did Lot suffer as the result of his incautious choice?

10. Who is Samson?

11. In what ways did Samson exhibit the Christian character trait of caution?

God's Work in Believers

Exercise caution in new or dangerous situations. For instance, teenagers often can't wait to get their driver's license. However, eagerly climbing behind the wheel and driving solo without understanding the vehicle's operation, knowing the rules of the road, or logging sufficient practice time exemplifies zeal without knowledge. The outcome can be tragic. Similarly, the avid lone hiker who heads down unfamiliar trails without compass or map shows careless desire or zeal. Hastiness to begin the trek exposes her to many dangers, including missed turns and the possibility of becoming lost. If she also neglected to check the weather or carry food, water, first aid supplies, adequate clothing, or a flashlight, her haste might lead to serious harm. Slow down when approaching new or potentially dangerous situations; don't plunge ahead too quickly. Unlike Lot, take time to think ahead, consider what's important, and plan things out. Ask God for grace to learn and exercise caution.

How do you know when you can trust someone? That's a difficult question. But spending time with a person and seeing her in different situations often leads to more (or, sometimes, less) trust. Ideally, you should have solid confidence in family and close friends. Recent or new acquaintances, in contrast, are more difficult to trust precisely because you haven't observed their behavior and disposition over time. You don't have to distrust everyone you meet openly. But you should remain cautious around those you barely know, especially if they ask you to trust them in some matter. Recall, for instance, how Hezekiah foolishly displayed Israel's wealth before the Babylonian envoy to the later detriment of his family and, indeed, the entire nation (Isa 39:1–7). Don't believe strangers simply because they look or sound kind or honest. Base trustworthiness on your experience with them rather than their appearance. Be doubly cautious when asked to trust someone you've never seen. People you meet online may not be who they say they are, so be wary about any digital interchange or correspondence. Don't disclose information through social media, over the phone, or anywhere else malevolent individuals might use to harm you. To guard against malware, think twice before visiting risky websites or clicking links within suspicious emails. Set strong passwords, and keep your anti-malware updated. Minimize opportunities for malicious people to hack into your online accounts, steal your identity, or learn details about your personal life. Pray the Lord will teach you to be cautious about such matters.

Maintaining a healthy skepticism about facts leads to sounder judgments and avoids hurting yourself or others unnecessarily. Exercise due care in reaching conclusions, waiting until all relevant facts are known. Too many people leap to wrong conclusions based on selective or false information. (Recall the trickling tidbits activity.) Indeed, overconfidence is the opposite of caution. Before drawing conclusions and acting on them, ask two questions: (a) How likely is it some relevant facts have not been revealed? (b) How likely is it some information presented as factual is false? Train yourself to ask these questions, developing cautiousness in your day-to-day thinking and judgments. But above all, seek the Holy Spirit's guidance anytime facts might be incomplete or incorrect; pray you will learn to exercise reasonable caution.

If the above admonitions create doubt about whether you will ever develop caution, don't despair. Do you have people in your life whom you really trust? Has God given them wisdom? If so, ask their advice whenever you need to be cautious but aren't sure how to proceed. Scripture teaches the immense value of good and wise counsel. "In an abundance of counselors there is safety" (Prov 11:14). "Without counsel plans fail, but with many advisers they succeed" (Prov 15:22). At the same time, be careful about counsel from the unwise or foolish. Remember that Adam listened to Eve about eating the forbidden fruit (Gen 3:17), Sarai counseled Abram to fulfill God's promise of descendants through Hagar (Gen 16:2), Rehoboam heeded the foolish advice of his young friends about crucial kingdom matters (1 Kgs 12 and 2 Chr 10), and Saul sought help from a medium contrary to God's law (1 Chr 10:13–14). Heeding unwise or foolish advice only increases careless tendencies.

Though wise advice from the trustworthy is good, counsel from the omniscient, all-wise Creator is far better. The loving Father longs for his children to learn caution, so seek his counsel above all others. Indeed, the act of seeking God's counsel about a matter is itself cautiousness. Stop and pray when facing new or dangerous situations, dealing with individuals of uncertain character or motives, or grappling with incomplete or unverified facts. Recall how that great man of God, Joshua, led Israel into the promised land and won one battle after another, carrying out the Lord's commands. And yet, on one occasion, Joshua forgot to be cautious. Seeing that Israel was unstoppable, Gibeonites living in Israel's midst deceived Joshua, pretending to be from a distant land and requesting a peace treaty with Israel. Joshua granted the treaty only to learn, a short time later, the men lived nearby. As a result, Joshua could not remove them from the promised land. How could Joshua, a brilliant military leader and faithful servant of the Lord, have made such a mistake? The answer is simple—he "did not ask counsel from the LORD" (Josh 9:14) in this matter. He was incautious about men he barely knew, men of uncertain character or motives.

God's Grace for Change

Complete the "Heart Assessment, Reflection, and Petition" (HARP) chart, assessing your own cautiousness. Reflect on times the Holy Spirit enabled or empowered you to be cautious in a situation, around certain people, or about drawing conclusions. Then, consider whether the Spirit might be revealing a need for you to become more cautious. If you want God to increase your cautiousness, put that desire in writing. This is a very important exercise that can help you respond to God's direction for your life. Plan to pray over your completed chart once or twice this next week.

Finally, talk to the Lord, using the words that follow or incorporating the thoughts into your own prayer: "Great Father of glory, I praise your holy name and bow before you in reverence and awe. Forgive my incautious moments and teach me to consider the consequences of not being careful. When I face new or dangerous situations, let me seek and understand your counsel. When I encounter people of uncertain character or motives, remind me to proceed cautiously and protect me. When I am tempted to draw conclusions from incomplete or unverified facts, cause me to proceed slowly, deliberately, and fairly. Thank you for giving me the power and desire to become cautious in my life. May I grow in grace and become more and more like my Savior each day. In his name, I pray. Amen."

Remember, the Lord's help is vital to cultivating Christian character. Only his power can enable you to change. When you fail to show the character trait of caution, confess it before God and ask for his forgiveness and help.

HARP Chart for Caution

Definition: Caution involves due care in dealing with new or dangerous situations, trusting people of uncertain character or motives, and drawing conclusions from incomplete or unverified facts.

Key verses: "Desire without knowledge is not good, and whoever makes haste with his feet misses his way" (Prov 19:2). "Whoever hates disguises himself with his lips and harbors deceit in his heart; when he speaks graciously, believe him not, for there are seven abominations in his heart" (Prov 26:24–25). "Every charge must be established by the evidence of two or three witnesses" (2 Cor 13:1).

Bible characters: When Abraham's negligent nephew acted incautiously, it exposed him and his family to danger. The wayward warrior's carelessness and unwariness around pagan women led to his capture and death.

How often do you show caution in your life: 5 = nearly always, 4 = most of the time, 3 = about half the time, 2 = less than half the time, or 1 = hardly ever? Your response is ____.
In what ways, if any, has the Holy Spirit enabled you to show caution?
In what ways, if any, has the Holy Spirit revealed to you a need to be more cautious?
What petition related to cautiousness, if any, would you like to bring before the throne of grace?

Compassion

Engage in one or more of these introductory activities:

1. Movie Night—Watch "The Blind Side" (2009, PG-13) or "Nicholas Nickleby" (2002, PG) as a class or individually. Based on a true story, the Touhy family in "The Blind Side" takes a quiet homeless teen, Michael Ohr, off the streets, eventually adopting him. Michael's huge bulk and protective instincts make him a formidable offensive lineman on the high school football team. Following graduation, Michael plays for Ole Miss, and, later, the Baltimore Ravens draft him in the first round. After the movie, cite instances in which the Touhy family showed warmth, tenderness, and concern for Michael and vice versa. Based on Charles Dickens' third novel, "Nicholas Nickleby" follows its 19-year-old namesake and protagonist as his father's death and the family's financial ruin force him to become a tutor at a boarding school. Wackford Squeers and his "enchanting" wife run the institution like a prison. A crippled servant boy named Smike, whom Nicholas befriends, receives the worst abuse from the sadistic couple. Meanwhile, Nicholas' sister receives a different sort of abuse from a two-faced uncle and his high-society friends. After this movie, explain why Nicholas cared so much about Smike and why the uncle cared so little about Nicholas and his family. What other characters showed concern for their fellow man?

2. Nature Study—Learn about African zebras[1] and share your findings through online photos or short video clips. As sociable animals, zebras travel in small harems but can band together in large herds, ranging from a few hundred to several thousand. Harems and herds slow their pace to accommodate the injured, elderly, and very

---

1. The initial idea of associating zebras' behavior with the character trait of compassion came from Carden and Carden, *Christian Character Curriculum* 2, 27.

young. Lions, hyenas, leopards, and cheetahs prey on zebras. When under attack, zebras form a semicircle defense, facing the predator as a community while shielding more vulnerable members behind them. Emphasize the concern strong, healthy zebras show towards weaker members.

As these activities illustrate, compassion for those who suffer or hurt is more than just a concerned feeling. The feeling instills a desire to help, and that desire often leads to action designed to alleviate the suffering. Compassion is like generosity (the topic of another lesson), but the latter, as defined, proceeds from an altruistic willingness to give or share things; it's not necessarily intended to relieve suffering. With this distinction in mind, what is this lesson's Christian character trait of compassion? Here's one way to define it:

> Compassion is pity, sympathy, or concern for those who suffer combined with a strong desire to relieve their hurt.

God desires his children to be soft and open towards those who hurt. From a biblical perspective, what does this character trait of compassion look like, and how can Christians improve it? This lesson addresses these points under the headings of "God's Word to Mankind," "God's Work in Believers," and "God's Grace for Change."

God's Word to Mankind

Key Verses

"Jesus went throughout all the cities and villages, teaching in their synagogues and proclaiming the gospel of the kingdom and healing every disease and every affliction. When he saw the crowds, he had compassion for them, because they were harassed and helpless, like sheep without a shepherd" (Matt 9:35–36). Seeing the throngs in their sin, misery, and brokenness, Jesus gently ministered to their spiritual, emotional, mental, and physical needs. All believers can't formally teach or preach; but, filled with compassion, they can share the good news and encourage others from God's Word. All Christians can't treat diseases and sicknesses; but compassionate hearts can encourage the weak and ill through word and deed.

"If anyone has the world's goods and sees his brother in need, yet closes his heart against him, how does God's love abide in him? Little children,

let us not love in word or talk but in deed and in truth" (1 John 3:17–18). Love for God expresses itself, at least partly, through compassion towards others; indifference to the needs of others suggests little or no love for God. "He who does not love his brother whom he has seen cannot love God whom he has not seen" (1 John 4:20). Thus, believers with material possessions beyond those necessary to meet their own needs and obligations should share with those having insufficient food, shelter, clothing, or medical attention. Compassion stirs the heart when needs arise, and the stirred heart often finds ways to relieve the needy.

Bible Characters

Sympathetic Samaritan (Luke 10:25–37)

Jesus' parable began with a lone traveler who was beaten, robbed, and left for dead. A priest and, later, a Levite saw the man but walked around him. Then, a Samaritan came down the road and pitied him. The man had serious injuries, no means of reaching shelter, and no money to pay for his own care. In merciful compassion, the Samaritan treated the wounds, took the man to an inn on his own donkey, and spent his own money towards the man's recovery.

Consider the three travelers who came upon the wounded man. The first two, though religious men knowing God's law, showed no compassion. Each, no doubt, possessed some means of alleviating the injured man's suffering but chose to ignore him. At a minimum, they could have stopped to check on him and, perhaps, offered food and water. But maybe they considered their engagements too pressing; this unfortunate man beside the road ranked low on their priority lists. The Samaritan, on the other hand, was the epitome of compassion. Interestingly, Israel's religious leaders looked down on Samaritans as a mixed-race people who were not true Israelites (e.g., see John 4:9). And yet, this despised Samaritan, not the priest and Levite, showed sympathy for the poor man whom thieves had beaten and robbed.

Pitying Patriarch (Luke 15:11–32)

The younger son took his inheritance and squandered it in riotous living abroad. But when the wealth ran out, famine struck the land, and this foolish young prodigal began to experience real need. Though Jewish, he took a job feeding unclean pigs, yet he still hungered. Deeply repentant, he headed home, hoping his father would hire him as a common servant. "But while he was still a long way off, his father saw him and felt compassion, and ran and embraced him and kissed him." The father saw how his son had suffered, instantly forgave his foolishness and waste, and took pity on him. Addressing the most immediate needs, the father brought clean clothes and prepared a feast for his younger son.

But the older son reacted quite differently. He became angry his younger brother had been restored so quickly. He felt little or no sympathy, failing to appreciate the father's compassion. In contrast, the older son wanted his brother to suffer the full consequences of his foolish ways; he had no desire to relieve his brother's hurt.

Review Questions

1. What is the Christian character trait of compassion?

2. What words are missing from these verses? "Jesus went throughout all the cities and villages, _____ in their synagogues and proclaiming the _____ of the kingdom and _____ every disease and every affliction. When he saw the crowds, he had _____ for them, because they were harassed and _____, like _____ without a shepherd" (Matt 9:35–36).

3. When Jesus showed compassion, what categories of needs did he meet?

4. What words are missing from these verses? "If anyone has the world's _____ and sees his brother in ____, yet _____ his heart against him, how does God's ____ abide in him? Little children, let us not love in ____ or talk but in ____ and in truth" (1 John 3:17–18).

5. According to 1 John 3:17–18, 4:20, what relationship exists between love of God and love of others?

6. What were priests and Levites?

7. Who were Samaritans?

8. How did the Samaritan in the parable show compassion?

9. In Jesus' parable, how did the younger son sin?

10. By returning home, did the younger son deserve his father's pity?

11. How did the father show compassion to his younger son?

12. How did the older son show compassion towards his brother?

13. When someone like the older son fails to show compassion, who gets hurt?

14. "As a father shows compassion to his children, so the LORD shows compassion to those who fear him" (Ps 103:13). "Our God is full of compassion" (Ps 116:5, NIV). "Can a woman forget her nursing child, that she should have no compassion on the son of her womb? Even these may forget, yet I [the LORD] will not forget you" (Isa 49:15). What do these verses teach about compassion?

God's Work in Believers

Compassion begins with a soft heart that hurts when others hurt. Whether expressed as pity, sympathy, or concern, it's being emotionally moved when others suffer. Perhaps your heart feels hard when you see others suffer; maybe you identify with the priest and Levite who ignored the man whom thieves beat and robbed. If so, ask the Lord to soften your spirit. God can make you compassionate like the sympathizing Samaritan; pray for this character trait.

But compassion requires more than just emotions. It includes strong desires to alleviate the hurt. Feeling concerned without any desire to help is not true compassion. Of course, it won't always be clear how to help. In those cases, ask for God's guidance. Remember that Jesus went about "teaching . . . and healing every disease and every affliction . . . [because] he had compassion on . . . the harassed and helpless" (Matt 9:35–36). Jesus is still like that even though he no longer walks the earth. Remember, the Almighty is full of compassion and can meet any need.

God desires you to be compassionate and alleviate the suffering of others to the extent you are able. In Jesus' sobering Olivet Discourse, the Lord tells the redeemed at the Last Judgment, "For I was hungry and you gave me food, I was thirsty and you gave me drink, I was a stranger and you welcomed me, I was naked and you clothed me, I was sick and you visited me, I was in prison and you came to me" (Matt 25:35–36). He was not saying acts of compassion save but the saved will be compassionate. If you lack this Christian character trait, confess your guilt to God and ask for the Holy Spirit to melt and remold your heart so it becomes full of compassion.

God's Grace for Change

Before examining your heart, considering how you might improve, and seeking divine help, ponder one last point—God's compassion towards you is unfathomable and unending. "Because of the LORD's great love [you] are not consumed, for his compassions never fail. They are new every morning; great is [his] faithfulness" (Lam 3:22–23, NIV). Let this brief reminder about and appreciation for God's undeserved grace prepare and motivate you to develop more of this lesson's character trait in yourself.

Then, complete the "Heart Assessment, Reflection, and Petition" (HARP) chart, assessing your own compassion. Reflect on times the Holy Spirit enabled or empowered you to show compassion as well as times God and others showed you compassion. Consider whether the Spirit might be revealing a need for you to become more compassionate. If you want God to increase your compassion, put that desire in writing. This is a very important exercise that can help you respond to God's direction for your life. Plan to pray over your completed chart once or twice this next week.

Finally, talk to the Lord, using the words that follow or incorporating the thoughts into your own prayer: "Holy triune God, I praise you for your great and abundant mercy. Taking pity on me in my lost estate, you saved me from sin and misery. Thank you, Jesus, for your compassionate, atoning sacrifice, making my salvation possible. Often, I see little of such compassion in my own life. Forgive and change me to be more like you. Father, give me a heart full of compassion that seeks to alleviate the physical, mental, emotional, and spiritual suffering of others. Without your help, my heart remains hard. But with your help, I cannot fail. Holy Spirit, make me compassionate like Jesus. Amen."

Remember, the Lord's help is vital to cultivating Christian character. Only his power can enable you to change. When you fail to show the character trait of compassion, confess it before God and ask for his forgiveness and help.

HARP Chart for Compassion

Definition: Compassion is pity, sympathy, or concern for those who suffer combined with a strong desire to relieve their hurt.

Key verses: "Jesus went throughout all the cities and villages, teaching in their synagogues and proclaiming the gospel of the kingdom and healing every disease and every affliction. When he saw the crowds, he had compassion for them, because they were harassed and helpless, like sheep without a shepherd" (Matt 9:35–36). "If anyone has the world's goods and sees his brother in need, yet closes his heart against him, how does God's love abide in him? Little children, let us not love in word or talk but in deed and in truth" (1 John 3:17–18).

Bible characters: Unlike the two religious leaders, the good Samaritan sympathized with the beaten and robbed man, providing medical care and shelter. The pitying patriarch compassionately forgave his prodigal son and then supplied clothes and food.

How often do you show compassion in your life: 5 = nearly always, 4 = most of the time, 3 = about half the time, 2 = less than half the time, or 1 = hardly ever? Your response is _____.
In what ways, if any, has the Holy Spirit enabled you to show compassion?
In what ways, if any, have God and others shown you compassion?
In what ways, if any, has the Holy Spirit revealed to you a need to be more compassionate?
What petition related to compassion, if any, would you like to bring before the throne of grace?

Contentment

Engage in one or more of these introductory activities:

1. Brainstorm—Discuss with others the meaning of "needs" and how needs relate to desire and contentment.[1] Begin with a simple question like this: "What kind of things do people need in life?" Answers might be wide-ranging and could even include electronic devices and internet services. Some responses may focus on necessities to sustain life like food, shelter, clothing, and maybe medical care. Next, query, "What needs does God promise to provide?" Answers may center around basic physical needs but also should include emotional, mental, social, and spiritual needs. Indeed, spiritual needs (especially salvation through faith in Christ) are more essential than others. Needs may vary over time (cf. needs of infants, young adults, and senior citizens) and among individuals. Remind believers that "God will supply every need of yours according to his riches in glory in Christ Jesus" (Phil 4:19). In this verse, "every need" doesn't include everything people may want or desire. As a final question, ask, "If God promises to provide all needs, why are his people oftentimes so discontent?" After allowing for discussion, end with this main point: Sometimes, God's people crave more than he provides; such cravings feed discontent.

2. Intriguing Insights—The quotations below make observations about contentment or its absence. Explain each quotation's meaning or otherwise comment about it.

   "You say, '. . . if I had a little more I should be very
   well satisfied.' You make a mistake, if you are

---

1. The initial idea of associating concepts of need with the character trait of contentment came from Carden and Carden, *Christian Character Curriculum* 1, 11.

not content with what you have, you would
not be satisfied if it were doubled."[2]

"The greater part of our happiness or misery
depends upon our dispositions and not upon
our circumstances."[3]

"Contentment is natural wealth; luxury, artificial
poverty."[4]

"Simplicity, simplicity, simplicity! I say, let your
affairs be as two or three, and not a hundred
or a thousand."[5]

"Discontent is like ink poured into water, which fills
the whole fountain full of blackness."[6]

These activities associate contentment and discontent with differing values, lifestyles, and desires. But what is this Christian character trait of contentment? Here's one way to define it:

Contentment entails being satisfied with God's provision.

God desires his children to be satisfied with their appearance, intellect, skills and abilities, family and friends, work and careers, recreational experiences, pains and discomforts, and property or wealth. From a biblical perspective, what does this character trait of contentment look like, and how can Christians improve it? This lesson addresses these points under the headings of "God's Word to Mankind," "God's Work in Believers," and "God's Grace for Change."

God's Word to Mankind

Key Verses

"I have learned in whatever situation I am to be content. I know how to be brought low, and I know how to abound. In any and every circumstance, I have learned the secret of facing plenty and hunger, abundance and need"

2. Spurgeon, "The Bed," 2.

3. Wharton, *Martha Washington*, 203-4.

4. Socrates as cited in Simmons, *A Laconic Manual*, 103.

5. Thoreau, *Walden*, 99.

6. Felltham, *Resolves*, 83.

(Phil 4:11–12). The apostle Paul learned contentment through many trials and God's enabling power amid each trial. No narrowly defined contentment this, Paul was satisfied "in whatever situation . . . in any and every circumstance." Whether penury or plenty, Paul was perpetually pleased with Providence's provision. What was the "secret" of being content? Perhaps it was knowing God (a) perfectly understood all his needs and (b) promised to supply every one of them fully. "Your heavenly Father knows that you need them all. But seek first the kingdom of God and his righteousness, and all these things will be added to you" (Matt 6:32–33).

"*Godliness with contentment is great gain, for we brought nothing into the world, and we cannot take anything out of the world. But if we have food and clothing, with these we will be content*" *(1 Tim 6:6–8)*. "Godliness" is being like God in thoughts, deeds, and attitudes; it's being devoutly Christ-like. True godliness subsumes contentment. As contentment develops and proceeds from godliness, "great [spiritual] gain" results. The gain is complete satisfaction in whatever God provides; it's an absence of worry about what God has supplied and whether God will continue supplying. Even if God provides only the basics needed to survive, the godly Christian remains calmly content.

Bible Characters

Disgruntled Descendant (Luke 15:11–32)

The family patriarch was a man of means, having servants, land, and livestock. He also had two sons. One day, the younger son said, "Father, give me the share of property that is coming to me." A world of meaning seems hidden beneath this terse statement. Whether clear to his father at the time, the younger son was saying, "I'm not happy living here anymore. Give me my inheritance now, so I can depart and live as I please. I want independence and freedom, not this lifeless drudgery day after day." He declared dissatisfaction with his father's provision and longed to direct his own affairs. What a paragon of discontent!

The patriarch yielded to his disgruntled descendant's demand, but the latter soon regretted his own foolishness. Leaving the structure of home life behind, the son immersed himself in wasteful spending and debauchery. He exchanged the light burden of family and home for the onerous, unforgiving yoke of abject poverty. His money soon evaporated, and the ensuing famine completed the double whammy. To survive, he slopped hogs, longing to eat husks the swine trampled.

But then, this foolish young man did something wise. Stopping to think, he realized he had been wrong and that his father might provide for him yet again, not as a son, of course, but as a servant. However, the younger son greatly underestimated the patriarch's love and pity. The father welcomed him home with open arms and celebrated his return. Though Jesus' parable does not reveal the entire aftermath, maybe the younger son learned contentment from this difficult, shameful episode in his life. Perhaps, in the years to come, he found satisfaction in his compassionate father's wise provision for his needs.

Tranquil Twosome (Acts 16:16–34)

Unjustly accused, beaten in public with rods, unlawfully jailed without trial, and fastened in an inner cell's stocks, many would have fretted, despaired, and perhaps even blamed God. And yet, the apostle Paul and his missionary companion, Silas, remained calm and satisfied. No doubt, this was one of the many situations through which Paul "learned the secret" of contentment (Phil 4:12). Around midnight, they prayed and sang hymns to God.

Suddenly, God made himself known to the tranquil twosome. A violent earthquake shook the prison's foundation, throwing open doors and loosening chains. The frightened jailer thought to kill himself, assuming his charges had escaped, and he would be held responsible. But Paul prevented him, and that night, God saved the jailer and his household. In addition, God provided for Paul and Silas' needs. The jailer took them home, cleaned their wounds, and fed them.

Review Questions

1. What is the Christian character trait of contentment?

2. What words are missing from these verses? "I have learned in _____ situation I am to be content. I know how to be brought ___, and I know how to _____. In ___ and _____ circumstance, I have learned the _____ of facing plenty and hunger, _____ and ____" (Phil 4:11–12).

3. What words are missing from this verse? "Your heavenly Father _____ that you ____ them. But ____ first his kingdom and his righteousness, and ___ these things will be _____ to you as well" (Matt 6:33).

4. What words are missing from these verses? "_____ with contentment is great gain, for we brought _____ into the world, and we cannot take _____ out of the world. But if we have ____ and _____, with these we will be _____" (1 Tim 6:6–8).

5. How did the younger son show discontent?

6. What consequences befell the younger son because of his discontent?

7. Who else did the younger son's discontent hurt?

8. What things might have led to Paul and Silas being discontent?

9. What did Paul and Silas do while in jail?

10. Who else did Paul and Silas' contentment benefit?

11. "Content[ment] makes poor men rich; discontent makes rich men poor."[7] How does this observation relate to the disgruntled descendant and the tranquil twosome?

God's Work in Believers

Do you feel a restless discontent in some areas of your life or during certain periods? That restlessness might be, at least partially, a lack of satisfaction with God's provision. Paul's contentment "in whatever situation" (Phil 4:11) is impossible apart from God. It takes the Holy Spirit's sanctifying power to develop this kind of restful satisfaction with his will. Ask God for contentment in all areas of your life. With his help, you can become satisfied with your appearance, intellect, abilities, family and friends, work, suffering, and property.

Why do people spend so much time and money on beauty products and the latest fashion? Why do they seem preoccupied with their appearance? Are they discontent with their looks? Why do so many marketers extol the wonders of that silky hair product, chic outfit, or some other item designed to make you look good or increase your popularity? One of the more difficult things with which to be satisfied is your appearance.

7. Franklin, *Poor Richard's Almanack*, 18.

Of course, contentment with your outward image does not mandate that you forgo soap, dress slovenly, or forswear grooming. Neither does it prevent you from dieting, exercising, or using makeup to improve your appearance. But it does mean you shouldn't fret because of the way God made you or devote inordinate time or money to the way you look. Thus, incessant attention to or persistent dissatisfaction with your clothes, height or weight, abnormalities or imperfections, nationality or ethnicity, skin color, or gender suggests a discontented spirit. Ask the Holy Spirit for contentment with how you look.

Strive to be content with the intellect with which God has blessed you. Just like your appearance, God deliberately fashioned your mind. Whether erudite, illiterate, or somewhere in between, you are special and important in his eyes. He fitted you with just the right number of brain cells, just the right amount of cerebral matter, so you can achieve his purpose for your life. This does not mean you should reject all opportunities for education and eschew learning. Improving your mind is a noble endeavor when done from the right motives. Indeed, don't waste your mind. At the same time, don't be dissatisfied with your brain's capacity to learn. God did not bestow on every person the rationality or creativity of an Einstein or Edison. Vigorously develop the mind God gave you for his glory, but don't be discontent with its limits. If doing your best, simply pray for contentment.

How exhilarating it can be to hear a philharmonic performance of Mozart's Symphony No. 40, view the Louvre's great masterpieces, see a perfectly executed double play end a World Series, observe a master mechanic diagnose and repair a 1966 Ford mustang, or listen as a well-known CPA explains retirement planning. It's good to appreciate the abilities of others. Yet occasionally, you might regret not having the talents they possess or, at least, not possessing them to the same degree. During those moments, remember your skills come from God, and you should develop and use them for his glory. Determine your primary talents—whether musical, athletic, artistic, mechanical, communicative, or some other—and improve those. While doing so, thank God for the level of skills and abilities he has seen fit to give you and ask for greater contentment. Everyone cannot be the best, but everyone can be the best they can be for God.

Have you ever felt discontent with your family or friends? How do you act and react towards those with whom you regularly deal? You love them, but, ever so often, perhaps you're just not very satisfied with them.

Maybe you even wish you could have been born into a different family or made better friends. If so, consider whether God may have had some purpose in bringing them into your life. Often, the Holy Spirit uses those nearest and dearest to sanctify. They can help knock off your rough edges and teach you to rely more and more on Jesus for strength, faith, and wisdom as you become more and more like him. Understanding this can provide a silver lining to what otherwise might be difficult, frustrating, or even bland relationships. If discontent still arises, confess your fault to God and ask him to restore your satisfaction with his provision. On the other hand, perhaps your discontent isn't related to unsatisfying relationships but from cherished family members or friends being too few or far away. You desire their warm company, but you see them so infrequently. If such is your case, accept your aloneness as God's provision and use it profitably to read good books, listen to edifying music, further your prayer life, help those in need, or redeem the time in other ways. Ask God for contentment when isolated or lonely. Also, remember that your nearest and dearest brother and friend is Jesus, and he "will never leave you nor forsake you" (Heb 13:5). Talk with him when alone, sharing your deepest thoughts with this "friend who sticks closer than a brother" (Prov 18:24).

Depending on your stage of life, you likely labor a great deal at school, work, or home. Many find fulfillment in these endeavors, but others do not and grow restless over time. For instance, those in school may find fault with classroom instruction, struggle with course assignments, or lack motivation. Those in the workplace may become dissatisfied with their tasks, compensation, status, or colleagues. Those laboring at home may grow weary of the thankless drudgery. Whether educational, vocational, or domestic settings, discontent is common. What to do? Pray to see purpose in your efforts, enjoy your accomplishments, and glorify God in how you approach each assignment and interact with others. Striving for these goals, with God's help, you likely will experience more contentment in the work he provides you to do.

Contentment can be elusive in the face of physical pain, mental anguish, or emotional sadness, whether due to chronic disease, financial collapse, family loss, or other suffering, anxiety, or grief. But, when your world falls apart, focus on God's commitments and assurances to comfort your spirit and foster contentment. Consider these unshakable declarations and promises: "The LORD is my shepherd, I shall not want" (Ps 23:1). "The LORD is my light and my salvation; whom shall I fear? The

LORD is the stronghold of my life; of whom shall I be afraid?" (Ps 27:1). "God is our refuge and strength, a very present help in trouble" (Ps 46:1). "The LORD is on my side; I will not fear. What can man do to me?" (Ps 118:6). "Behold, I [Jesus] am with you always, to the end of the age" (Matt 28:20). "For those who love God all things work together for good, for those who are called according to his purpose" (Rom 8:28). "I will never leave you nor forsake you" (Heb 13:5). Notwithstanding these and other ironclad pledges, hardship may hinder your mind from focusing on God sometimes. Amid physical, emotional, and mental troubles, the soul may fall into spiritual distress, wondering why God seems distant and why it's so difficult to pray. In those dark seasons, it's essential to remember God's promises depend on his faithfulness and truthfulness, not your anxious thoughts and feelings. Your emotions might oscillate and bewilder you, but God remains true to all he vows. He will act on his declarations, helping and delivering you even if your mind and soul are confused, fearful, doubting, or discontent. When peril keeps you from focusing on God, remember that he is, without a doubt, always focusing on you. Beseech the Holy Spirit for contentment with and trust in God's faithfulness and truthfulness.

Finally, find contentment in the things you own and consume, whether much or little. As Paul said, "In any and every circumstance, I have learned the secret of facing plenty and hunger, abundance and need" (Phil 4:12). It's good to work hard for a better life, studying diligently in school or striving to advance in your career, trade, or calling. But are you routinely dissatisfied with your current income and the things it can buy? Do you often crave things you can't afford such as a bigger home, newer vehicles, the latest and greatest gadgets, fancier clothes, and exotic vacations? Do you routinely spend more than you earn like the disgruntled descendant? These may be signs of discontent. There's nothing wrong, per se, with being rich or poor. But if you have much, don't constantly long for more. If you have little, strive to live happily within your means. If you "have food and clothing, with these . . . be content" (1 Tim 6:8). The bottom line is this—pray for contentment with your income and wealth since God supplies them and desires your satisfaction with his gracious provision.

To sum up, find your contentment in God alone and the things he supplies. Resist comparing yourself to other people and what they have; don't covet their appearance, intellect, abilities, family, friends, work, income, or property. Such comparisons breed discontent. Instead, measure yourself against what God wants you to become and strive heartily to attain it. As you do so, be content with all God provides along the way. True contentment banishes restlessness and fills the human spirit with joy and peace. Indeed, "those who seek the LORD lack no good thing" (Ps 34:10). So, take brimful delight in knowing God has provided for every need and will continue providing for every need in this life and the life to come. Then, let that knowledge content you just like it did the tranquil twosome—Paul and Silas.

God's Grace for Change

Before examining your heart, considering how you might improve, and seeking divine help, ponder one last point—Jesus contentedly left heaven's splendor for a meager, earthly existence, all for your sake. "Foxes have holes, and birds of the air have nests, but the Son of Man has nowhere to lay his head" (Luke 9:58). Let this brief reminder about and appreciation for God's undeserved grace prepare and motivate you to develop more of this lesson's character trait in yourself.

Then, complete the "Heart Assessment, Reflection, and Petition" (HARP) chart, assessing your own contentment. Reflect on times the Holy Spirit enabled or empowered you to be content as well as times Jesus showed contentment during his earthly life. Consider whether the Spirit might be revealing a need for you to become more content. If you want God to increase your contentment, put that desire in writing. This is a very important exercise that can help you respond to God's direction for your life. Plan to pray over your completed chart once or twice this next week.

Finally, talk to the Lord, using the words that follow or incorporating the thoughts into your own prayer: "Dear God, how marvelous is your name in all the earth. Great is your faithfulness to all your promises. Yet, despite your constant faithfulness, I often distrust your declarations and assurances, becoming discontent with your provision for my life. Forgive me this sin and sanctify me so that I honor you more. Grant me contentment in all areas of my life at all times. Teach me to find all my satisfaction in you; teach me to rejoice in your provision. Thank you for what you will accomplish in my life. Help me to glorify your name through my day-to-day contentment and, thus, do your perfect and holy will. Amen."

Remember, the Lord's help is vital to cultivating Christian character. Only his power can enable you to change. When you fail to show the character trait of contentment, confess it before God and ask for his forgiveness and help.

HARP Chart for Contentment

Definition: Contentment entails being satisfied with God's provision.

Key verses: "I have learned in whatever situation I am to be content. I know how to be brought low, and I know how to abound. In any and every circumstance, I have learned the secret of facing plenty and hunger, abundance and need" (Phil 4:11–12). "Godliness with contentment is great gain, for we brought nothing into the world, and we cannot take anything out of the world. But if we have food and clothing, with these we will be content" (1 Tim 6:6–8).

Bible characters: The disgruntled descendant's discontent led to financial ruin, but he sought forgiveness and experienced the father's compassion. In the most trying times, the tranquil twosome—Paul and Silas—learned contentment.

How often do you show contentment in your life: 5 = nearly always, 4 = most of the time, 3 = about half the time, 2 = less than half the time, or 1 = hardly ever? Your response is ____.
In what ways, if any, has the Holy Spirit enabled you to be content?
How did Jesus model contentment during his earthly life in ways benefiting you?
In what ways, if any, has the Holy Spirit revealed to you a need to be more content?
What petition related to contentment, if any, would you like to bring before the throne of grace?

Courage

Engage in one or more of these introductory activities:

1. John Knox—Do background research on this Scottish theologian.[1] Focus on one or two incidents that illustrate the bold courage of Knox in standing for God's truth. For example, Mary, Queen of Scots, once summoned Knox to Holyrood Palace where she confronted him. Mary accused Knox of teaching the populace religious beliefs differing from hers, which she characterized as sedition or treason. She also reasoned that Scripture required people to follow their rulers; since his teaching encouraged people to disobey her, he sinned. Not backing down, Knox observed the queen claimed authority belonging only to God and, thus, blasphemed. Such was his staunch courage and commitment to truth in menacing situations. His life illustrated how the fear of God overcomes the fear of man. Scotland's regent reportedly eulogized Knox as a "man who never feared any flesh."[2]

2. Movie Night—Watch "The Scarlet and the Black" (1983, NR), "A Man for All Seasons" (1966, G), or "Mr. Smith Goes to Washington" (1939, NR) as a class or individually. Based on true events, "The Scarlet and the Black," tells how an Irish priest in the Vatican, Monsignor O'Flaherty, saved thousands of Jews, Allied downed pilots, and escaped POWs from the Nazis during World War II. Of course, the title refers to the dominant colors of the Roman Catholic cassock as well as the Nazi regalia. The cat-and-mouse drama features O'Flaherty hiding refugees and leading them to safety while an SS Lieutenant Colonel, Herbert Kappler, desperately seeks to stop him. The stakes are high, but O'Flaherty never flinches in the face of

1. The initial idea of associating John Knox with the character trait of courage came from Carden and Carden, *Christian Character Curriculum* 3, 71.

2. Warfield, "John Knox," 378.

extreme danger. When and how did O'Flaherty or others show courage? In "A Man for All Seasons," Sir Thomas More, the principled Lord Chancellor of England, refuses to support King Henry VIII's request to divorce and remarry, which might give him a male heir to the throne. Eventually, More's staunch position leads to his execution. What pressures did More feel to capitulate, and what made him stand firm? How might things have turned out differently for all involved if More had acceded to the king's request? In "Mr. Smith Goes to Washington," crooked politicians try to destroy a well-meaning, newly appointed senator. However, everyone misjudges the mild-mannered idealist's integrity and spunk. In the dramatic conclusion of a 25-hour filibuster, the young senator brings down a major graft scheme and the powerful people involved. Through what means did politicians try to manipulate and coerce Mr. Smith, and why did the latter stand his ground at great peril?

3. Nature Study—Learn about wolverines[3] and share your findings through online photos or video. Wolverines live primarily in northern Canada, Alaska, Siberia, and the Nordic countries. Resembling small bears, adults typically weigh fifteen to thirty pounds. Though small, their frame is stocky and muscular. Wolverines usually catch small prey or scavenge for food, but their fierce courage when challenged is legendary. They'll fearlessly fight a cougar or wolves over a carcass. Also, they've been known to take down much larger game like caribou, reindeer, and even moose that deep snow impedes. For perspective, one wolverine expert likened such encounters to a domestic cat killing a deer.

These activities provide insight into the nature of true Christian courage. Here's one way to define that character trait biblically:

> Courage is the strength of mind or heart that allows people to face threats, pains, dangers, or other difficulties without fear overwhelming them.

God desires his children to stand firm before threats, patiently endure pains, confront dangers, rise above difficulties, and overcome fears in doing what is right. From a biblical perspective, what does this character trait of courage look like, and how can Christians improve it?

3. The initial idea of associating wolverines' behavior with the character trait of courage came from Carden and Carden, *Christian Character Curriculum* 3, 71.

This lesson addresses these points under the headings of "God's Word to Mankind," "God's Work in Believers," and "God's Grace for Change."

God's Word to Mankind

Key Verses

"Be strong and courageous and do it. Do not be afraid and do not be dismayed, for the LORD God, even my God, is with you. He will not leave you or forsake you, until all the work for the service of the house of the LORD is finished" *(1 Chr 28:20)*. King David spoke these words to his son, Solomon, who would succeed him as ruler over Israel. The "work" involved constructing and furnishing the palatial temple in Jerusalem, which would become the resting place for the ark of the covenant. The Holy Spirit gave David the temple plans, and David gathered many of the building materials. But God designated Solomon to carry out the plans. The daunting, arduous project would require many skilled craftsmen and laborers, careful attention to precise details, and punctilious management over many years. Solomon might easily feel overwhelmed, fearful, and discouraged at the enormity of the task, but David instructed him to continue until the temple stood complete. David gave Solomon two reasons to "be strong and courageous." First, God would be with him. Second, God would not leave or forsake him.

"The wicked flee when no one pursues, but the righteous are bold as a lion" *(Prov 28:1)*. The wicked see specters of immediate peril where none exists; they panic and "flee when no one pursues." The wicked, no matter how bold their outward bearing, secretly fear and inwardly anguish over this life and the next. Their conscience afflicts with a haunting, undefined, ever-present dread. Like Raskolnikov's fear for his undiscovered villainy, it tortures and terrorizes the soul at every turn.[4] In contrast, the righteous conscience rests easy, knowing God's forgiveness and its secure hope in Christ. A spirit of calmness and guiltlessness allows the righteous to be "bold as a lion" before any threat, pain, danger, or difficulty. It gives the upright person inner strength and courage the wicked never know.

---

4. Dostoevsky, *Crime and Punishment*, 85.

Bible Characters

Lionhearted Leader (Josh 1:1–11)

Moses had recently died, and Joshua became Israel's new leader. But the formidable task before him was impossible by human standards. God wanted the Israelis, ragtag descendants of Egyptian slaves, to enter the promised land and conquer seven nations with more numerous warriors and more powerful weapons than them (Deut 7:1). Many might tremble and quake at the prospect; some might consider it a suicide mission. And yet, God gave his marching orders. In three days, Israel would cross the Jordan River and begin its military campaign.

How could Joshua lead, and how could this timid nation follow in the face of such overwhelming odds? How could Joshua be a strong and courageous leader against seven mighty nations living in fortified cities? Was God telling him to "man up" and find the inner strength and indomitable spirit that would propel Israel to victory? Indeed, didn't God say, "Be strong and very courageous"? He did, but that wasn't the entire message. Intertwined with the directive to be strong and courageous was the admonition to trust and obey. As to trust, God promised Joshua that "no man shall be able to stand before you all the days of your life. . . . I will not leave you or forsake you." As to obedience, God said to "do according to all the law . . . . Do not turn from it to the right hand or to the left." In other words, God said trust and obey me, and I will give you strength and courage for the difficult, dangerous things I ask you to do.

Audacious Apostles (Acts 4:1–31)

Through the power of Jesus, Peter and John miraculously healed a crippled beggar near the temple gate (Acts 3:1–11). Then, to the gathering crowd, Peter boldly proclaimed Jesus as Christ, Lord, and Savior (Acts 3:12–26). His words agitated the priests, temple guards, and Sadducees. The guards arrested Peter and John, threw them into prison, and, the next day, brought the apostles before the Sanhedrin. This Jewish assembly consisted of "rulers and elders and scribes" of the law. It included conniving, power-hungry men who intimidated and threatened their opponents. From a human perspective, Peter and John were in a difficult, nay dangerous, pickle.

The Sanhedrin began the proceeding: "By what power or by what name did you do this?" More timid men might have mumbled some weak excuse and buckled before so great an assemblage. But Peter and John had not been cut from that cloth; the Holy Spirit gave them much power and courage to speak the Word of God without flinching (Acts 1:8, 2:1–4). And, so, Peter stood and preached to the Sanhedrin and its influential religious leaders. He didn't pull any punches either. Listen to his plucky, fearless words: "Let it be known to all of you and to all the people of Israel that by the name of Jesus Christ of Nazareth, whom you crucified, whom God raised from the dead—by him this man is standing before you well. . . . There is salvation in no one else [than Jesus], for there is no other name under heaven given among men by which we must be saved."

The apostles' audacious courage startled the Sanhedrin. Knowing Peter and John to be unschooled, they wondered at their boldness and whether it had something to do with Jesus. So, they took time to gather their wits and strategize. Then, dismissing Peter and John, the Sanhedrin commanded them not to teach about Jesus any longer. But that didn't end the matter; the apostles weren't done. As a parting shot, Peter and John replied, "Whether it is right in the sight of God to listen to you rather than to God, you must judge, for we cannot but speak what we have seen and heard." Recall how the apostles fled from Gethsemane on the night of Jesus' betrayal and how Peter denied knowing Jesus a few hours later. Compare those earlier, shameful times of weakness with the great courage the apostles showed on this day. After leaving, the apostles met with other believers and prayed, "Now, Lord, look upon their threats and grant to your servants to continue to speak your Word with all boldness." Then, the Holy Spirit empowered them to resume speaking openly about Jesus.

Review Questions

1. What is the Christian character trait of courage?

2. What words are missing from this verse? "Be _____ and _____ and do it. Do not be _____ and do not be _____, for the LORD God, even my God, is ____ you. He will not _____ you or _____ you, until ___ the work for the service of the house of the LORD is _____" (1 Chr 28:20).

3. Who spoke the words in 1 Chr 28:20, and to whom did he speak them?

4. To what "work" does 1 Chr 28:20 refer?

5. In 1 Chr 28:20, what two reasons did David give Solomon for being courageous?

6. What words are missing from this verse? "The wicked _____ when no one _____, but the righteous are _____ as a _____" (Prov 28:1).

7. After Moses died, what task did God call Joshua to accomplish?

8. What reasons might have argued against Joshua's ability to conquer the promised land?

9. Where did Joshua find the courage to do what God commanded?

10. According to Acts 1:8, to what task had God called Peter and John?

11. In Jerusalem, to whom did Peter and John witness?

12. From where did Peter and John receive the courage to witness?

13. When the Sanhedrin forbid Peter and John to teach about Jesus in the future, what did the audacious apostles say?

God's Work in Believers

Some consider courage and fear to be opposites—courage equates to no fear, and petrifying fear means zero courage. But that's not the view here. Though courage often assuages and calms fear, courage isn't necessarily fear's absence. People sometimes perform courageously despite inward, lurking fear. Acting boldly, even as fear rises, can itself be courageous. So, courage is the inner fortitude of mind or heart that allows Christians to deal with threats, pains, dangers, or other difficulties without fear overwhelming or paralyzing them.

Think about times when you felt unjustly threatened. Whether from school bullies, tyrannical bosses, autocratic leaders, or common ruffians, most people feel intimidated, imperiled, vulnerable, or oppressed on occasion. Threats can be verbal or consist of cutting looks. Threats can be physical like a raised fist or malevolent glare. Or, threats can be veiled, insinuating that recipients might be fired, demoted, sanctioned, excluded, shunned, coerced, harassed, or canceled. Recall how the Sanhedrin threatened the audacious apostles, Peter and John, with more harassment if they continued speaking the truth. Recall their courageous response to that threat.

Like receiving threats, dealing with pain also requires courage. In this life, many people experience agonizing or prolonged pain at some point. The anguish may be physical, mental, emotional, spiritual, or some combination. Moreover, the pain can be attributable to disease, injury, poor relationships, financial setbacks, depression, or backsliding. With so many types and sources of pain, the need for courage is ongoing and frequent.

People often associate the word "danger" with unexpected catastrophes, unprovoked attacks, or other emergencies that threaten harm. Indeed, danger can arise from diverse phenomena such as natural disasters, criminal activity, wild animals, and even Satan. Close encounters with tornados, floods, earthquakes, burglars, active shooters, timber rattlers, mountain lions, and malevolent spirits all involve danger. Also recall the danger young David faced from the giant warrior Goliath (1 Sam 17:37); Shadrach, Meshach, and Abednego faced from King Nebuchadnezzar and the fiery furnace (Dan 3:16–18); and Daniel faced from the king's decree forbidding prayer to God (Dan 6:10). When suddenly confronted with such things, courage is needed.

Difficulties in life beyond those involving actual threats, pains, or dangers include dealing with common phobias. Many people fear things like failure, flying, spiders, public speaking, heights, darkness, rejection, germs, solitude, or death. Still other difficulties relate to complex or perplexing projects at school, work, or home. Recall how God gave the lion-hearted leader, Joshua, the gargantuan task of conquering the promised land. Solomon also had a difficult assignment—building and furnishing the temple according to God's specifications.

Whether dealing with threats, pains, dangers, or other difficulties, the question is, "How can you develop courage?" First, understand courage as a character trait whereas fear is an emotion. When present, courage mitigates fear, so the latter does not overwhelm or paralyze you; but courage does not necessarily extinguish fear. You may show courage while simultaneously experiencing fear; the trait and the emotion can coexist within you at the same moment and often does. Second, know that courage comes from God. Believers do not develop courage through their own sheer will and determination. Gideon had the seemingly impossible assignment of defeating the Midianite hordes with only three hundred soldiers. Knowing his fear, God gave him the means of courage

(Judg 7:10–12). Similarly, those trying to acquire courage solely through self-effort shortchange themselves; they end up with some cheap, unreliable counterfeit of true courage. Third, remember that the Lord desires you to trust and obey him as a pathway to courage. When you depend on the omnipotent, omniscient God and serve him through difficult circumstances, he gives you a calm, guileless spirit, enabling you to face all obstacles or challenges boldly. Fourth, remember that God promises to be with you and never leave or forsake you, no matter the difficulty. "The LORD is my light and my salvation; whom [or what] shall I fear? The LORD is the stronghold of my life; of whom [or what] shall I be afraid?" (Ps 27:1). "The LORD is my helper; I will not fear. What can man [or anything] do to me?" (Heb 13:6). Fifth, regularly ask the Holy Spirit for help whenever threats, pains, dangers, or difficulties arise in your life and depend on him again and again to give you fresh courage.

God's Grace for Change

Before examining your heart, considering how you might improve, and seeking divine help, ponder one last point—Jesus courageously atoned for your sin even though it involved great suffering and sorrow. "My Father, if it be possible, let this cup pass from me; nevertheless, not as I will, but as you will" (Matt 26:39). Let this brief reminder about and appreciation for God's undeserved grace prepare and motivate you to develop more of this lesson's character trait in yourself.

Then, complete the "Heart Assessment, Reflection, and Petition" (HARP) chart, assessing your own courage. Reflect on times the Holy Spirit enabled or empowered you to be courageous in the face of threats, pains, dangers, or other difficulties as well as times Jesus showed courage during his earthly life. Consider whether the Spirit might be revealing a need for you to show more courage. If you want God to increase your courage, put that desire in writing. This is a very important exercise that can help you respond to God's direction for your life. Plan to pray over your completed chart once or twice this next week.

Finally, talk to the Lord, using the words that follow or incorporating the thoughts into your own prayer: "My Father, I praise and exalt your righteous name. But I am frail, weak, and sinful. How often and how great I have sinned against you. Please forgive and heal me. How thankful I am, Jesus, for your incarnation. How thankful I am that you faced and endured grave threats, pains, dangers, and other difficulties on my behalf to win my salvation and make me righteous. Conform me now to your image through the Holy Spirit for your glory and my good. Cast out my fear as I contemplate that the Father reigns, Christ mediates, and the Holy Spirit comforts. Grant me much boldness to face threats, pains, dangers, and other difficulties in my life. Give me much courage to do your will without shrinking away. Amen."

Remember, the Lord's help is vital to cultivating Christian character. Only his power can enable you to change. When you fail to show the character trait of courage, confess it before God and ask for his forgiveness and help.

HARP Chart for Courage

Definition: Courage is the strength of mind or heart that allows people to face threats, pains, dangers, or other difficulties without fear overwhelming them.

Key verses: "Be strong and courageous and do it. Do not be afraid and do not be dismayed, for the LORD God, even my God, is with you. He will not leave you or forsake you, until all the work for the service of the house of the LORD is finished" (1 Chr 28:20). "The wicked flee when no one pursues, but the righteous are bold as a lion" (Prov 28:1).

Bible characters: Joshua received the strength and courage to be a lionhearted leader through trusting and obeying God. The audacious apostles spoke boldly before the temple crowd and the Sanhedrin through the Holy Spirit's power and courage.

How often do you show courage in your life: 5 = nearly always, 4 = most of the time, 3 = about half the time, 2 = less than half the time, or 1 = hardly ever? Your response is ____.
In what ways, if any, has the Holy Spirit enabled you to show courage?
How did Jesus model courage during his earthly life in ways benefiting you?
In what ways, if any, has the Holy Spirit revealed to you a need to be more courageous?
What petition related to courage, if any, would you like to bring before the throne of grace?

Decisiveness

Engage in one or more of these introductory activities:

1. Critical Choices—Read Scripture passages involving some good and some bad choices.[1] After each reading, ask four questions: (a) What did _____ chose? (b) Why did _____ make that decision? (c) What consequence followed because of this decision? (d) If _____ had chosen differently, what do you think the consequences might have been instead? Some sample passages appear below with suggested responses.

> Adam (Gen 3:1–19)—(a) Adam (and Eve) chose to disobey God by eating the forbidden fruit. (b) Eve ate the fruit because it was good for food, pleasing to the eye, and, according to the serpent, desirable for wisdom. Adam ate the fruit because Eve gave it to him and in rebellion against God. (c) The human race fell into sin, and God expelled Adam and Eve from the Garden of Eden. (d) Mankind might have gained eternal life without suffering from sin and misery.

> Moses (Exod 2:11–15; Heb 11:24–27)—(a) Moses chose to suffer reproach with God's people rather than enjoy the pleasures of sin for a season. (b) Moses reasoned that suffering disgrace for Christ's righteousness was worth more than Egypt's riches. (c) God used Moses to lead Israel out of Egypt. (d) God would

---

1. The initial idea of associating decisions from the Bible with the character trait of decisiveness came from Carden and Carden, *Christian Character Curriculum* 3, 39.

have delivered Israel through other means, according to his promise, but history likely would have known nothing about Moses.

Balaam (Num 22:1–31; 2 Pet 2:15–16)—(a) Balaam chose to disobey God when he went to the Moabite king, Balak, after being summoned. (b) He coveted the sordid fee Balak offered him to curse Israel. (c) The angel of the Lord blocked his path three times as he went to Balak. After arriving, Balaam blessed Israel three times rather than cursing them (Num 24:10). (d) This is hard to say, but here's one possible answer. Israel later slew Balaam because he sought knowledge through illegitimate means (Josh 13:22). Balaam may have lived a more righteous life and died peacefully if he had not been temporarily swayed to curse Israel for a fee nor dabbled in the dark arts.

Israel (Deut 30:1–20)—(a) Arguably, looking at Israel's later history, many chose against "loving the LORD [their] God, . . . walking in his ways, and . . . keeping his commands and his statutes and his rules." (b) Many in Israel loved the world more than God. (c) Israel suffered many times because of their rebellion and disobedience. But the culmination must have been when the Assyrians led the Northern Kingdom into exile in 722 BC and when the Babylonians captured the Southern Kingdom and led it away in 586 BC. (d) If Israel had loved the Lord their God with their whole being, obeyed his commands, and served only him, they would have prospered in the land, enjoyed God's great favor, and never experienced captivity and exile.

Judas Iscariot (Luke 22:1–6, 47–53)—(a) Judas chose to betray Jesus to the chief priests. (b) Satan tempted and overcame Judas, who agreed to receive money for his betrayal. (c) The temple guards arrested Jesus, the Sanhedrin tried and convicted him, and Roman soldiers crucified him. (d) Judas might not have met a violent, shameful end (Acts 1:18–19).

Peter and John (Acts 4:13–31)—(a) The apostles chose to obey God rather than the Sanhedrin and, thus, continued speaking about Jesus. (b) It was right to obey God, and they feared him more than the misguided religious leaders. (c) They prayed for protection and power. Then, the Holy Spirit filled them, and they spoke boldly about Jesus. (d) God had commanded them to teach; if they had not obeyed, God likely would have chastised them.

God (Eph 1:3–5)—(a) God chose a people for salvation before creation. (b) He predestined the elect because he loved them. (c) As a result, he also committed to call, regenerate, justify, adopt, sanctify, and glorify the elect. (d) If God had not chosen some to be saved, all would have died in their sins without hope.

2. Movie Night—Watch "Hoosiers" (1986, PG) as a class or individually. In the film, loosely based on a true story, Norman Dale comes to a small Indiana high school in 1951 to coach basketball. His emphasis on fundamentals and teamwork rubs locals the wrong way, especially when his six players experience early losses. But eventually, Coach Dale's disciplined approach produces wins, taking the team to the state finals. What decisions did Coach Dale; Myra Fleener, the female teacher; "Shooter" Flatch, the assistant coach; Jimmy Chitwood, the star player; and Strap Purl, the prayerful player, make, and what caused each choice to be either good or bad?

3. Would You Rather?—Most people make many decisions every day. Answer the questions below, involving binary decisions, and follow up each question with two more queries: (a) Why would this be good? (b) Why might this turn out badly? The point of the two

follow-up questions is to focus on consequences—whether probable or merely possible, whether positive or negative. As phrased, several of the questions involve common daily or periodic decisions in which the binary span is wide and inflexible to facilitate a discussion of long-term consequences. For instance, the first sample question provides a wide span (10:00 PM or 2:00 AM) and inflexibility ("every night" and "each morning").

> Would you rather go to bed at 10:00 PM every night or 2:00 AM each morning?
>
> Would you rather sleep six hours every night or ten hours?
>
> Would you rather skip breakfast each morning or be late for school or work?
>
> Would you rather eat only salad every night or just pizza?
>
> Would you rather exercise three hours every day or never exercise?
>
> Would you rather go to the doctor for an annual physical exam or only visit the doctor when you get sick?
>
> Would you rather buy medical insurance or just hope you never get too sick or have a bad accident?
>
> Would you rather floss and brush twice a day or just brush every other day?
>
> Would you rather go to school fifty weeks a year or only four weeks a year?
>
> Would you rather work twenty hours every week or fifty hours?
>
> Would you rather drive each morning in heavy traffic to a high-paying job or walk to a nearby job that pays a lot less?
>
> Would you rather have a job you love but that barely pays the bills or a job you sometimes hate that pays well?

> Would you rather spend everything you earn and
> have lots of fun or spend half your earnings
> and save the rest for retirement?
>
> Would you rather have many so-so friends or just
> one close friend?
>
> Would you rather live alone with few responsibilities
> or get married and have kids?

These activities show how important it is to make sound decisions throughout life. Indeed, a wise decision today forestalls needless regrets and much heartache tomorrow. A later lesson deals with discernment, a key element in decision-making. But what is this Christian character trait of decisiveness? Here's one way to define it:

> Decisiveness involves timely choices that wisely consider future consequences.

God desires his children to make decisions that glorify him. From a biblical perspective, what does this character trait of decisiveness look like, and how can Christians improve it? This lesson addresses these points under the headings of "God's Word to Mankind," "God's Work in Believers," and "God's Grace for Change."

God's Word to Mankind

Key Verses

"Choose this day whom you [Israel] will serve . . . . But as for me [Joshua] and my house, we will serve the LORD" (Josh 24:15). Just before this call for decisiveness and declaration of his own decision, Joshua recounted God's faithfulness in doing everything he promised to Israel, namely giving them land and making them into a great nation. First, God led Abraham, Isaac, and Jacob throughout Canaan, the land promised but not yet given. Next, God took Israel's family down to Egypt where they were enslaved but became numerous. Then, the Lord led them out of bondage via Moses and Aaron, defeating Pharaoh and his army. After forty years in the wilderness, God brought Israel back to Canaan, destroying seven nations more powerful than them. Indeed, the Lord reminded Israel that its successes were "not by [its] sword or by [its] bow" (Josh 24:12) but through his power. In this context of God fulfilling all he promised to

Israel, Joshua chose to obey the only living and true God, knowing the Lord would continue showing steadfast love, abundant mercy, and great faithfulness to his chosen people. But now, Israel also had to choose. If Israel decided to forsake God, disaster awaited (Josh 24:20).

"If your right eye causes you to sin, tear it out and throw it away. . . . If your right hand causes you to sin, cut it off and throw it away" (Matt 5:29–30). This passage does not require, endorse, nor, in any way, encourage self-mutilation. Instead, the Lord taught the importance of personal holiness, especially in the face of strong, persistent temptation or recurring sin. Jesus commanded saints to take whatever steps necessary to avoid or resist unrelenting or vexatious temptation or to purge cherished, deep-seated, or besetting sin. They should do so even if they must take radical steps, likened to gouging out an eye or cutting off a hand (though, again, actual mutilation is not in view). They must do so even if the steps prove costly. Ignoring Jesus' command and allowing sin to reign only leads to more hardship in life, exacting a much higher cost later. In contrast, making the hard decision to deal sharply with temptation and sin leads to eternal rewards that dwarf any fleeting pleasures from disobedience.

Bible Characters

Contra Choice (Dan 1:1–20)

Nebuchadnezzar, king of Babylon, besieged Jerusalem in 605 BC, and Judah became a vassal state. The invading army carried away the noblest and most skilled Judeans, among them, Daniel. In Babylon, Nebuchadnezzar acculturated the captives to their new home and then used their talents to strengthen his kingdom. Placing his chief official in charge of the most-promising young exiles, the king ordered them given the best food and wine. However, Daniel and three others—Shadrach, Meshach, and Abednego—resolved not to eat the king's choice fare. Instead, they asked for a contrary, herbaceous diet.

Their strange request risked the chief official's and, possibly, even King Nebuchadnezzar's displeasure. But consuming the king's food and drink would have violated God's dietary laws for Jews. So, in obedience to God, Daniel and his three friends suggested a trial run of vegetables and water. Reluctantly, the chief official agreed. After ten days, however, these four men looked healthier than all the other captives who had feasted on the royal food and wine. As time passed, Daniel and his friends continued to prosper and brought much glory to God.

Dream Decision (Matt 1:18–26)

While a virgin engaged to be married, Mary became pregnant with Jesus, not through relations with a man, but through the mysterious operation of the Holy Spirit. As a result, a decision confronted her fiancé. As a kind and righteous man, Joseph did not want to humiliate Mary publicly for what he assumed to be unfaithfulness. So, he purposed to break off their engagement quietly.

But, before he could do so, an angel came to him in a dream. The heavenly messenger told Joseph to continue with the marriage, explaining how Mary had remained faithful. Indeed, God had chosen his betrothed to birth and raise the long-awaited Messiah. This new information changed Joseph's decision, bringing it into conformity with God's will.

Review Questions

1. What is the Christian character trait of decisiveness?

2. What words are missing from this verse? "_____ this day whom you will _____ . . . . But as for me and my house, we will _____ the LORD" (Josh 24:15).

3. Why did Joshua choose to follow the Lord?

4. What two things had God promised Israel?

5. What words are missing from these verses? "If your right ___ causes you to ___, tear it out and throw it away. . . . If your right _____ causes you to ___, cut it off and throw it away" (Matt 5:29–30).

6. What consequences result from decisions about temptation and besetting sin?

7. Where did Daniel live?

8. What is the first decision the Bible records that Daniel and his three friends made?

9. Why did Daniel and his three friends make this decision?

10. How did Daniel and his friends make this decision and, at the same time, show respect to those in authority over them?

11. How did God bless their resolve to obey him?

12. When Joseph found out Mary was pregnant, what did he resolve to do?

13. What new information changed Joseph's decision?

God's Work in Believers

Decisions, decisions, most people make countless choices every day. Ranging from the mundane or commonplace (e.g., what to eat for breakfast) to those affecting the world economy and geopolitics (e.g., how to negotiate a trade agreement), it's nearly impossible to avoid decisions. So, how can you develop the Christian character trait of decisiveness? Regardless of your station in life, the choices confronting you, or your natural abilities, God can help you (a) make timely decisions that (b) wisely consider future consequences.

Being decisive requires timely choices. Of course, many situations and opportunities require quick or even immediate action. For example, what should you do when caught outdoors in a lightning storm? Should you accept a ride home from a recent acquaintance? What, if anything, should you order for dessert? Other decisions, especially those with far-reaching or long-term consequences, may not need resolving right away. Whether circumstances require quick or more contemplative action, God stands ready to hear your prayer for assistance.

When time to choose, however, some people can't pull the decision trigger. All the options have been laid on the table, all the pros and cons have been fully examined, and the deadline draws near. But whoever must decide can't or won't do it. At times, a lack of good choices explains this hesitancy or unwillingness to decide. If just bad choices exist, the decision-maker might hold out for an unknown better alternative that doesn't exist and, thus, not choose. Of course, many decisions in life involve choices between the lesser of two or more evils. Not deciding is itself a choice and, often, an unwise one at that. When you can't or won't decide, other people or circumstances inevitably choose for you. If you regularly find yourself unable to choose when decisions must be made, ask the Holy Spirit to teach you.

Of course, timeliness alone doesn't make you decisive; it doesn't infuse your choices with wisdom. Indeed, people make many unwise decisions in life. Choices lacking wisdom occur for a variety of reasons. Some people habitually make snap decisions in rapid-fire succession, and that's not necessarily bad. But being too quick to draw conclusions and decide a matter may be the result of not identifying or adequately considering all the options. It also might reflect a failure to think carefully about future consequences. Particularly if you've made impulsive or hasty judgments in the past that proved unwise, slow down your decision-making process if time permits.

How can you bring more wisdom into your decision-making? Consider whether you might not have identified all possible options, investigate or research all alternatives, lay complex decisions out in table format with pros and cons for each option, note future consequences associated with each choice, and seek wise counsel from others you trust. Then, search the Scriptures and bring the decision into the throne room of grace, laying it as an urgent petition before God. Ask that his will be done rather than your own will. After that, decide and act on it in a timely manner, trusting God to help you choose. Regularly approaching life choices in this way leads to better decision-making; it will develop within you the Christian character trait of decisiveness.

God's Grace for Change

Before examining your heart, considering how you might improve, and seeking divine help, ponder one last point—The Father timely decided to send a Redeemer, and Jesus chose to pay the ransom for your sin, making you a child of God. "When the fullness of time had come, God sent forth his Son . . . to redeem those who were under the law, so that we might receive adoption as sons" (Gal 4:4–5). Let this brief reminder about and appreciation for God's undeserved grace prepare and motivate you to develop more of this lesson's character trait in yourself.

Then, complete the "Heart Assessment, Reflection, and Petition" (HARP) chart, assessing your own decisiveness. Reflect on times the Holy Spirit enabled or empowered you to make timely, wise choices as well as times God and others made wise decisions that benefited you. Consider whether the Spirit might be revealing a need for you to become more decisive. If you want God to increase your decisiveness, put that desire in writing. This is a very important exercise that can help you respond to God's direction for your life. Plan to pray over your completed chart once or twice this next week.

Finally, talk to the Lord, using the words that follow or incorporating the thoughts into your own prayer: "Omniscient Father, I praise and lift high your name. Forgive my sins though they are many and great. Forgive me even though my choices in life often have been to do my own will in rejection of your will. How much I must displease and grieve you at times. And yet, you chose me in Christ before the foundation of the world, and, for that, I am eternally grateful. Thank you for Jesus, who chose to lay down his life as a sacrifice for my sin. As one of your chosen and forgiven people, help me to make good choices in my life. Through the Holy Spirit, develop within me the ability to make timely decisions that wisely consider your law, your will, and future consequences to myself and others. In the name of Christ, my Savior, amen."

Remember, the Lord's help is vital to cultivating Christian character. Only his power can enable you to change. When you fail to show the character trait of decisiveness, confess it before God and ask for his forgiveness and help.

HARP Chart for Decisiveness

Definition: Decisiveness involves timely choices that wisely consider future consequences.

Key verses: "Choose this day whom you [Israel] will serve . . . . But as for me [Joshua] and my house, we will serve the LORD" (Josh 24:15). "If your right eye causes you to sin, tear it out and throw it away. . . . If your right hand causes you to sin, cut it off and throw it away" (Matt 5:29–30).

Bible characters: To honor God, four Judean captives decided against consuming the king's choice fare. Joseph decided to wed Mary only after God told him to do so in a dream.

How often do you show decisiveness in your life: 5 = nearly always, 4 = most of the time, 3 = about half the time, 2 = less than half the time, or 1 = hardly ever? Your response is ____.
In what ways, if any, has the Holy Spirit enabled you to show decisiveness?
In what ways, if any, have God and others made wise decisions from which you benefited?
In what ways, if any, has the Holy Spirit revealed to you a need to be more decisive?
What petition related to decisiveness, if any, would you like to bring before the throne of grace?

Deference

Engage in one or more of these introductory activities:

1. Hudson Taylor—Do background research on this British missionary to China.[1] Present a brief overview of his life, perhaps using a short, online video. But then, focus on how his deference to Chinese culture created opportunities for sharing the gospel. For example, unlike other missionaries of the day, he wore Chinese clothing, ate with chopsticks, shaved his forehead, and braided his remaining hair into a single pigtail or queue. In effect, Hudson Taylor became like the Chinese people so he might teach them about Jesus (1 Cor 9:22). During his 51 years of missionary work, he started the China Inland Mission and recruited hundreds of missionaries.

2. Movie Night—Watch "The Princess Bride" (1987, PG) or "Driving Miss Daisy" (1989, PG) as a class or individually. In an early segment of "The Princess Bride," Buttercup enjoys asserting her will over the farm boy, Westley. But every time she does, he responds with three simple words and does what she asks. At a minimum, watch a short video clip of this scene. What one-word descriptions can you give of Buttercup's requests and Westley's singular response? For example, the words "demanding," "bossy," or "assertive" might come to mind for Buttercup. For Westley, "amenable," "obliging," "congenial," "yielding," "respectful," or "deferential" might be mentioned. Buttercup wanted certain things done, and Westley always complied in a quiet, agreeable manner. Responding as he did developed their friendship and love for each other. How might their relationship have evolved differently if Westley had responded harshly or defensively? In "Driving Miss Daisy," the friendship between an

---

1. The initial idea of associating Hudson Taylor with the character trait of deference came from Carden and Carden, *Christian Character Curriculum* 3, 7.

elderly Jewish woman and her somewhat younger African American chauffeur, Hoke, starts rocky but then steadily improves over the years. The catalyst for change came from Hoke's kind responses to the woman's constant irritability. What specific things did Hoke say to or do for Miss Daisy that, over time, developed their long-term friendship?

These activities show, in appropriate circumstances, the importance of deferring. Deference involves yielding to others, while two later lessons deal with humility (or the proper view of self) and respectfulness (or the proper view of others). Viewing self and others correctly makes yielding easier. So, what is this Christian character trait of deference? Here's one way to define it:

> Deference is the volitional yielding to another person's opinion, judgment, need, wish, preference, or will.

God desires his children to consider others more important than themselves. From a biblical perspective, what does this character trait of deference look like, and how can Christians improve it? This lesson addresses these points under the headings of "God's Word to Mankind," "God's Work in Believers," and "God's Grace for Change."

God's Word to Mankind

Key Verses

"Be devoted to one another in brotherly love. Honor one another above yourselves" (Rom 12:10, NIV). Being devoted to others means committing time, energy, thoughts, and resources to them, implying less of these things for personal use. Such devotion involves sacrifice. In one of the great "one another" verses of the Bible, believers are commanded to prefer and honor others (especially fellow Christians) above themselves and to do so in kindness and tender affection that flows from brotherly love. Unlike the world, which often craves preeminence and self-honor, believers should consider others worthier than themselves. Without using the word, this verse paints a beautiful picture of what it means to show deference. Remember that Jesus told his disciples, "Love one another: just as I have loved you, you also are to love one another. By this all people will know that you are my disciples, if you have love for one another" (John 13:34–35). Deference is an expression of such love.

"If food makes my brother stumble, I will never eat meat, lest I make my brother stumble" (1 Cor 8:13). Pagans sacrificed animals to false gods, and local markets sold the leftover meat. Paul knew meat offered to idols was the same as other meat; buying and eating either was okay. However, some weaker believers (perhaps new converts) did not understand and associated the sacrificial meat with idol worship, tempting them to sin against their consciences. Out of loving concern for their spiritual well-being, Paul abstained from eating meat sacrificed to false gods. He yielded to and respected the feelings, opinions, and judgments of his weaker brethren, acting out of deferential love rather than from his knowledge.

Bible Characters

Amenable Abraham (Gen 13:5–13, 19:1–38)

The expanding herds of Abraham and his nephew, Lot, proved too great for the land, causing their herdsmen to quarrel over the limited grass and water. So, Abraham suggested they separate. As elder statesman, Abraham could have insisted on his rights, choosing the land he preferred and letting Lot take what was left. But instead, he proffered an amenable solution: "If you take the left hand, then I will go to the right, or if you take the right hand, then I will go to the left." In other words, Abraham deferred to Lot.

Presumably, Lot didn't hesitate to choose first. He departed for the lush and well-watered Jordan plain, which lay near the wicked city of Sodom. Later, he moved into Sodom itself but had to flee when God destroyed it. While fleeing, Lot's wife disobeyed God and died. Fearful of the cities, Lot relocated to a mountain cave with his two daughters. Ironically, after having chosen the best land, Lot ended up afraid to live in it.

Selfless Servant (Phil 2:3–8)

The self-absorbed person provides a stark contrast with the individual focused on others. Out of self-centered desire and empty pride, the former pushes opinions and judgments, gratifies self, and follows personal wishes and preferences. But the selfless servant yields humbly to the will of family, friends, and, indeed, people in general, prioritizing their needs when possible.

Jesus provides the supreme example of this latter person. Though "in the form of God," he "emptied himself, by taking the form of a servant." Though God, he became man and "humbled himself by becoming obedient to the point of death, even death on a cross." Jesus relinquished heaven's privileges to live a lowly human life and suffer a painful end. In divine love, he surrendered his own will to save the elect. He placed his people's needs and interests above his own.

Review Questions

1. What is the Christian character trait of deference?

2. What words are missing from this verse? "Be devoted to one _____ in brotherly love. _____ one another _____ yourselves" (Rom 12:10, NIV).

3. What words are missing from this verse? "If ____ makes my brother _____, I will _____ eat meat, lest I make my _____ stumble" (1 Cor 8:13).

4. What's wrong with eating meat offered to idols?

5. Regarding meat offered to false gods in 1 Cor 8:13, did the apostle Paul advocate acting out of love or based on knowledge?

6. How did Abraham defer to Lot?

7. What does Phil 2:3 say to do in humility?

8. Besides conducting their own affairs, what does Phil 2:4 instruct believers to do?

9. How did Christ Jesus provide the supreme example of deferential love?

God's Work in Believers

Deference often means not seeking your own self-interest. Don't be like "Diotrephes, who likes to put himself first" (3 John 9). Instead, in deference, become a servant, placing the needs of others before your own (Mark 10:44). Recall how the apostle Paul commended Timothy: "I have no one like him, who will be genuinely concerned for your welfare. For they all seek their own interests, not those of Jesus Christ" (Phil 2:20–21).

You will have many opportunities in life to show deference, including interchanges with those in authority over you. Except when doing so would be morally wrong, respectfully yield to parents, teachers, church leaders, employers, police, and others in authority. Deferring to these individuals doesn't mean you can't politely express an opinion or disagree. But after doing so, yield to the judgment or will of the person in authority. Show support for the decision in your demeanor, attitude, and words; don't pout, undermine, or otherwise signal your disagreement with the one in authority. Instead, respectfully and willingly defer to that individual's decision. This can be a very difficult thing to do, but don't rely on your own strength. Ask the Holy Spirit to empower you for the task.

Beyond authority figures, learn and practice deference with your peers: "Be devoted to one another in brotherly love. Honor one another above yourselves" (Rom 12:10, NIV). You can even defer to those under your charge if doing so doesn't abdicate your responsibilities. Recall how amenable Abraham gave preference to Lot on the matter of grass and water rights. Also, remember how Jesus became a selfless servant to others, even though he held the divine right of sovereign command. Pray for wisdom in how and when to defer to peers and subordinates.

In casual conversation, deferring sometimes means keeping silent after someone expresses an opinion differing from your own. People who regularly correct those around them, especially in inconsequential matters, lack deference. That doesn't mean you always must agree with everyone or you can't express your own opinion. However, deference may require withholding your opinion at times for the sake of maintaining peace, showing respect, or building up the body of Christ. Remaining quiet during such times can be extraordinarily hard, but the Holy Spirit can teach you deference.

God's Grace for Change

Before examining your heart, considering how you might improve, and seeking divine help, ponder an earlier point one last time—Jesus put your needs above his own, showing deference. He "emptied himself, by taking the form of a servant . . . [and] humbled himself by becoming obedient to the point of death, even death on a cross" (Phil 2:7–8). Let this brief reminder about and appreciation for God's undeserved grace prepare and motivate you to develop more of this lesson's character trait in yourself.

Then, complete the "Heart Assessment, Reflection, and Petition" (HARP) chart, assessing your own deference. Reflect on times the Holy Spirit enabled or empowered you to yield voluntarily to another person's opinion, judgment, need, wish, preference, or will as well as times Jesus showed deference during his earthly life. Consider whether the Spirit might be revealing a need for you to be more deferential. If you want God to increase your deference, put that desire in writing. This is a very important exercise that can help you respond to God's direction for your life. Plan to pray over your completed chart once or twice this next week.

Finally, talk to the Lord, using the words that follow or incorporating the thoughts into your own prayer: "Dear Father, I praise you for your steadfast love, great faithfulness, and abundant mercy. You are worthy of my obedience, submission, and deference. Forgive my many failures to honor you. Thank you for sending a Redeemer and Savior to pay for my sins and save me. Just as Jesus humbled himself and took on the nature of a servant, develop in me this character trait of deference. Holy Spirit, give me the power to yield willingly and graciously to others in my daily life and, so, become more and more like Jesus. Amen."

Remember, the Lord's help is vital to cultivating Christian character. Only his power can enable you to change. When you fail to show the character trait of deference, confess it before God and ask for his forgiveness and help.

HARP Chart for Deference

Definition: Deference is the volitional yielding to another person's opinion, judgment, need, wish, preference, or will.

Key verses: "Be devoted to one another in brotherly love. Honor one another above yourselves" (Rom 12:10, NIV). "If food makes my brother stumble, I will never eat meat, lest I make my brother stumble" (1 Cor 8:13).

Bible characters: Though the elder statesman, amenable Abraham offered Lot first choice of the land. Leaving heaven, the selfless servant surrendered his own will to save the elect and placed their needs above his own.

How often do you show deference in your life: 5 = nearly always, 4 = most of the time, 3 = about half the time, 2 = less than half the time, or 1 = hardly ever? Your response is ____.
In what ways, if any, has the Holy Spirit enabled you to show deference?
How did Jesus model deference during his earthly life in ways benefiting you?
In what ways, if any, has the Holy Spirit revealed to you a need to be more deferential?
What petition related to deference, if any, would you like to bring before the throne of grace?

Diligence

Engage in one or more of these introductory activities:

1. Movie Night—Watch "October Sky" (1999, PG) as a class or individually. The main character, young Homer Hickam, grows up in coal-mining country. After viewing Russia's Sputnik, he and three friends design and launch homemade rockets, making many mistakes along the way. What reasons might Homer have had for quitting? Why didn't he quit, and what benefits resulted from Homer's persistence?

2. Nature Study—Learn about ants and share your findings through online photos or short video clips. Perhaps the most populous and ubiquitous species on earth, the lowly ant demonstrates how steadfast effort and a never-say-die attitude accomplish great things over time. If available, display an ant farm (or an online video of one) and describe its operation, noting the colony's constant motion as each ant diligently carries out its assigned task. Read Aesop's Fable, "The Ant and the Grasshopper," and note how the ant worked hard while the grasshopper took it easy and procrastinated. "Go to the ant, O sluggard; consider her ways, and be wise. Without any chief, officer, or ruler, she prepares her bread in summer and gathers her food in harvest" (Prov 6:6–8). "Ants are a people not strong, yet they provide their food in the summer" (Prov 30:25). These passages expound further on the diligence of ants and contrast the nature of ants with that of slothful people, whom the Bible dubs sluggards.

3. Noah's Ark—Take a field trip to one of the life-size replicas: Ark Encounter in Williamstown, Kentucky; Creation Evidence Museum in Glen Rose, Texas; or Ark of Noah Foundation in Pasadena, California. Otherwise, use photos or video from their websites and other online resources to understand and appreciate the diligence

required to build the ark. Estimates vary, but one apologetics ministry says the vessel was 510 feet long (i.e., about 1½ times the length of a football field), 85 feet wide, and 51 feet tall.[1] The same organization estimates Noah built the ark in 55 to 75 years.[2]

For success, many endeavors require a firm commitment, hard work, and persistence. In a word, they call for diligence. A later lesson about responsibility draws on this character trait. But what is diligence? Here's one way to define it:

> Diligence means the persistent, steadfast pursuit of a worthwhile objective or purpose.

God desires his children to work hard and persevere in worthwhile endeavors throughout life. From a biblical perspective, what does this character trait of diligence look like, and how can Christians improve it? This lesson addresses these points under the headings of "God's Word to Mankind," "God's Work in Believers," and "God's Grace for Change."

God's Word to Mankind

Key Verses

"How long will you lie there, O sluggard? When will you arise from your sleep? A little sleep, a little slumber, a little folding of the hands to rest, and poverty will come upon you like a robber, and want like an armed man" (Prov 6:9–11). No matter how long the sleep nor how sufficient the rest, the sluggard desires more; he resists all inward misgivings and outward pressures to rise and get busy. Through long habit, indolence supplants all vestiges of diligence. The eventual outcome is poverty. Just as an armed robber steals a man's wallet, so inactivity and idleness lead to penury.

"Whatever you do, work heartily, as for the Lord and not for men" (Col 3:23). This command applies to all categories of work, whether school studies, employment, business and professional activities, home chores, church service, or random acts of kindness. Whatever the physical or mental labor, God desires it to be done with hearty vigor and enthusiasm. The key to fulfilling this command consistently involves a proper perspective. All work should be done predominantly for the Lord and

1. Answers in Genesis, "Noah's Ark," n.p.
2. Hodge, "How Long Did It Take?" n.p.

only secondarily for teachers, bosses, clients, family, fellow Christians, and other earthly masters and beneficiaries. This viewpoint or attitude incentivizes and promotes diligence.

Bible Characters

Resolute Ruth (Ruth 2:1–23)

Naomi, her husband, and their two sons lived in Bethlehem of Judah until famine forced them beyond the Dead Sea to Moab. In this foreign land, Naomi's husband died, her sons married Moabite women, and then her two sons died. Afterwards, Naomi heard Judah's famine was over and decided to return home. With nothing to offer her daughters-in-law, however, she urged them to remain in Moab. One indeed stayed, but the other, Ruth, embraced Naomi and said, "Where you go I will go, and where you lodge I will lodge" (Ruth 1:16). So, Naomi and Ruth traveled to Bethlehem, arriving just as barley harvest began.

In an agrarian society with little means of support, how could these two widowed women survive? Understanding their plight, Ruth went into the fields to gather any remaining grain after the reapers passed through. Day after day, Ruth picked up scraps, resolute in her purpose and diligent in her work. What she gleaned in daylight, she threshed in the evening and shared with her mother-in-law. Every day, she repeated her labors and, thus, provided for herself and Naomi until the barley and wheat harvests ended. Then, God rewarded Ruth's diligence, providing for her and Naomi through a man named Boaz.

Industrious Israelites (Neh 4:1–23, 6:1–16)

In 586 BC, Babylon destroyed Jerusalem and took many Judeans captive. But years later, some exiles returned to Judah. The first group returned in 539 BC under Zerubbabel and rebuilt the temple. In 458 BC, a second group returned under Ezra, the priest. Nehemiah led a third group back to Judah in 444 BC. He purposed to rebuild the wall around Jerusalem and, thus, provide for the returned exiles' protection and defense.

Wasting no time, Nehemiah inspected what little remained of the wall within three days of his arrival. To conceal his objective, he reconnoitered the once-glorious city's perimeter after dark, finding the wall in ruins and the city gates burned. But rather than being discouraged, Nehemiah formed a plan and presented it to the Israelites, who wholeheartedly agreed to begin the daunting project. So, Nehemiah divvied up the work, assigning different groups to rebuild gates while other groups constructed or repaired adjacent walls. Thus, the rebuilding effort progressed simultaneously at many points around the city. "We built the wall. And all the wall was joined together to half its height, for the people had a mind to work" (Neh 4:6). In short, the Israelites showed themselves industrious or diligent.

The Jews' steadfastness and persistence alarmed the land's non-Jewish inhabitants and their leaders—Sanballat, Tobiah, and Geshem—who schemed and threatened at every turn. However, Nehemiah responded strategically to each new danger. For example, he posted armed guards around the clock and instructed all workers to sleep within the city. When the vexatious trio requested a meeting outside the city, Nehemiah responded, "I am doing a great work and I cannot come down. Why should the work stop while I leave it and come down to you?" (Neh 6:3). When they accused Nehemiah of rebellion against Babylon, he prayed to God for strength (Neh 6:9). When they tried to frighten Nehemiah, he would not be intimidated (Neh 6:11). In the face of these troubles, did the diligence of Nehemiah and the Israelites pay off? It most certainly did since they completely rebuilt the wall around Jerusalem in just fifty-two days (Neh 6:15).

Review Questions

1. What is the Christian character trait of diligence?

2. What words are missing from these verses? "How long will you lie there, O _____? When will you arise from your _____? A little sleep, a little _____, a little folding of the hands to rest, and _____ will come upon you like a robber, and _____ like an armed man" (Prov 6:9–11).

3. What words come to mind that describe someone who is not diligent?

4. What words are missing from this verse? "_____ you do, work _____, as for the _____ and not for ___" (Col 3:23).

5. What words in Colossians 3:23 convey the idea of diligence?

6. How did Ruth show diligence?

7. How did Nehemiah show diligence?

8. How did the Israelites show diligence?

God's Work in Believers

Diligent people reveal their character in the way they approach and undertake assignments, projects, duties, chores, and other tasks. First, they firmly commit to the endeavor at hand and get busy. Second, they work steady and hard. Third, they persist through all obstacles and timely finish the job.

A firm commitment means, among other things, not procrastinating. Those who say they will do something but then find excuses not to begin may lack sincere commitment. Faltering at the starting gate, in turn, lessens the likelihood of finishing on time or even at all. Indeed, "procrastination is the thief of time."[3] So, as the old cliché goes, "Never do tomorrow what you can do today." Like Ruth and Nehemiah, hasten to start any new task. People who start timely often finish timely. As a bonus, they typically experience much less stress in their lives from impending deadlines. Indeed, procrastination and stress are inseparable first cousins. Therefore, with God's help, spurn and unlearn any ingrained habit to procrastinate so you might take the first step towards developing the Christian character trait of diligence.

Once you begin, work steady and hard like the ants in the nature study. Don't let every little hindrance and distraction sidetrack you; imitate Nehemiah who stayed on the job despite his enemies' attempts to delay, discourage, or stop him. Labor hard even when no one is watching or supervising. Strive to accomplish every task—even if routine, mundane, or menial—with excellence and on time; faithfulness and care in small things often carry over into large matters. Finally, don't work grudgingly or out of compulsion but wholeheartedly with alacrity and good cheer. Work principally for the Lord rather than to impress or please people (Col 3:23), relying on his strength rather than your own.

Starting promptly and working hard doesn't always assure success; you still must finish. Some people begin well but then falter when unexpected setbacks occur, difficult people discourage them, or life's little

---

3. Young, *The Complaint*, 12.

mishaps demand their attention. Then, feeling overwhelmed or helpless, they neglect to finish. Over time, this outcome repeats itself, becoming habit and a defeatist mindset. If this describes you, ask the Holy Spirit to change your heart and mind. Then, try pushing through each difficulty and accomplishing your goal despite unforeseen situations that, in the past, defeated you. With God's help, you'll learn to accomplish more than you expected and succeed where you thought it impossible. Finding out you can complete tasks, despite barriers, is a key element in becoming diligent. Indeed, diligent people expect obstacles and overcome them as a normal part of accomplishing worthwhile endeavors. Remember Noah, whom God strengthened and encouraged through many years as he completed an enormous ark to save his family and the animals.

Diligence can be a very difficult trait to cultivate, especially for someone with a deep-rooted tendency to procrastinate, dilly-dally, or quit. Nonetheless, God can do all things. If you lack diligence, approach the throne of grace humbly, confess your inability to complete tasks on time, and express your desire to develop this character trait.

God's Grace for Change

Before examining your heart, considering how you might improve, and seeking divine help, ponder one last point—God diligently searched for you amid sin's darkness and degradation. "As a shepherd [diligently] seeks out his flock when he is among his sheep that have been scattered, so will I seek out my sheep, and I will rescue them from all places where they have been scattered on a day of clouds and thick darkness" (Ezek 34:12). Let this brief reminder about and appreciation for God's undeserved grace prepare and motivate you to develop more of this lesson's character trait in yourself.

Then, complete the "Heart Assessment, Reflection, and Petition" (HARP) chart, assessing your own diligence. Reflect on times the Holy Spirit enabled or empowered you to be diligent in some assignment or task as well as times God and others worked diligently for your benefit. Consider whether the Spirit might be revealing a need for you to become more diligent. If you want God to increase your diligence, put that desire in writing. This is a very important exercise that can help you respond to God's direction for your life. Plan to pray over your completed chart once or twice this next week.

Finally, talk to the Lord, using the words that follow or incorporating the thoughts into your own prayer: "Great triune God, all your works are glorious and majestic. Indeed, you created the world in the space of six days and made everything very good. You also planned and carried out my salvation. I remember Christ's words on the cross—"It is finished"—and thank you that Jesus did not leave my redemption unfinished but persevered to the end through painful suffering and humiliation to save me from sin. My Father, many times in my life I have not been diligent in the work you have given me. Please forgive. Help me to overcome procrastination, work steady and hard, and persevere through and finish each task no matter the obstacles or difficulties. I need and ask for your grace to accomplish such things. Hear my voice and answer. I pray in Christ's name, who was diligent in his great work of redemption. Amen."

Remember, the Lord's help is vital to cultivating Christian character. Only his power can enable you to change. When you fail to show the character trait of diligence, confess it before God and ask for his forgiveness and help.

HARP Chart for Diligence

Definition: Diligence means the persistent, steadfast pursuit of a worthwhile objective or purpose.

Key verses: "How long will you lie there, O sluggard? When will you arise from your sleep? A little sleep, a little slumber, a little folding of the hands to rest, and poverty will come upon you like a robber, and want like an armed man" (Prov 6:9–11). "Whatever you do, work heartily, as for the Lord and not for men" (Col 3:23).

Bible characters: Resolute Ruth entered the fields day after day to glean behind the harvesters and, thus, provided food for herself and Naomi. Under Nehemiah's leadership, the industrious Israelites worked with all their hearts and finished building Jerusalem's walls in just 52 days.

How often do you show diligence in your life: 5 = nearly always, 4 = most of the time, 3 = about half the time, 2 = less than half the time, or 1 = hardly ever? Your response is ____.
In what ways, if any, has the Holy Spirit enabled you to show diligence?
In what ways, if any, have God and others worked diligently in ways benefiting you?
In what ways, if any, has the Holy Spirit revealed to you a need to become more diligent?
What petition related to diligence, if any, would you like to bring before the throne of grace?

Discernment

Engage in one or more of these introductory activities:

1. Intriguing Insights—The quotations below make observations about discernment. Explain each quotation's meaning or otherwise comment about it.

    "The supreme end of education, we are told, is expert discernment in all things."[1]

    "Let a man talk loudly and prettily, and many hearers will believe anything he says. Dear brothers and sisters, we must have discernment, or we shall be found aiding and abetting error!"[2]

    "The discernment of the Holy Spirit is not for the purposes of criticism, but for purposes of conversion [or intercession]."[3]

    "Everyone is prejudiced in favour of his own powers of discernment, and will always find an argument most convincing if it leads to the conclusion he has reached for himself."[4]

2. Nature Study—Learn about rufous hummingbirds and share your findings through online photos or video. In the fall, these tiny birds migrate from southern Alaska, western Canada, Washington, and Oregon to as far away as southern Mexico, a journey often exceeding three thousand miles. To survive, they fly through mountainous regions where wildflower nectar provides nourishment and energy.

1. Samuel Johnson as cited in Osgood, *Boswell's Life of Johnson*, xviii.
2. Spurgeon, "The Ear Bored," 7.
3. Chambers, "Studies in the Sermon," 81.
4. Pliny the Younger, *Letters*, 53.

In the spring, they return to their breeding grounds in Alaska and Canada but follow the Pacific coastline where they find different wildflowers from which to feed. Rufous hummers must discern the right time to migrate and the proper route. Leaving at the wrong time on such a long journey or selecting a route without sufficient flowers along the way can prove fatal.

3. Shapes and Sequences—In a class setting, select age- and skill-appropriate online exercises that ask individuals to identify, from among a group of shapes (or items), the one (a) differing from the others or (b) completing a pattern sequence. Such exercises commonly appear in intelligence, reasoning, or aptitude tests that require participants to distinguish between shapes (or items) meeting the specified requirement and those that don't. These exercises, in one sense, are like life—distinguishing between right and wrong choices sometimes proves challenging.

These activities show how important it is to assess situations correctly and how difficult that can be at times. In fact, an earlier lesson dealt with decisiveness, an attribute depending heavily on discernment. What is this Christian character trait of discernment? Here's one way to define it:

> Discernment is the keen ability to distinguish between right and wrong, truth and error, and good and evil.

God desires his children to discern the morality of their own choices, motives, actions, and opinions and, in many cases, those of others also. From a biblical perspective, what does this character trait of discernment look like, and how can Christians improve it? This lesson addresses these points under the headings of "God's Word to Mankind," "God's Work in Believers," and "God's Grace for Change."

God's Word to Mankind

Key Verses

"Give your servant therefore an understanding mind to govern your people, that I may discern between good and evil" (1 Kgs 3:9). The enormous responsibilities confronting the young, inexperienced Solomon daunted him. How could he administer justice when God's people were

so numerous, their disputes were so complex, and he was so unproven? In this apprehensive state, God asked Solomon what he most desired. Solomon could have requested longevity, riches, triumph over enemies, honor, or fame. But instead, confessing ignorance and uneasiness in civic matters, he requested the ability to distinguish right from wrong. This request for discernment pleased God.

"Do not despise prophecies, but test everything; hold fast what is good. Abstain from every form of evil" (1 Thess 5:20–22). The apostle Paul admonishes believers to listen respectfully to preaching but test whether what they hear squares with Scripture (cf. Acts 17:11, which mentioned the Thessalonians). Stated differently, the elect should avoid two extremes—they should not scorn genuine attempts to preach truth, but neither should they automatically accept every word as absolute truth simply because it came from a preacher's lips, even if spoken passionately or eloquently. Indeed, those teaching error from the pulpit come in two forms. Some are false prophets who seek to deceive while others are well-meaning servants who sometimes miss the bullseye of complete truth. In fact, even the most erudite, sincere, and meticulous Bible expositors speak amiss at times. Therefore, the elect should test every sermon's opinions, assertions, interpretations, and applications against the only legitimate touchstone—God's infallible Word. In so doing, believers seek to discern between doctrines that are (a) true and, thus, to be embraced and followed and (b) erroneous and, thus, to be rejected or dismissed.

Bible Characters

Astute Abigail (1 Sam 25:1–35)

On the run from King Saul, David respectfully asked Nabal to share provisions from his bounty, especially since David and his six hundred men had protected Nabal's sheep. Nabal could have shared from his great abundance or, if not, politely declined. But instead, he rebuffed David's request with a particularly churlish, disparaging response, stinging David's ego. Though a man after God's own heart, David lost his temper and, lacking discernment at that moment, set out to kill Nabal and those near him.

Panicked over Nabal's surly, foolish treatment of David, the servants alerted Nabal's wife, Abigail. She, in turn, loaded donkeys with food and wine and intercepted David. Showing discernment, she acknowledged her husband's wicked folly and yet gently advised David to forgo revenge and avoid "grief or pangs of conscience for having shed blood without cause or . . . working salvation himself." In short, she discerned her husband's evil temperament and words while, at the same time, gently entreated David not to respond in kind, which also would have been wrong. Recognizing the truth of her words, David said, "Blessed be you, who have kept me this day from bloodguilt and from working salvation with my own hand!"

Sagacious Solomon (1 Kgs 3:16–28)

God granted King Solomon's request for a discerning heart (1 Kgs 3:9). Then, one day, a particularly difficult situation put Solomon's God-given discernment on full display. Two prostitutes and a baby appeared before the king with a troubling tale. Both women bore a male child just three days apart. However, one baby died during the night, and, in the morning, each woman claimed the living child as her own. To whom did the baby belong?

Solomon listened carefully to both women before deciding what to do. Noting the passion of each, Solomon called for a sword and ordered the living child to be divided between the two mothers. The surprising edict, no doubt, caught the two women unawares, resulting in outbursts that revealed the truth. One immediately changed her plea to one of sparing the little boy: "Oh, my lord, give her the living child, and by no means put him to death." But the other pronounced the king's order just: "He shall be neither mine nor yours; divide him." Solomon discerned the first woman, who desired above all else to spare the child, was the true mother.

Review Questions

1. What is the Christian character trait of discernment?

2. What words are missing from this verse? "Give your servant therefore an _____ mind to _____ your people, that I may _____ between good and evil" (1 Kgs 3:9).

3. Why did Solomon ask God for a discerning heart?

4. What words are missing from these verses? "Do not despise _____, but ____ everything; hold fast what is ____. Abstain from every form of ____" (1 Thess 5:20–22).

5. "Now these Jews [in Berea] were more noble than those in Thessalonica; they received the word with all eagerness, examining the Scriptures daily to see if these things were so" (Acts 17:11). How does this verse relate to 1 Thess 5:20–22?

6. Who lacked discernment, David or Nabal?

7. How did Abigail show discernment?

8. What was it about the case before Solomon that required him to be discerning?

9. How did Solomon show discernment in adjudicating the case of the two prostitutes?

God's Work in Believers

As a character trait, discernment yields several benefits. First, it promotes good and wise moral decisions. As the quintessential human example, King Solomon discerned the baby's true mother in a case that would have stumped other judges. Second, a person of discernment profits from the advice and reproof of others, not rejecting good counsel or appropriate correction through undue defensiveness, denial, or pride. "By insolence comes nothing but strife, but with those who take advice is wisdom [including discernment]" (Prov 13:10). "A rebuke goes deeper into a man of understanding [or discernment] than a hundred blows into a fool" (Prov 17:10). Third, the discerning spirit responds wisely to evil influences, thoughts, and deeds. Recall how Abagail understood her husband's wrong and the likelihood that David also might react indefensibly, which led her to avert much wrong and harm. Fourth, discernment protects the elect from deceivers and falsehoods. "Do not believe every spirit, but test the spirits [through discernment] to see whether they are from God, for many false prophets have gone out into the world" (1 John 4:1).

But these benefits beg the question: How can you acquire or increase discernment? As with other character traits, you can't simply try harder and get the sought-after results. Though good to desire and seek discernment, any gains ultimately depend on God.

To begin, regularly study and obey the Scriptures. Don't just nibble at the crumbs of elementary truths but feed deeply on the meat of solid doctrine, noting particularly the Bible's demarcation line between right and wrong, truth and error, good and evil. The "solid food [of God's Word] is for the mature, for those who have their powers of discernment trained by constant practice to distinguish good from evil" (Heb 5:14).

Also, ask the Holy Spirit for spiritual insight into your own choices, motives, actions, and opinions. "Who can discern his errors? Declare me innocent from hidden faults" (Ps 19:12). Honestly, carefully, and habitually discerning things about yourself can be humbling, but this personal introspection provides an essential and solid foundation for judging the choices, motives, actions, and opinions of other people. Indeed, neglecting the former while specializing in the latter runs the risk of base hypocrisy. Pray for a keen ability to distinguish between right and wrong, truth and error, and good and evil in all aspects of your life and then, as appropriate and necessary, the lives of others. Of course, the Holy Spirit bestows discernment on some believers more than others. Thus, when lacking discernment, seek counsel from saints whom God has made especially wise.

God's Grace for Change

Complete the "Heart Assessment, Reflection, and Petition" (HARP) chart, assessing your own discernment. Reflect on times the Holy Spirit enabled or empowered you to be discerning. Then, consider whether the Spirit might be revealing a need for you to become more discerning. If you want God to increase your discernment, put that desire in writing. This is a very important exercise that can help you respond to God's direction for your life. Plan to pray over your completed chart once or twice this next week.

Finally, talk to the Lord, using the words that follow or incorporating the thoughts into your own prayer: "Heavenly Father, how righteous are your ways, how pure your truth, how perfect your goodness, and how wise your thoughts. Thank you for being my God and allowing me to be one of your people. Though you have made me a new creature in Christ, I often show little discernment in my choices, motives, actions, and opinions. Holy Spirit, teach me to distinguish between right and wrong, truth and error, good and evil. In doing so, help me to obey and serve you better. Day by day, conform me to the image of Christ. In his holy name, amen."

Remember, the Lord's help is vital to cultivating Christian character. Only his power can enable you to change. When you fail to show the character trait of discernment, confess it before God and ask for his forgiveness and help.

HARP Chart for Discernment

Definition: Discernment is the keen ability to distinguish between right and wrong, truth and error, and good and evil.

Key verses: "Give your servant therefore an understanding mind to govern your people, that I may discern between good and evil" (1 Kgs 3:9). "Do not despise prophecies, but test everything; hold fast what is good. Abstain from every form of evil" (1 Thess 5:20–22).

Bible characters: Astutely assessing the conflict, Abagail prevented vengeful bloodshed with gifts and sound words. Using his God-given discernment, Solomon determined which of two women was a baby's true mother.

How often do you show discernment in your life: 5 = nearly always, 4 = most of the time, 3 = about half the time, 2 = less than half the time, or 1 = hardly ever? Your response is _____.
In what ways, if any, has the Holy Spirit enabled you to show discernment?
In what ways, if any, has the Holy Spirit revealed to you a need for more discernment?
What petition related to discernment, if any, would you like to bring before the throne of grace?

Endurance

Engage in one or more of these introductory activities:

1. Movie Night—Watch "Iron Will" (1994, PG) as a class or individually. Seventeen-year-old Will Stoneman competes in a 522-mile dogsledding competition to save the family business. Battling the elements, his lead dog, vicious competitors, an initially skeptical public, a snide reporter, sleep deprivation, and his own inexperience, the young, indomitable musher shows inspiring courage and perseverance. What obstacles did Will face, and how did he overcome each one?

2. Nature Study—Learn about camels[1] and share your findings through online photos or short video clips. Native to Africa, Asia, and the Middle East, these even-toed ungulates have become mostly domesticated pack or saddle animals, valued for their great endurance. As "ships of the desert," they plod long distances in extreme heat. Their humps store fat for energy, and several physical features allow them to preserve water, avoiding dehydration. For instance, thirsty camels can binge drink thirty or more gallons of water, storing it in their digestive and circulatory systems many days. Their thick coats provide so much insulation that they rarely lose moisture through sweating. Also, when exhaling, some moisture becomes trapped in their nostrils and is reabsorbed into the body.

3. Physical Challenge—Choose an appropriate physical event that would be moderately challenging like running an obstacle course, climbing a steep hill, or hiking a few miles. If done as a class, encourage everyone to complete the event, enduring to the end, even

---

1. The initial idea of associating camels' abilities with the character trait of endurance came from Carden and Carden, *Christian Character Curriculum* 3, 3.

if they must stop to rest. Who completes the event first (or last) is unimportant but whether each person finishes. Explain afterwards that enduring through life's mental, emotional, and spiritual challenges can be difficult too.

These activities introduce the concept of endurance or persevering through tasks or experiences until their completion. Endurance bears some resemblance to a later lesson's trait—patience. But whereas patience involves calm amid difficulties, endurance requires persistence through difficulties. More specifically, this lesson's Christian character trait can be defined like this:

> Endurance is the capacity to withstand or accept prolonged or intense pain, hardship, misfortune, persecution, affliction, testing, discipline, or other adversity without quitting or losing heart.

God desires his children to endure through difficult times to accomplish worthwhile tasks, achieve honorable objectives, and glorify Christ. From a biblical perspective, what does this character trait of endurance look like, and how can Christians improve it? This lesson addresses these points under the headings of "God's Word to Mankind," "God's Work in Believers," and "God's Grace for Change."

God's Word to Mankind

Key Verses

"It is for discipline that you have to endure. God is treating you as sons. For what son is there whom his father does not discipline?" (Heb 12:7). God sometimes sends hardship that must be endured to discipline his people, either as chastisement for unrepentant sin or a trial to strengthen and improve character. At the time, these hardships seem unpleasant and painful. However, in sending them, God acts as a benevolent, loving Father to his adopted sons and daughters. Far from being the harsh punishment associated with God's wrath, this discipline restores those who stray, prepares and strengthens others for future service, and produces holiness, righteousness, and peace (Heb 12:11).

"This is a gracious thing, when, mindful of God, one endures sorrows while suffering unjustly. For what credit is it if, when you sin and are beaten for it, you endure? But if when you do good and suffer for it you endure,

this is a gracious thing in the sight of God" (1 Pet 2:19–20). It is a "gracious" or commendable thing when saints endure unjust pain because of their awareness of or focus on the Lord. Note the three essential conditions resulting in divine approval. First, the discomfort or misery must be undeserved; pain attributable to the sufferer's wrongdoing is not praiseworthy but justice. Second, the individual must bear up under or endure the pain without rebelling or grumbling. Third, the motive or influence behind the endurance must be "mindful[ness] of God." That is, the sufferer must view the endurance as the Father's will, a duty to him, and an act that brings him glory. In effect, the sufferer's conscience must look to God for approval and wait on him for justice or deliverance. This uncommon kind of endurance magnifies the Lord.

Bible Characters

Silent Sufferer (Matt 26:57–67 and 27:11–14, 27–50)

The Christian's quintessential example of submissive endurance is Jesus. During his three-year earthly ministry, Jesus often experienced privation, conflict, derision, persecution, and rejection. But the hostility against him reached fever pitch during the evil mockery and torture surrounding his so-called trial. From the Sanhedrin's illegal proceedings to the undeserved beatings and abuse, he endured severe mental, emotional, and physical anguish. Then, following the unjust sentence, Jesus submitted to the cruel death of a Roman crucifixion amid the disdain and callous taunts of the soldiers and Jewish leaders.

How did Jesus bear this intense suffering? Strikingly, he bore much of the injustice in silence. "When he was reviled, he did not revile in return; when he suffered, he did not threaten, but continued entrusting himself to [the Father] who judges justly" (1 Pet 2:23). At trial, Jesus responded to some queries, but he kept quiet whenever the religious leaders and their unscrupulous witnesses hurled false accusations at him, refusing to defend or acquit himself. He also remained silent when Pilate tried unsuccessfully to release him. "He was oppressed, and he was afflicted, yet he opened not his mouth; like a lamb that is led to the slaughter, and like a sheep that before its shearers is silent, so he opened not his mouth" (Isa 53:7). Even while on the cross, he declined to summon legions of angelic warriors to rescue him (Matt 26:53).

Why did Jesus endure this painful suffering when he could have mustered heaven's host? Why did Jesus never give up, quit, or lose heart? He endured to save the elect through his substitutionary atonement for sin; without his endurance, they would have been lost. Moreover, he set the perfect example of how to endure this life's pains, hardships, misfortunes, persecutions, afflictions, tests, and other adversities. "[Jesus] endured the cross, despising the shame, and is seated at the right hand of the throne of God. Consider him who endured from sinners such hostility against himself, so that you may not grow weary or fainthearted" (Heb 12:2–3).

Tenacious Toilers (2 Tim 2:3–12)

Telling Timothy to expect and bear adversity in gospel ministry, the apostle Paul gave three examples of endurance that require intense, focused labor. Soldiers devotedly follow their commanding officers, leaving little time for civilian pursuits or entanglements; their military lives involve sacrifice, strict discipline, fatigue, deprivation, and peril. Likewise, successful athletes train often and hard for their competitive events, and tireless farmers spend many long days preparing soil, planting seeds, and tending crops.

Those engaged in all three occupations tenaciously toil for worthwhile goals. Soldiers train for battle, athletes prepare to win competitive events, and farmers seek bountiful harvests. To succeed, they must not quit, get sidetracked, or lose heart. Similarly, Paul instructed his young protégé to endure earthly hardship for the elect's sake, pursuing heavenly rewards.

Review Questions

1. What is the Christian character trait of endurance?

2. What words are missing from this verse? "It is for _____ that you have to _____. God is treating you as ____. For what son is there whom his _____ does not discipline?" (Heb 12:7).

3. For what reasons does God discipline the saints through hardship?

4. What four truths help believers endure hardship without resisting, murmuring, or complaining?

5. Sometimes, the correct response to chastisement is silence. In the context of Heb 12:7, what does this mean?

6. What words are missing from these verses? "This is a _____ thing, when, mindful of ___, one _____ sorrows while suffering _____. For what credit is it if, when you ___ and are beaten for it, you _____? But if when you do good and _____ for it you _____, this is a _____ thing in the sight of God" (1 Pet 2:19–20).

7. According to 1 Pet 2:19–20, what three conditions must exist before a believer in pain is commendable before God?

8. "If you are insulted for the name of Christ, you are blessed, because the Spirit of glory and of God rests upon you. But let none of you suffer as a murderer or a thief or an evildoer or as a meddler. Yet if anyone suffers as a Christian, let him not be ashamed, but let him glorify God in that name" (1 Pet 4:14–16). How do these verses relate to 1 Pet 2:19–20?

9. Generally, when and how did Jesus suffer hardship?

10. How did Jesus endure the hardship surrounding his trial and crucifixion?

11. What words are missing from this verse? "He was _____, and he was _____, yet he opened not his _____; like a lamb that is led to the _____, and like a sheep that before its shearers is _____, so he _____ not his mouth" (Isa 53:7).

12. What two reasons explain why Jesus never gave up but, instead, endured the pain of crucifixion?

13. What three occupations does the apostle Paul give Timothy as examples of endurance?

14. In Paul's three examples, what evidences the respective endurance of each occupation or calling?

15. In Paul's three examples, what are the worthwhile goals of each occupation or calling?

16. What did Paul's three examples teach Timothy about endurance?

God's Work in Believers

At times, the Christian life entails prolonged or intense pain, hardship, misfortune, persecution, affliction, testing, discipline, or other adversity. How should you think about and respond to such difficulties? Some people lash out at God or others and may even sink into depression or self-pity. But you should: (a) consider the adversity's origin, (b) understand that a biblical response involves endurance, (c) apprehend the nature of biblical endurance, and (d) remain confident in the outcome of godly endurance. Only God provides power to endure the many difficulties in this life; seek his help before the throne of grace.

First, consider the adversity's origin. In his perfect wisdom, God sent your difficulty or allowed it to occur. "In the day of prosperity be joyful, and in the day of adversity consider: God has made the one as well as the other" (Eccl 7:14). Moreover, the Lord has a purpose in each difficulty you experience. "For those who love God all things [including adversities] work together for good, for those who are called according to his purpose" (Rom 8:28).

Second, understand that a biblical response to adversity involves endurance. "It is for discipline that you have to endure" (Heb 12:7). This does not mean, of course, you cannot pray for relief, nor does it preclude you from taking righteous and just steps to alleviate your pain, hardship, misfortune, persecution, or other adversity. It does mean, however, that, while praying or taking proper steps, you should endure. Furthermore, if God delays long in his answer, you should continue enduring. Indeed, as noted below, waiting for God goes to the very nature of endurance.

Third, apprehend the nature of biblical endurance. Don't confuse it with mere Stoicism, which is only a philosophical indifference to adversity or mental repression of emotions. True biblical endurance requires a spiritual focus rather than one involving only the mind. Neither is endurance just hopeless resignation to fate. But if endurance does not mean these things, what does it mean? True biblical endurance requires you to be "mindful of God" (1 Pet 2:19), understanding your adversity as loving discipline. "Shall we not . . . be subject to the Father of spirits and live?" (Heb 12:9). Quietly wait on the Father's justice and timing, just as the Lamb of God silently suffered through his painful trial and death. Resist grumbling and murmuring even if you must suffer long and wrongfully. Like the three tenacious toilers, bear up, don't quit, and never lose heart. As the struggle prolongs or unexpected setbacks occur, return your focus to God and plunge ahead with renewed vigor to do his will. "We do not lose heart. Though our outer self is wasting away, our inner self is being renewed day by day. For this light momentary affliction is preparing for us an eternal weight of glory beyond all comparison, as we look not to the things that are seen but to the things that are unseen. For the things that are seen are transient, but the things that are unseen are eternal" (2 Cor 4:16–18).

Fourth, remain confident in the outcome of godly endurance. "In due season we will reap, if we do not give up" (Gal 6:9). "You have need of endurance, so that when you have done the will of God you may receive what is promised" (Heb 10:36). Specifically, God promises endurance will develop your overall character. "Suffering produces endurance, and endurance produces character" (Rom 5:3–4). "Let steadfastness [endurance] have its full effect, that you may be perfect and complete, lacking in nothing" (Jas 1:4). "After you have suffered a little while, the God of all grace . . . will himself restore, confirm, strengthen, and establish you" (1 Pet 5:10). As the apostle Paul put it, "I am content with weaknesses, insults, hardships, persecutions, and calamities. For when I am weak, then I am strong" (2 Cor 12:10).

God's Grace for Change

Before examining your heart, considering how you might improve, and seeking divine help, ponder one last point—To stop his suffering, Jesus could have summoned thousands of angels (Matt 26:53). But his deep love for you compelled him to endure, finishing redemption's work (John 19:30). Let this brief reminder about and appreciation for God's undeserved grace prepare and motivate you to develop more of this lesson's character trait in yourself.

Then, complete the "Heart Assessment, Reflection, and Petition" (HARP) chart, assessing your own endurance. Reflect on times the Holy Spirit enabled or empowered you to endure some adversity as well as times Jesus showed endurance during his earthly life. Consider whether the Spirit might be revealing a need for you to show more endurance. If you want God to increase your endurance, put that desire in writing. This is a very important exercise that can help you respond to God's direction for your life. Plan to pray over your completed chart once or twice this next week.

Finally, talk to the Lord, using the words that follow or incorporating the thoughts into your own prayer: "Great is the Lord and greatly to be praised. I bow before you, confessing that I often sin in many ways, asking again for your grace—please forgive me. How thankful I am that you called me to salvation and that, even now, you prepare me for my heavenly home. As part of this process, I understand that you often send or allow pain, hardship, misfortune, persecution, affliction, testing, discipline, and other adversities. I am thankful for these because they come from your hand, my loving Father. Enable me to endure these difficulties without grumbling, complaining, or giving up. Use them to develop my character and make me spiritually mature. Use them to make me more like Jesus, the silent sufferer who redeemed me. In his name, amen."

Remember, the Lord's help is vital to cultivating Christian character. Only his power can enable you to change. When you fail to show the character trait of endurance, confess it before God and ask for his forgiveness and help.

HARP Chart for Endurance

Definition: Endurance is the capacity to withstand or accept prolonged or intense pain, hardship, misfortune, persecution, affliction, testing, discipline, or other adversity without quitting or losing heart.

Key verses: "It is for discipline that you have to endure. God is treating you as sons. For what son is there whom his father does not discipline?" (Heb 12:7). "This is a gracious thing, when, mindful of God, one endures sorrows while suffering unjustly. For what credit is it if, when you sin and are beaten for it, you endure? But if when you do good and suffer for it you endure, this is a gracious thing in the sight of God" (1 Pet 2:19–20).

Bible characters: During his trial and crucifixion for the elect, Jesus often suffered in silence. Just as soldiers, athletes, and farmers tenaciously toil for their goals, so Paul instructed Timothy to endure hardship with his eyes focused on eternity.

How often do you show endurance in your life: 5 = nearly always, 4 = most of the time, 3 = about half the time, 2 = less than half the time, or 1 = hardly ever? Your response is ____.
In what ways, if any, has the Holy Spirit enabled you to show endurance?
How did Jesus model endurance during his earthly life in ways benefiting you?
In what ways, if any, has the Holy Spirit revealed to you a need to be more enduring?
What petition related to endurance, if any, would you like to bring before the throne of grace?

Fairness

Engage in one or more of these introductory activities:

1. Brainstorm—Think of several people in the Bible who showed themselves fair-minded towards others, giving reasons for your selections. You might mention how Moses desired fairness when disputes arose between individuals and judged these matters himself, later appointing honest judges to rule in his place (Exod 18). Next, consider biblical characters who were unfair and, again, mention reasons. For instance, King Ahab and his wife, Jezebel, had Naboth murdered so they could steal his vineyard (1 Kgs 21). Likewise, Laban dealt deceitfully with Jacob in the nuptial matter of Leah and Rachel (Gen 29:15–28).

2. Movie Night—Watch "To Kill a Mockingbird" (1962, NR) as a class or individually. Atticus Finch, a small-town lawyer, represents a black client, Tom Robinson. Due to racial prejudice, Tom is falsely accused and, later, wrongly convicted of raping a white woman. Atticus' children, Jem and Scout, confront a different kind of bias involving their reclusive neighbor, "Boo" Radley. Give specific instances in which people treated Tom and Boo justly or unjustly. What other examples of equity or inequity appeared in the video?

These activities show the varied contexts in which issues of fairness or unfairness might arise. But what is this Christian character trait of fairness? Here's one way to define it:

> Fairness occurs when people apply the same rules and standards in the same way to everyone and treat others as they would themselves like to be treated.

God desires his children to treat everyone fairly. From a biblical perspective, what does this character trait of fairness look like, and how can Christians improve it? This lesson addresses these points under the headings of "God's Word to Mankind," "God's Work in Believers," and "God's Grace for Change."

God's Word to Mankind

Key Verses

"You shall not be partial to the poor or defer to the great, but in righteousness shall you judge your neighbor" (Lev 19:15). In all matters, be fair and just. Favor neither the poor nor the rich, the weak nor the great. Don't let pity for the poor nor awe of the great signify. Instead, assess everyone impartially on each situation's facts. Base decisions on a cause's merits, not the people involved. Only then are judgments true, righteous, and fair.

"Whatever you wish that others would do to you, do also to them, for this is the Law and the Prophets" (Matt 7:12). Often, people act in thoughtless ways, failing to consider sensitivities, needs, and desires beyond their own. For such neglectful proclivities, the practical remedy involves a mental swap, placing yourself in the position of others and carefully considering what is fair and just from the latter's perspective. Known as the Golden Rule, this moral precept closely parallels the second greatest commandment—"Love your neighbor as yourself." Indeed, Jesus characterized both rule and commandment as summarizing everything the Law and Prophets teach about proper human relationships and interactions (Matt 22:39–40).

Bible Characters

Just Jonathan (1 Sam 20)

Early in their acquaintance, Jonathan became steadfast friends with the young shepherd and brave warrior named David (1 Sam 18:1–4). However, David's military victories stoked a spiteful, unjust jealousy in Jonathan's father, King Saul (1 Sam 18:15–16, 30). The king feared David's battlefield exploits would overshadow his own accomplishments and eventually lead to David replacing him on Israel's throne. On several occasions, Saul even tried to kill him (1 Sam 18:10—19:15).

Jonathan's natural love for and devotion to his father could have diminished or, perhaps, ended his friendship with David. His familial inclinations could have prejudiced Jonathan, causing him to view David like his father did, as a potential threat or usurper. Yet, that never happened. When David said Saul wished to kill him, Jonathan wondered if his best friend might be mistaken. Nonetheless, he listened and devised ways to test the legitimacy of David's fear. When circumstances proved Saul's murderous intent, Jonathan helped David escape and sorrowed greatly to see him go. Without doubt, Jonathan treated David the way he would have wanted David to treat him if their roles had been reversed. Jonathan treated David fairly.

Prejudiced Placements (Jas 2:1–9)

Jesus is all glorious in his person and work. He is worthy of all glory and praise because of marvelous things like his steadfast love, great faithfulness, absolute truth, pure holiness, eternal greatness, genuine goodness, and saving work of redemption. With such solid reasons for exalting his name, why should believers ever become smarmy and wheedling around the rich? How can such a temporal, fleeting characteristic such as wealth compare with the glorious attributes and work of Christ? On what basis and under what circumstances should Christians extol or lionize mere humans based on their money? Believers must beware of glorifying earthly things like property and carefully examine their motives whenever such temptations arise.

Of course, it's okay to respect and honor the rich in some ways if the poor, under similar circumstances, receive the same respect and honor. To do otherwise discriminates; it acts on evil thoughts such as (a) the rich are good people, but the poor are not, and (b) currying favor with the rich can benefit me, while doing so with the poor cannot. It distinguishes between people based on their wallet's bulk or void and, thus, betrays rank favoritism. In addition, it breaks the "royal law," which instructs, "Love your neighbor [e.g., the poor] as yourself." In short, prejudiced placements of guests around a table and similar discriminations based on economic means violate the moral law.

Review Questions

1. What is the Christian character trait of fairness?

2. What words are missing from this verse? "You shall not be _____ to the poor or defer to the _____, but in _____ shall you judge your neighbor" (Lev 19:15).

3. What words are missing from this verse? "_____ you wish that _____ would do to you, do also to them, for this is the ___ and the _____" (Matt 7:12).

4. What is the principle found in Matt 7:12 commonly called?

5. How are the Golden Rule and the second greatest commandment similar?

6. Why did Saul treat David unfairly?

7. How did Jonathan prove himself fair?

8. Why does Jas 2:1–9 begin with a reference to the glorious nature of the Lord Jesus Christ?

9. What kind of evil thoughts might someone harbor who unjustly discriminates between the rich and poor?

God's Work in Believers

Fairness (or its lack) permeates and influences all segments of society. Where it abounds, relationships flourish, and society prospers. Conversely, where the populace neglects or rejects it, much misery and heartache result. Fairness affects legal proceedings, business matters, civil discourse, and personal interactions. But regardless of what course the culture or community at large takes, God expects individual believers to deal fairly in all aspects of their lives. "Blessed are they who observe justice, who do righteousness at all times!" (Ps 106:3). Of course, biblical fairness depends on the Holy Spirit's work in your life rather than your own self-effort; pray for the grace to be always just.

Being fair means (a) applying the same rules to everyone in the same way and (b) treating others as you wish to be treated. The first yardstick considers how you would treat others in a similar situation; it bridles prejudice, partiality, and favoritism. The second requires an introspective contemplation of how you'd like to be treated if roles were reversed. Generally, both notions of fairness lead to the same result for mature Christians. But sometimes, you might find one easier to apply than the other.

Consider the first notion—applying the same rules to everyone in the same way. With God's help, hate and eschew all prejudiced placements and other unfair, discriminatory acts. Don't treat someone better or worse based on their race, gender, ethnicity, age, wealth, appearance, fame, or other irrelevancy. Remember the impartiality of Jesus who ate with sinners and touched lepers (Matt 8:2–3; 9:10–11). He treated people even-handedly, and so should you. Recall how he disconcerted the hypocritical religious leaders, not pulling his oratorical punches through either fear of offending or desire for gain (e.g., Matt 23:27; John 8:44). Jesus did not show favoritism to the high and mighty, and neither should you. In all situations, Jesus treated people according to their words and deeds, not according to artificial contrivances that do not really matter. Focus on the worth of people, not the magnitude of their earnings or capital. Never let earthly grandeur bedazzle nor a distorted sense of social justice legitimize unfair harm to another. Instead, glorify God in all things, including your treatment of others. "You shall not be partial to the poor or defer to the great, but in righteousness shall you judge your neighbor" (Lev 19:15).

The second notion, known as the Golden Rule, is pure genius in its potent brevity—treat others as you desire to be treated. Closely resembling the admonition to love others as you love yourself, it appraises fairness through a mental role reversal, providing moral guidance in myriad daily situations. This requires God's grace also. For example, suppose someone callously embarrassed Lee in front of others, and Lee feels disgraced and humiliated. At the very least, the Golden Rule would restrain you from doing anything to embarrass Lee further. But you might ask yourself, "If I was Lee, would I want someone to encourage me privately or, perhaps even, publicly assist me?" Your answer will help guide what you say or do. Here's another example. Assume you find someone's wallet in a parking lot on Monday morning. It contains an ATM card, four credit cards, $140 cash, a driver's license, a list of usernames and passwords, and several retail and identification cards. How quickly would you try to find the owner, and how hard would you try? Would you wait until Tuesday to seek the wallet's owner? If you could not locate anyone within an hour, would you stop trying? Does the Golden Rule suggest you seek sooner and search longer? What would you desire if someone found your lost wallet?

Hear one final word about the Golden Rule—apply it with some measure of common sense. Suppose you are a judge who must pronounce sentence on a man guilty of first-degree murder. Mentally switching roles, you might wish for a very light sentence in his situation, say, one year parole with no prison time. However, you cannot pronounce such a lenient sentence when all sense of justice forbids it and the citizenry whom you serve would strongly oppose it. More appropriately, you might cast yourself in society's role and ask how the populace would want you to pronounce sentence or what they might deem fair and just. Would they desire you to release someone who has committed murder and might do so again, perhaps harming those near and dear to them? Thus, the Golden Rule must be applied only after considering proper legal boundaries as well as the welfare of everyone affected. Consider another example. If a friend is having a bad day and you wish to cheer her, would you think, "A cup of coffee would lift my spirits, so I'm going to fix her a piping hot cup of joe," even though you know she dislikes coffee but loves iced chai? Of course, not—you'd chill some chai for her! So, the Golden Rule must be applied with a sensible dose of levelheadedness. You must consider not only what you would want in the other person's situation but also what you would want if you had all her likes and dislikes.

God's Grace for Change

Complete the "Heart Assessment, Reflection, and Petition" (HARP) chart, assessing your own fairness. Reflect on times the Holy Spirit enabled or empowered you to be equitable, impartial, or just towards others. Then, consider whether the Spirit might be revealing a need for you to be fairer in some dealings or situations. If you want God to increase your fairness, put that desire in writing. This is a very important exercise that can help you respond to God's direction for your life. Plan to pray over your completed chart once or twice this next week.

Finally, talk to the Lord, using the words that follow or incorporating the thoughts into your own prayer: "Great Father of glory, your judgments are always righteous and perfect. In striking contrast, I often treat others unfairly. Forgive me when I show partiality, display favoritism, make prejudiced placements, or fail to heed the Golden Rule. Conform me to the image of Jesus, who was impartial and fair in all his dealings with mankind. Make me quick to listen and slow to judge, treating others as I wish to be treated. Keep me from discriminating against or unduly favoring anyone based on race, gender, ethnicity, age, resources, appearance, or popularity. Thank you for the victories you grant me, the times you have caused me to be fair and just. Through your continued grace, sanctify me more and more in the days ahead. Holy Spirit, teach me to be fair with others. Amen."

Remember, the Lord's help is vital to cultivating Christian character. Only his power can enable you to change. When you fail to show the character trait of fairness, confess it before God and ask for his forgiveness and help.

HARP Chart for Fairness

Definition: Fairness occurs when people apply the same rules and standards in the same way to everyone and treat others as they would themselves like to be treated.

Key verses: "You shall not be partial to the poor or defer to the great, but in righteousness shall you judge your neighbor" (Lev 19:15). "Whatever you wish that others would do to you, do also to them, for this is the Law and the Prophets" (Matt 7:12).

Bible characters: Just Jonathan treated David the way he would have wanted David to treat him if their roles had been reversed. Prejudiced placements based on wealth come from evil thoughts that glorify the wrong things, unfairly discriminating.

How often do you show fairness in your life: 5 = nearly always, 4 = most of the time, 3 = about half the time, 2 = less than half the time, or 1 = hardly ever? Your response is ____.
In what ways, if any, has the Holy Spirit enabled you to show fairness?
In what ways, if any, has the Holy Spirit revealed to you a need for more fairness?
What petition related to fairness, if any, would you like to bring before the throne of grace?

Faith

Engage in one or more of these introductory activities:

1. Hymn Sing—Find hymns about faith.[1] Possible selections include: "I Know Whom I Have Believed," "Jesus, I Am Resting, Resting," "Leaning on the Everlasting Arms," "My Faith Has Found a Resting Place," "My Faith Looks Up to Thee," "'Tis So Sweet to Trust in Jesus," "Trust and Obey," and "Trusting Jesus." Sing (or read aloud) one or more verses of two or more hymns. Alternatively, play online recordings of the hymns. What does each hymn say about faith? What different words did the songs use for "faith" or the phrase "have faith in"?

2. Movie Night—Watch "Chariots of Fire" (1981, PG) as a class or individually. Based on a true story, the film contrasts two Olympic runners—Eric Liddell, a Christian Scotsman, and Harold Abrahams, a Jewish Englishman. The protagonist, Liddell, runs to glorify God. In the end, his strong, solid faith trumps his love of country and self. What evidence indicates Liddell's Christian faith was genuine? Read 2 Kgs 6:8–18. What is the difference between chariots of the enemy in verse 15 and chariots of fire in verse 17?

These activities emphasize various aspects of biblical faith. A later lesson addresses the complementary trait of repentance, which involves sorrowing for and turning from sin. But what is this Christian character trait of faith? Here's one way to define it:

> Faith is belief and trust in God and his Word, especially regarding the finished work of Christ for salvation.

---

1. The initial idea of using hymn sings to introduce the character trait of faith came from Carden and Carden, *Christian Character Curriculum* 1, 33.

God desires his children to believe and trust in him completely. From a biblical perspective, what does this character trait of faith look like, and how is it improved? This lesson addresses these points under the headings of "God's Word to Mankind," "God's Work in Believers," and "God's Grace for Change."

God's Word to Mankind

Key Verses

"We walk by faith, not by sight" (2 Cor 5:7). When believers die, they can look forward to "an eternal home in heaven" (2 Cor 5:1). Though myriad burdens encumber this life, faith allows saints to rest confidently in the pledge of everlasting comfort, yea, bliss, which the Holy Spirit guarantees (2 Cor 5:5). Christians should evince daily faith in their earthly pilgrimages, focusing on what God says the future holds and pursuing his will rather than shortsightedly fixating on what their human intellect and senses perceive and suggest. Along the path of life with its many dangers, God's people should discount what their minds and eyes reveal since faith provides much greater insight and light. Indeed, the Christian's faith should overlay and influence all aspects and dimensions of life. In the Old Testament, God expressed the same truth to the Judeans as they contemplated a future Babylonian captivity and exile. Despite the coming hardship, God declared, "The righteous shall live by his faith" (Hab 2:4).

"A person is not justified by works of the law but through faith in Jesus Christ" (Gal 2:16). In justification, God declares a sinner to be righteous, permanently removing sin's guilt and penalty from that moment throughout eternity. So, how does someone become righteous in God's sight? It's not through faithfulness to any institution, ritual keeping, obedience to the moral law, personal merit, good deeds, painful penance, or anything else a sinner can do, nor is salvation through Jesus plus any of these things. The only way to become right with God is through faith alone in Christ alone, believing and trusting in Jesus as Savior and Lord. "By grace you have been saved through faith. And this is not your own doing; it is the gift of God, not a result of works, so that no one may boast" (Eph 2:8–9).

Bible Characters

Summoned Saint (Gen 5:21-24; Heb 11:5-6)

The Bible provides few details about Enoch's life. He lived 365 years, not a particularly long time vis-à-vis his contemporaries. More noteworthy, "Enoch walked with God." What tremendous meaning those few words convey! Walking with God doesn't refer to the occasional garden stroll with an acquaintance but to a daily way of life with a close friend, a life of faith. Enoch believed God exists and rewards those who earnestly seek him; he pleased the Lord, trusting, obeying, worshiping, and glorifying him. As with New Testament saints, God saved Enoch through faith, and Enoch walked by faith.

Interestingly, Enoch never died; he did not suffer the normal pangs of physical death. Instead, God beckoned him, and, in that moment, he vanished from the earth and entered heaven. Why would the Lord summon this saint in such an unusual manner? Perhaps God was rewarding Enoch while calling others' attention to his quintessential faith.

Trusting Trekker (Gen 12:1-9, 15:1-7, 22:1-19; Heb 11:8-12, 17-19)

Abraham's faith in God led to great obedience and blessing. When Abraham (known then as Abram) lived in Ur of the Chaldeans, the Lord told him to migrate hundreds of miles and sojourn in Canaan, promising to make him the father of a great nation. Abraham obeyed, and God elaborated on his promised blessing—his descendants would (a) become numerous like the stars and (b) possess the land of Canaan. At times, God tested Abraham's faith in these promises. For example, the Lord commanded him to offer his only son, Isaac, as a burnt sacrifice. As before, Abraham showed his willingness to trust and obey God completely. Knowing the Lord promised him many descendants, Abraham believed that, if Isaac died, the Almighty would resurrect him.

Centuries later, God miraculously fulfilled his two promises to Abraham. Moses brought a vast multitude, Abraham's descendants known now as Israel, out of Egyptian bondage to the very brink of the promised land (Deut 32:48-52; 34:1-4). Then, Joshua led Israel on a brilliant military campaign, vanquishing the wicked inhabitants, occupying Canaan, and establishing God's people as a great nation (Josh 1—12).

But Abraham's blessing included, not just the promise of many descendants and much land but also, righteousness for himself. How did Abraham become right in God's sight? Was it through keeping ceremonial or moral laws or, perhaps, through service or obedience? No, Abraham "believed the Lord, and he counted it to him as righteousness" (Gen 15:6). Just like believers today, God justified Abraham through faith, crediting the righteousness of a Redeemer, albeit yet future, to Abraham's account. Once justified, he obeyed and served God, not vice versa.

Review Questions

1. What is the Christian character trait of faith?

2. What words are missing from this verse? "We walk by _____, not by _____" (2 Cor 5:7).

3. What words are missing from this verse? "The righteous shall ____ by his _____" (Hab 2:4).

4. What words are missing from this verse? "A person is not _____ by works of the ___ but through _____ in Jesus Christ" (Gal 2:16).

5. What words are missing from these verses? "By _____ you have been saved through _____. And this is not your own doing; it is the ____ of God, not a result of _____, so that no one may boast" (Eph 2:8–9).

6. What words are missing from this verse? "Enoch _____ with God, and he was ___, for God ____ him" (Gen 5:24).

7. What does it mean to walk with God?

8. What instrument or mechanism did God use to justify Enoch?

9. Why did God take Enoch to heaven without him physically dying?

10. What two things did God promise Abraham?

11. What was Abraham thinking when he prepared to offer his son, Isaac, as a burnt sacrifice?

12. When did God fulfill the two promises he made to Abraham?

13. Did God justify Abraham, declaring him to be righteous, through his obedience, works, or moral life?

God's Work in Believers

Faith is belief and trust in God and his Word, especially regarding the finished work of Christ for salvation. "Belief" and "trust" normally mean the same thing as faith. Indeed, Scripture often uses the three words interchangeably. Thus, to believe in Christ typically means to have faith or trust in Christ. There is a sense, however, in which belief can refer only to head knowledge or intellectual assent. Such belief might posit, for example, that God exists, created all things, and speaks to mankind through the Bible. But simply believing these things about God, without any engagement of the heart or will, is not true faith. "You believe that God is one; you do well. Even the demons believe—and shudder!" (Jas 2:19). Consider biblical characters who, arguably, just believed in God superficially, never possessing true saving faith, such as King Saul, Judas Iscariot, and Simon the sorcerer.

For salvation, not only must belief proceed beyond mere head knowledge, but its focus must be on the revealed Savior, Jesus Christ. "God so loved the world, that he gave his only Son, that whoever believes in him should not perish but have eternal life. . . . Whoever believes in the Son has eternal life; whoever does not obey the Son shall not see life, but the wrath of God remains on him" (John 3:16, 36). As Paul and Silas succinctly declared, "Believe in the Lord Jesus, and you will be saved" (Acts 16:31). Since the Father and Son are one, belief in the Son necessarily means belief in the Father and vice versa (John 8:19, 10:30). Conversely, refusing or neglecting to believe in the "only Son" amounts to rejection of the Father as well. But what exactly should you believe about Jesus? The most important thing to believe is that "Christ died for [y]our sins in accordance with the Scriptures, . . . he was buried, [and] . . . he was raised on the third day" (1 Cor 15:3–4). "If you confess with your mouth that Jesus is Lord and believe in your heart that God raised him from the dead, you will be saved" (Rom 10:9).

Unlike superficial belief, genuine trust involves the heart and will, presupposing and proceeding beyond head knowledge. Novice skydivers seated comfortably at twelve thousand feet can believe, in theory, their parachutes will open, but trust spurs the actual leap into nothingness. Just like trusting your parachute in the momentous matter of freefalls, trusting God means relying on him and his Word in the important matter of life. "Trust in the LORD with all your heart, and do not lean on your own understanding" (Prov 3:5).

True faith, which only God can give, provides wondrous benefits. For instance, it brings rest to the inner man. "Find rest, O my soul, in God alone; my hope comes from him" (Ps 62:5, NIV). "Come to me, all who labor and are heavy laden, and I will give you rest. Take my yoke upon you, and learn from me, for I am gentle and lowly in heart, and you will find rest for your souls" (Matt 11:28–29). Trust brings calm and tranquility to saints who depend on God rather than self. When you trust God, you rest in his promises rather than your own feelings, intellect, or desires. You trust that God works all things together for your good and his glory and, thus, rest serenely in that truth (Rom 8:28). The rest from such trust dispels mental or spiritual anxieties such as worry, fear, and doubt; it gives your soul a deep, satisfying peace, even amid great trouble.

Faith also provides strength and victory for daily living. "Some trust in chariots and some in horses, but we trust in the name of the LORD our God" (Ps 20:7). "Take up the shield of faith, with which you can extinguish all the flaming darts of the evil one" (Eph 6:16). "Who is it that overcomes the world except the one who believes that Jesus is the Son of God?" (1 John 5:5). Moreover, faith provides confidence in God's promises even though evidence of their fulfillment is currently unobservable. "Now faith is the assurance of things hoped for, the conviction of things not seen" (Heb 11:1).

As a permanent gift, faith does not justify the elect and then go dormant or fade away. To the contrary, God grants faith for justification, and then it persists and grows. Yes, it might weaken at times or ebb and flow, but its long-term trajectory tends upward. Faith can vary in degree or intensity, at some points in life being strong and at other times weak, but nothing can extinguish it completely in the true believer. Faith doesn't just justify; it also plays a role in sanctification, supporting and sustaining the elect as they become more and more holy during their lives. It strengthens the saints to walk with God, believe his promises, and hope in the future. Genuine, biblical faith is the most precious of all Christian character traits.

So, how is your faith? Have you accepted Jesus intellectually but not deep within your soul? Do you believe in him as Savior but not as Lord and King, not as someone to be obeyed or served? Do you believe God exists but, at the same time, don't find him particularly relevant or important in your daily life? In short, do you believe in your head but not trust in your heart? Hopefully, you believe in Jesus from your heart and live daily by faith, walking with God. If this describes you, thank the Lord for his abundant grace and pray for continued spiritual growth. But, if your faith is weak, ask the Holy Spirit to increase and strengthen it. If your faith is just head knowledge and doesn't involve real trust, ask the Holy Spirit for saving faith. Furthermore, whatever your condition, meditate privately on the words of Scripture and listen to solid, expository preaching since "faith comes from hearing, and hearing through the word of Christ" (Rom 10:17).

God's Grace for Change

Complete the "Heart Assessment, Reflection, and Petition" (HARP) chart, assessing your own faith. Reflect on times the Holy Spirit enabled or empowered you to show faith. Then, consider whether the Spirit might be revealing a need for you to have more or stronger faith. If you want God to increase your faith, put that desire in writing. This is a very important exercise that can help you respond to God's direction for your life. Plan to pray over your completed chart once or twice this next week.

Finally, talk to the Lord, using the words that follow or incorporating the thoughts into your own prayer: "My Father, how great and glorious is your name in all the earth. From a heart of deepest gratitude, I thank you for giving me saving faith. You enable me to believe in the Lord Jesus Christ. Indeed, I confess and know that Jesus, the divine Son of God, walked upon the earth, lived a sinless life, performed miracles, taught people about the Father, fulfilled Old Testament prophecies, suffered beatings and ridicule in unjust trials, died through crucifixion on a Roman cross, rose from a sealed tomb where he had been buried, and ascended to the Father where he ever lives to intercede for the saints. I believe all these things through the faith you have given me, the faith that justifies me, the faith that saves me from my sins. Forgive my past, present, and future sins whether small or great, unintentional or intentional, careless or presumptuous, forgotten or remembered. Through faith, I believe Jesus paid the ransom for all my sins as the sacrificial Lamb of God. Jesus, thank you for paying the dreadful cost of my sin and giving me faith and, thus, your righteousness. Now, help me to live by faith every day, trusting you with my life rather than depending on my own feelings, thoughts, or desires. Enable me to trust in you more consistently, rest in you more calmly, depend on you more completely, and walk with you more faithfully. Indeed, give me more and more faith until that day when you call me away to my eternal, heavenly home. In my great and glorious Savior's name, I pray. Amen."

Remember, the Lord's help is vital to cultivating Christian character. Only his power can enable you to change. When you fail to show the character trait of faith, confess it before God and ask for his forgiveness and help.

HARP Chart for Faith

Definition: Faith is belief and trust in God and his Word, especially regarding the finished work of Christ for salvation.

Key verses: "We walk by faith, not by sight" (2 Cor 5:7). "A person is not justified by works of the law but through faith in Jesus Christ" (Gal 2:16).

Bible characters: Enoch trusted God, walking daily with him until God summoned him home. God justified Abraham through faith, crediting the righteousness of Jesus to his account.

How often do you show faith in your life: 5 = nearly always, 4 = most of the time, 3 = about half the time, 2 = less than half the time, or 1 = hardly ever? Your response is _____.
In what ways, if any, has the Holy Spirit enabled you to show faith?
In what ways, if any, has the Holy Spirit revealed to you a need for more faith?
What petition related to faith, if any, would you like to bring before the throne of grace?

Forgiveness

Engage in one or more of these introductory activities:

1. Hymn Sing—Find hymns about God's forgiveness. Possible selections include: "Forgive Our Sins as We Forgive," "From Out the Depths, I Cry, O Lord, to Thee," "My Sins, My Sins, My Savior!" "No, Not Despairingly Come I to Thee," and "Though Your Sins Be as Scarlet." Sing (or read aloud) one or more verses of two or more hymns. Alternatively, play online recordings of the hymns. What does each song say about God's forgiveness or human forgiveness? In addition to singing or listening to hymns, view an online video of Kevin LeVar singing "A Heart that Forgives" (2009), which emphasizes the importance of forgiving others. Even better, save LeVar's video and use it as this lesson's capstone just preceding or following the closing prayer.

2. Movie Night—Watch "Amish Grace" (2010, PG) or "Unbroken: Path to Redemption" (2018, PG-13) as a class or individually. Based on true stories, both movies involve long, painful struggles to forgive brutal wrongs. Afterwards, consider these five questions: (a) Why was it so hard for Ida Graber (or Louis Zamperini) to forgive? (b) Was Ida (or Louis) wrong not to forgive? (c) In what ways did Ida (or Louis) suffer because she (or he) could not or would not forgive? (d) What turning point in Ida's (or Louis') life helped her (or him) forgive? (e) How could Ida (or Louis) forgive someone who was no longer alive? If not used to introduce this lesson, consider viewing one or both movies later when the biblical concept of forgiveness is better understood.

These activities highlight God's wondrous grace in forgiving sinners, the difficulty people sometimes experience in forgiving great wrongs, and the relief those who forgive others experience. But what is this Christian character trait of forgiveness? Here's one way to define it:

> Forgiveness is an attitude that waives or surrenders feelings of bitterness, anger, or vengeance for wrongs suffered.

Another character trait, repentance, merits some mention for its relationship to forgiveness. A person who wrongs another and then repents, admitting fault and sorrowing for the harm done, may induce the wronged party to forgive. Thus, repentance and forgiveness often occur contemporaneously and lead to reconciliation. Nonetheless, repentance can occur without the other person's forgiveness and vice versa. Regarding this lesson, God always desires his children to forgive those who have harmed or hurt them. From a biblical perspective, what does this character trait of forgiveness look like, and how can Christians improve it? This lesson addresses these points under the headings of "God's Word to Mankind," "God's Work in Believers," and "God's Grace for Change."

God's Word to Mankind

Key Verses

"If you forgive others their trespasses, your heavenly Father will also forgive you, but if you do not forgive others their trespasses, neither will your Father forgive your trespasses" (Matt 6:14–15). These verses underscore the imperative to forgive others. All believers sin, and one sin they sometimes commit involves grudges. An unwillingness to forgive should be a matter for serious prayer and repentance. When Christians refuse or neglect to forgive, the Father may withhold his forgiveness from them. Not forgiving others leaves believers with a sense of unresolved guilt for their own sins, distancing them from the Father's merciful pardon and loving communion. "Judgment is without mercy to one who has shown no mercy" (Jas 2:13).

"Be kind to one another, tenderhearted, forgiving one another, as God in Christ forgave you" (Eph 4:32). The Father forgives the elect every sin through Jesus' atoning work on Calvary. Likewise, believers should freely forgive every offense or hurt, emulating God's grace to them. Forgiveness should proceed promptly and willingly from kind and compassionate hearts, not through gritted teeth or feigned forbearance. Christians should forgive others just like God forgave them.

Bible Characters

Reassuring Ruler (Gen 50:15–21)

One day in the land of Canaan, 17-year-old Joseph suffered a great wrong from his ten older brothers that would shape his remaining life. Out of jealous hatred, several brothers thought about murdering him outright. But instead, they stripped off his ornamented robe, cast him into a dry cistern, and sat down to eat. When a caravan of Midianite merchants passed, destined for Egypt, the brothers sold Joseph into bondage, never expecting to see him again (Gen 37). Soon, he became the slave of an Egyptian official, managing his household and property. But later, after the official's wife lodged a false accusation against him, Joseph served a long prison term. Yet, God never forsook Joseph and, through divine providence, brought about a big change in his life (Gen 39). When two nightmares troubled Pharaoh, God revealed to Joseph the meaning of each dream's imagery—seven years of agricultural abundance would precede seven years of widespread famine—which Joseph, in turn, disclosed to Pharaoh. Sensing Joseph's great wisdom and skill, Pharaoh made him, at age thirty, second in command over all Egypt, instructing him to manage the realm's economy so it survived the famine (Gen 40—41). Thus, God miraculously delivered Joseph from prison, giving him a position of great responsibility and authority.

When the famine came, it struck Canaan also, and the ten brothers traveled to Egypt seeking grain to buy. Standing before Joseph, they did not recognize their younger sibling. Instead, they saw an austere ruler who questioned and threatened them (Gen 42—44). When Joseph finally revealed his identity, however, it frightened them even more; they assumed Joseph would take vengeance for the wrongs suffered at their hands. But their younger brother had forgiven them in his heart. Seeing their fear, he reassured them of his forgiveness: "I am your brother, Joseph, whom you sold into Egypt. And now do not be distressed or angry with yourselves because you sold me here, for God sent me before you to preserve life" (Gen 45:4–5). Years later when their father died, the brothers worried again about the tremendous pain they had caused. However, Joseph never wavered in his forgiveness but kindly reassured his ten brothers once more.

Merciful Martyr (Acts 7:51–60)

God gave Stephen, one of the first deacons, great faith and much grace so he performed wondrous miracles. Jealous of his influence, the Jewish leaders hauled him before the Sanhedrin or great council, accusing him falsely of wanting to destroy the Jerusalem temple and disparaging the law of Moses (Acts 6:5—7:1). In his defense, Stephen reviewed Israel's history, beginning with Abraham, proceeding through Moses, and touching on Solomon's temple. He emphasized God's faithfulness and provision as well as the nation's persistent stubbornness (Acts 7:2–50).

But then, Stephen became very direct with the Jewish leaders, saying they differed little from their rebellious ancestors. They even killed the prophesied Messiah, Jesus the Righteous One. In a blind rage, the Jews dragged him outside Jerusalem and stoned him to death. But his last words are telling: "Lord, do not hold this sin against them." In asking for God's mercy, Stephen showed he already had forgiven these men from his heart. He surrendered all feelings of bitterness and anger for the baneful wrong he suffered. Though a martyr for the faith, Stephen died desiring forbearance for his murderers.

Review Questions

1. What is the Christian character trait of forgiveness?
2. What words are missing from these verses? "If you _____ others their _____, your heavenly _____ will also forgive you, but if you do ___ forgive others their trespasses, _____ will your Father forgive your trespasses" (Matt 6:14–15).
3. What words are missing from this verse? "Judgment is without _____ to one who has shown no _____" (Jas 2:13).
4. What words are missing from this verse? "Be ____ to one another, tenderhearted, _____ one another, as God in _____ _____ you" (Eph 4:32).
5. According to Eph 4:32, what feelings or qualities generally accompany forgiveness?
6. How did Joseph's ten older brothers wrong him?
7. What suggests Joseph forgave his brothers?
8. How did the Jewish leaders wrong Stephen?
9. Did Stephen forgive these Jewish leaders?

God's Work in Believers

People wrong others in many ways. Harm may be physical, mental, emotional, spiritual, or financial. Individuals may wound through bodily pain, uncaring neglect, or dismissive, belittling, or scolding speech; they may steal or damage property, malign reputations, or tempt to sin. Some wrongs are relatively small and quickly forgotten, while grievous injuries can prove difficult to overlook. Yet, Christians are commanded to forgive all wrongs, so it's essential to understand what this character trait is and is not. What does it look or feel like to forgive, and what does forgiveness not involve or require?

When you permit anger or resentment to arise and continue, you harm yourself. As others have observed, only fools ingest poison, supposing the dose will wound their enemies. In contrast, forgiving means you cease to feel anger, resentment, or bitterness for injuries received, letting go of negative desires and emotions stemming from others' harmful or thoughtless actions or neglect. You may feel those causing offense owe you something, and, in a sense, they do. But, in forgiveness, you proactively cancel their debt. Though wronged, you give up any supposed right to return the hurt. You don't keep score to pay people back or upbraid them later. You bear no malice for past grievances and nurse no desire for revenge; you make no attempt to get even. In brief, your soul releases all the negativity for wrongs suffered whether large or small, intended or unintended, recurrent or isolated. Ideally, forgiveness becomes a way of life, so you enjoy a constant state of waiving every detrimental emotion flowing from every offense and doing so almost immediately. "It is . . . glory to overlook an offense" (Prov 19:11).

Consistent triumphs in this area occur only through much prayer and God's power. Nonetheless, it helps to adopt a right perspective that motivates, one that focuses on your own sinfulness and God's forgiveness. "Be kind to one another, tenderhearted, forgiving one another, as God in Christ forgave you" (Eph 4:32). How many times have you offended God? How many times, intentional or not, have your words or actions hurt others? Stop to reflect over the great multitude and seriousness of your own offenses; then remember, dear believer, that Jesus paid with his lifeblood for them all, and God forgave you everything. Thus, does it make sense to hold a grudge, especially over the paltry sins of others and the often-minor harm to you? Heed Jesus' parable in which the servant forgiven a great debt refused, in turn, to extend the small bill of another.

As a result, the master reinstated the unmerciful servant's entire debt, imprisoning him until he satisfied it all. Jesus concluded, "So also my heavenly Father will do to every one of you, if you do not forgive your brother from your heart" (Matt 18:35). The apostle Paul makes the same point: "Bear . . . with one another and, if one has a complaint against another, forgiv[e] . . . each other; as the Lord has forgiven you, so you also must forgive" (Col 3:13).

These admonitions extend beyond single slights and other easily overlooked infractions. They also apply to repeated, deliberate, injurious wrongs that, initially, might seem impossible to pardon. How can you forgive the one who badgers, belittles, or bullies you almost daily? Again, reflect on the repeated, injurious wrongs you have committed against your heavenly Father. To whom God gives much, he requires much in return. So, plead with the Holy Spirit for more grace to forgive and, through divine power, strive to do so as often as you receive injury.

Some who have been hurt badly may struggle with forgiveness because they mistakenly believe it requires (a) the wrongdoer, first, to repent, (b) the wrongdoer to receive pardon from all consequences, or (c) themselves to act as though the offense never occurred. But consider again the way this lesson defines forgiveness: It is an attitude that waives or surrenders feelings of bitterness, anger, or vengeance for wrongs suffered. The three results mentioned above (and discussed below) are not essential nor even necessarily appropriate in all cases. Whether these things happen or not, the injured saint still should forgive from the heart.

First, consider whether forgiveness can or should occur without the person at fault repenting. Some believers refuse to forgive, absent the offender's repentance, relying on this verse: "If your brother sins, rebuke him, and if he repents, forgive him" (Luke 17:3). Indeed, many learned this transactional notion of forgiveness early in life. "Brad, apologize to George for [whatever the infraction]. George, forgive Brad. Now, boys, shake hands." Reconciliations became nice, tidy, bilateral exchanges that were repeated over and over throughout youth, some spoken in earnest and others lacking sincerity. Brad gave George a verbal apology in return for an oral expression of forgiveness, and then they shook on the deal. However, repentance and forgiveness are both unilateral matters of the heart. Indeed, whether words are exchanged or not, one person might genuinely repent without the other party forgiving, or one individual might sincerely forgive even though the other person never repents. Granted, repentance and forgiveness often transpire in near proximity, and repentance expressed out loud as an apology may prompt or help along the forgiveness or vice versa. But each remains an internal matter of the heart. Christians who are hurt should forgive even if the wrong-doer hasn't repented and, from all appearances, is never likely to repent. Of course, when people repent and apologize for harm done, seeking forgiveness, believers should express aloud the forgiveness that already has taken place within their hearts and do so graciously. Returning to Luke 17:3, the verse, at first glance, seems to make forgiveness contingent on repentance. Yet, it doesn't explicitly deal with those who do not repent. Importantly, most other Bible passages suggest forgiveness always should occur, such as the two key verses appearing earlier in this lesson.

Second, sincere forgiveness can occur without pardoning the offender from reasonable consequences. Through forgiveness, Christians let go of negative feelings and desires, but pardon may be a different matter. Some offenses warrant an authority figure imposing disciplinary or precautionary measures, especially when no remorse or repentance occurs. Moreover, legal consequences might be appropriate in grievous cases. Of course, none should adopt a forgive-but-not-pardon mantra for every minor offense, pretending to forgive without doing so and always insisting on a pound of flesh as payback. But whether you forgive is separate from any question of pardon; you should always forgive regardless of consequences, if any, flowing from the offense. Here are three examples of forgiveness without pardon:

1. Ten-year-old Josh loves hiking with his dad. Normally, they stay close together, but occasionally, Dad allows his young son to run ahead. One day, Josh disappears down the path. When his dad sees him next, Josh is leaning over a dangerous precipice. He did not mean to venture so near the edge and, in fact, had told his dad earlier he would not, but his enthusiasm got the best of him. Josh sincerely apologizes for his carelessness, and Dad forgives his son. However, as a precaution, Dad no longer permits Josh to venture ahead by himself.

2. Kaye is supposed to complete her homework right after school before going outside to play. However, for the past month, she's been sneaking outside before finishing her assignments. When Mom confronts her, Kaye gets irritated. In loving wisdom, Mom forgives Kaye for disobeying but still grounds her for one week, forbidding

her to play outside after school. Mom hopes this discipline brings repentance and keeps Kaye from neglecting her studies again.

3. Gracie gets hooked on opioids following surgery and, later, steals money from a friend to support her habit. The friend forgives Gracie but still expects repayment. After recovering, however, Gracie earns a decent income but neglects to repay the amount she owes. So, the friend sues her in civil court to recover the stolen funds and then forgives her for the legal hassle.

Third, forgiveness doesn't always mean a friendship or trust must be immediately and completely restored; things sometimes do not return to what they once were. Indeed, after great wrongs causing much harm, extending affection or confidence too quickly or fully may be imprudent if not foolish. Christians can sincerely forgive others while also being careful to avoid hurtful, abusive, or vulnerable situations going forward; forgiveness should not make it easier to be victimized again. You may have heard someone say forgiving is forgetting. But how can it be? Forgiveness removes anger from the heart, not memories from the brain. After egregious harm, it's wise to be more guarded around the wrongdoer, at least for a while. That's especially true if the culprit lacked repentance, making the harmful behavior more likely to recur. For the offender, earning back friendship or trust might require considerable time. However, the individual should not have to earn a Christian's forgiveness.

Sometimes, forgiveness is a process rather than a once-and-done decision or commitment. You might have genuinely forgiven a person. But later, some unexpected stirring of the soul, rather than a repeated offense, resurrects the bitter feelings you assumed buried. And, just like that, resentment bubbles to the surface, disturbing your peace, as if you'd never dealt with it. When bitter and angry feelings return, forgive anew and as many times as the negative emotions recur. Plead with the Holy Spirit to grant you lasting forgiveness and trust him to do so.

Unless a hermit, you'll never lack opportunities to forgive others, even within communities of believers. Family, friends, acquaintances, and strangers will do things that hurt you at times. But here's the question: Would you rather go through life having the Christian character trait of forgiveness and enjoying God's peace, or would you prefer to hold grudges, experiencing frequent or, perhaps, continual anger, resentment, and bitterness? Too many people live in the latter condition. How much better families, churches, and societies would be if Christians consistently forgave others from their hearts. Live in "all humility and gentleness, with patience, bearing with one another in love, eager to maintain the unity of the Spirit in the bond of peace" (Eph 4:2–3). Pray for the grace to forgive.

God's Grace for Change

Before examining your heart, considering how you might improve, and seeking divine help, ponder one last point—God's forgiveness of you is radical. "As far as the east is from the west, so far does he remove [your] transgressions from [you]" (Ps 103:12). Let this brief reminder about and appreciation for God's undeserved grace prepare and motivate you to develop more of this lesson's character trait in yourself.

Then, complete the "Heart Assessment, Reflection, and Petition" (HARP) chart, assessing your own tendency to forgive. Reflect on times the Holy Spirit enabled or empowered you to forgive as well as times God and others forgave you. Consider whether the Spirit might be revealing a need for you to forgive someone now. If you want God to increase your grace to forgive, put that desire in writing. This is a very important exercise that can help you respond to God's direction for your life. Plan to pray over your completed chart once or twice this next week.

Finally, talk to the Lord, using the words that follow or incorporating the thoughts into your own prayer: "God of all love, compassion, and mercy, how great your awesome works and wondrous name! And yet, I often sin against you and others, refusing to forgive and holding grudges. Teach me to forgive when people wrong me; empower me to forgive my debtors for the small and large ways they sometimes hurt me. Cause me to emulate Stephen who prayed, 'Lord, do not hold this sin against them,' as I genuinely forgive from my heart. Through the Holy Spirit, give me the ability to forgive others consistently, remembering that you often have forgiven me great and grievous sins and will do so yet again and again until you receive me into glory. Thank you for forgiving all my past, present, and future sins through Jesus my Redeemer in whose name I pray. Amen."

Remember, the Lord's help is vital to cultivating Christian character. Only his power can enable you to change. When you fail to show the character trait of forgiveness, confess it before God and ask for his forgiveness and help.

HARP Chart for Forgiveness

Definition: Forgiveness is an attitude that waives or surrenders feelings of bitterness, anger, or vengeance for wrongs suffered.

Key verses: "If you forgive others their trespasses, your heavenly Father will also forgive you, but if you do not forgive others their trespasses, neither will your Father forgive your trespasses" (Matt 6:14–15). "Be kind to one another, tenderhearted, forgiving one another, as God in Christ forgave you" (Eph 4:32).

Bible characters: The reassuring ruler forgave his ten older brothers for selling him into slavery. The merciful martyr forgave his executioners, asking God not to hold their sin against them.

How often do you show forgiveness in your life: 5 = nearly always, 4 = most of the time, 3 = about half the time, 2 = less than half the time, or 1 = hardly ever? Your response is _____.
In what ways, if any, has the Holy Spirit enabled you to show forgiveness?
In what ways, if any, have God and others forgiven you?
In what ways, if any, has the Holy Spirit revealed to you a need to be more forgiving?
What petition related to forgiveness, if any, would you like to bring before the throne of grace?

Generosity

Engage in one or more of these introductory activities:

1. Nature Study—Learn about meerkats, those lissome tunnelers of "The Lion King" (1994, G) fame, and share your findings through online photos or short video clips. Native to southern Africa, meerkats live communally in mobs (aka clans or gangs). A dominant male and female breed to provide most of the mob's pups. This alpha pair rules the mob, which may include up to fifty subordinate members. Meerkats forage for food, primarily insects. But when predators approach, they dive into "bolt holes" for safety. Interestingly, subordinates exhibit three altruistic behaviors in which they give generously of their time and resources for the mob's benefit. First, subordinate females babysit and nurse young pups belonging to the alpha pair and other meerkats. Second, foraging adults feed hungry pups that, again, often don't belong to them. Third, meerkats take turns on sentry duty to protect the foraging mob, watching for predators that include martial eagles and other birds of prey; cobras, puff adders, and other snakes; and jackals. Though some researchers believe other factors explain meerkats' apparent altruism, their behavior, nonetheless, illustrates what generosity looks like.

2. Temporal Treasure—In a group setting, act out parables, lessons, or events from the Bible involving material possessions. Use a few coins or dollar bills for props as needed. Others should try to guess what you are acting out. Consider using biblical passages like these: (a) "Cast your bread upon the waters, for you will find it after many days. Give a portion to seven, or even to eight, for you know not what disaster may happen on earth" (Eccl 11:1–2). (b) "Do not lay up for yourselves treasures on earth, where moth and rust destroy and where thieves break in and steal, but lay up for yourselves treasures in heaven, where neither moth nor rust destroys and where

thieves do not break in and steal. For where your treasure is, there your heart will be also" (Matt 6:19–21). (c) "Jesus looked up and saw the rich putting their gifts into the offering box, and he saw a poor widow put in two small copper coins. And he said, 'Truly, I tell you, this poor widow has put in more than all of them. For they all contributed out of their abundance, but she out of her poverty put in all she had to live on'" (Luke 21:1–4).

These activities illustrate and encourage generosity, which resembles compassion, the topic of a prior lesson. But compassion focuses on ministry to hurting people, whereas generosity benefits everyone. More specifically, what is this Christian character trait of generosity? Here's one way to define it:

> Generosity reflects an altruistic willingness to give time, money, or other resources to people or causes without expecting something in return.

God desires his children to be unselfish and openhanded about things with which he has blessed them. From a biblical perspective, what does this character trait of generosity look like, and how can Christians improve it? This lesson addresses these points under the headings of "God's Word to Mankind," "God's Work in Believers," and "God's Grace for Change."

God's Word to Mankind

Key Verses

"One man gives freely, yet gains even more; another withholds unduly, but comes to poverty. A generous man will prosper; he who refreshes others will himself be refreshed" (Prov 11:24–25, NIV). Strange paradox! Worldlings cannot understand how subtraction increases the whole. However, God assures the growth or refreshment, whether material or spiritual, and controls its timing. True generosity, of course, requires a proper motive—the benefactor must give "freely" with no expectation of value in return. Giving time, money, or other resources primarily to become richer is not generous but transactional; the stimulus, instead, should be to share God's goodness with others gratis. On the flip side, those who unduly withhold temporal means, whether out of covetousness or fear, should expect material or spiritual "poverty" and emptiness.

"In a severe test of affliction, [the Macedonian churches'] abundance of joy and their extreme poverty have overflowed in a wealth of generosity on their part. For they gave according to their means, as I can testify, and beyond their means, of their own accord, begging us earnestly for the favor of taking part in the relief of the [Jerusalem] saints" (2 Cor 8:2–4). The Jerusalem church was hurting, perhaps due to persecution or the famine Agabus foretold (Acts 11:28). The apostle Paul commended the Macedonian churches—primarily Philippi, Thessalonica, and Berea—for their "wealth of generosity" to the suffering saints in Jerusalem. The Macedonian assemblies, though themselves subject to "a severe test of affliction" and "extreme poverty," had given richly from cheerful hearts of "abundan[t] . . . joy." Paul had not pushed them to give. Instead, they begged for the privilege and gave sacrificially "beyond their means." Now, Paul admonished the more wealthy and affluent believers in Corinth to follow the Macedonian example; he sought to stir up their magnanimity for the poor Jerusalem saints. "One such poor Macedonian might well shame a hundred rich Corinthian curmudgeons."[1] But Paul may have been angling for more than shame to incentivize the Corinthians. He also observed how God's favor rested on the Macedonian believers because of their liberality and how Jesus Christ set the quintessential example of generosity (2 Cor 8:1, 9).

Bible Characters

Surly Stinginess (1 Sam 25:1–11)

Mistrustful of King Saul, David and his six hundred armed men fled to a desert region. In nearby Carmel, a wealthy man named Nabal sheared sheep. Such was a festive occasion; once workers had shorn the sheep, great joy and feasting followed. David sent ten men to Nabal, greeting him respectfully, wishing him long life and good health, and requesting provisions. His entreaty seemed reasonable on three grounds. First, sharing one's bounty after sheepshearing was customary. Second, David's men had lived honorably near Nabal's shepherds; unlike other armed bands, they had not forcefully taken any sheep. Third, David's men had been a protective wall to Nabal's shepherds and sheep, shielding them against wild predators and marauding Arabs. Arguably, this guardianship saved many sheep from being killed or plundered, preserving Nabal's wealth.

1. Trapp, *Commentary*, 566.

Nabal could have politely refused to help. But instead, he responded with unnecessary vitriol, insulting David and his men. His surly stinginess, already known to his wife and servants, revealed an unthankful, ungenerous heart. Someone whom God had blessed so greatly with material wealth refused to refresh his fellow man. Because of his foolish self–centeredness, God took Nabal's life (1 Sam 25:38).

Kingly Kindness (2 Sam 9:1–13)

David became deeply devoted friends with King Saul's oldest son, Jonathan. They admired, respected, and trusted each other. Because of their mutual love and concern, Jonathan and David entered a covenant. Jonathan promised to warn David of harm that might come his way from Saul. David, in turn, promised to show kindness to Jonathan's family, even after he became king (1 Sam 20:14–17). The Philistines later killed Saul and Jonathan at Mount Gilboa (1 Sam 31:1–6).

Several years after Saul's death, all Israel made David king, and he sought some tangible way to fulfill his covenant with Jonathan. He discovered Jonathan's crippled son, Mephibosheth, living in Transjordan. Summoned to Jerusalem, Mephibosheth may have feared David planned to kill him, crushing a possible usurper to the throne. But the covenant dominated David's thoughts; he wished to show kingly kindness to Jonathan's son and did so in three ways. First, he restored Saul's land to Mephibosheth. Second, he commissioned Ziba and his sons as Mephibosheth's personal steward and staff, establishing him like royalty. Third, David invited Mephibosheth to eat permanently at the king's table. The first and second kindnesses were but just; the third was pure generosity.

Review Questions

1. What is the Christian character trait of generosity?

2. What words are missing from these verses? "One man _____ freely, yet _____ even more; another _____ unduly, but comes to _____. A _____ man will prosper; he who _____ others will himself be refreshed" (Prov 11:24–25, NIV).

3. Which group of Christians did Paul say had given generously?

4. To whom had these saints sent gifts and for what purpose?

5. What words are missing from these verses? "In a severe ____ of affliction, their abundance of joy and their extreme _____ have overflowed in a wealth of _____ on their part. For they ____ according to their _____, as I can testify, and beyond their means, of their own accord, begging us earnestly for the _____ of taking part in the _____ of the saints" (2 Cor 8:2–4).

6. Was David wrong in asking Nabal for provisions?

7. How did Nabal show his generosity?

8. What covenant did David enter with Jonathan?

9. How did David keep this covenant and show generosity?

God's Work in Believers

Few can match the tightfisted miserliness of Ebenezer Scrooge. In all literature, perhaps no character less magnanimous ever existed than the old moneygrubbing skinflint springing from the mind and pen of Charles Dickens: "Oh! but he was a tight-fisted hand at the grindstone, Scrooge! a squeezing, wrenching, grasping, scraping, clutching, covetous, old sinner! Hard and sharp as flint, from which no steel had ever struck out generous fire; secret, and self-contained, and solitary as an oyster."[2] You may know real-life Scrooges who rarely, if ever, warm others with "generous fire." What makes them that way? What trait or emotion underlies their lack of generosity? Consider two possibilities—selfishness and fear.

Selfishness involves an inordinate concern for one's own comforts and wants, which naturally leads to very little interest in whether others secure or enjoy those things. As inversely related character traits, selfishness and generosity occupy opposing ends of the spectrum; the more selfish a person, the less generous, and vice versa. Selfishness shows itself in numerous ways—the child who refuses to share a toy, the mother who pays more attention to an electronic device than her toddler, the brother who will not temporarily forgo morning lattes to help his sister through a difficult financial stretch, the family who will not invite a lonely neighbor to join them for Thanksgiving Dinner, the father who sleeps late on Sunday rather than taking his wife and kids to church, the believer who gives

2. Dickens, *A Christmas Carol*, 10.

negligibly to his church even though he is financially able to tithe, and the surly sheepshearer named Nabal who shows no hospitality to those who have done him good. In short, the opportunities for selfishness are endless, but so are those to show its antithesis—generosity. To become more generous, pray for a caring heart and the Holy Spirit's grace and power to shift the focus from yourself to others.

Like selfishness, fear can impede generosity. Many people lack generosity, not because they don't care about others, but because they fear not having enough time, money, or other resources to meet their own needs. For instance, demanding careers can leave little time for family and friends. Professionals and small business owners may fear the consequences of giving time to others when they lack sufficient hours to complete their work. Consider also that many living through the 1930s' Great Depression acquired the habit of life-long frugality to protect themselves against another crippling financial disaster. They knew what it was like to suffer, so they hoarded, scrimped, and saved to lessen the chance of it happening to them again. But even people born after the Great Depression can experience macro-fears like economic collapse or micro-fears like the financial demands of their personal retirement and long-term care. Prudently planning for such anticipated needs is not wrong. But, at the same time, an inordinate fear that prevents or stifles generosity goes too far. If fear keeps you from being generous, ask the Holy Spirit for wisdom in allocating your time and planning your finances. Then, place your trust increasingly, not in your own abilities and provision, but in God's.

Having addressed generosity's two major impediments—selfishness and fear—consider now the attitude that should accompany generosity. Don't simply give but do so willingly and cheerfully, like the Macedonian believers. "You shall give to [your poor brother] freely, and your heart shall not be grudging" (Deut 15:10). "Each one must give as he has decided in his heart, not reluctantly or under compulsion, for God loves a cheerful giver" (2 Cor 9:7). As you give, pray for a willing and cheerful spirit.

Stay alert for opportunities to show generosity. Particularly look for occasions to help hurting or destitute believers. "As we have opportunity, let us do good to everyone, and especially to those who are of the household of faith" (Gal 6:10). "Visit orphans and widows in their affliction" (Jas 1:27). Help the "brother or sister [who] is poorly clothed and lacking in daily food" (Jas 2:15). "If anyone has the world's goods and sees his brother in need, yet closes his heart against him, how does God's love abide in him?" (1 John 3:17). The Holy Spirit can direct you to such opportunities calling for both compassion and generosity.

Does the Bible's frequent admonishment to help the poor and distressed mean the disadvantaged need not show generosity? No, impoverished, disadvantaged, or hurting believers often can and should develop this positive trait as well through giving their time and even sharing their meager resources. Consider how the poor widow of Zarephath shared her last bit of food amid great famine (1 Kgs 17:7–16). The Bible admonishes all believers to practice this virtue, not just those with free time, extra money, or abundant resources. For example, "Whoever gives one of these little ones even a cup of cold water because he is a disciple, truly, I say to you, he will by no means lose his reward" (Matt 10:42). And, once more, recall how the poor Macedonians gave generously to their Judean brethren (2 Cor 8:2–4).

As one expression of generosity, don't forget to practice hospitality (Rom 12:13). Hospitality is the warm, friendly, and generous opening of one's home to guests for lodging, meals, entertainment, or fellowship. David showed great hospitality to Mephibosheth in letting him always eat meals at the king's table. You also might invite people into your own home, whether it be friends to enjoy conversation, visiting missionaries to stay in a spare bedroom, or church members to eat Sunday dinner. If hospitality has not been your practice, ask the Holy Spirit to teach you how to begin.

Beyond thankfulness for God's grace, consider two other aspects of generosity. First, God loves and rewards the generous heart. "Give, and it will be given to you. Good measure, pressed down, shaken together, running over, will be put into your lap. For with the measure you use it will be measured back to you" (Luke 6:38). "Whoever sows sparingly will also reap sparingly, and whoever sows generously will also reap generously" (2 Cor 9:6, NIV). "Do not neglect to do good and to share what you have, for such sacrifices are pleasing to God" (Heb 13:16). Second and more importantly, generosity glorifies God. "You will be enriched in every way to be generous in every way, which through us will produce thanksgiving to God. . . . By their approval of this service, they will glorify God because of . . . the generosity of your contribution for them and for all others" (2 Cor 9:11, 13).

God's Grace for Change

Before examining your heart, considering how you might improve, and seeking divine help, ponder one last point—In addition to redemption from sin and misery, God graciously gives many other good gifts to you. "If any of you lacks wisdom, let him ask God, who gives generously to all without reproach, and it will be given him" (Jas 1:5). Let this brief reminder about and appreciation for God's undeserved grace prepare and motivate you to develop more of this lesson's character trait in yourself.

Then, complete the "Heart Assessment, Reflection, and Petition" (HARP) chart, assessing your own generosity. Reflect on times the Holy Spirit enabled or empowered you to be generous as well as times God and others showed generosity to you. Consider whether the Spirit might be revealing a need for you to become more generous. If you want God to increase your generosity, put that desire in writing. This is a very important exercise that can help you respond to God's direction for your life. Plan to pray over your completed chart once or twice this next week.

Finally, talk to the Lord, using the words that follow or incorporating the thoughts into your own prayer: "My Father, how glorious and praiseworthy your name and all your works! Thank you for extending your divine generosity to me through your marvelous grace and great salvation. However, though blessed so abundantly, I still sin; I fail to show generosity to others; I fail to share my time and resources. Too often, I display the surly stinginess of Nabal. Too often, I fear letting go of time and money. Too often, I neglect to show hospitality in opening my home. Too often, I do not refresh others with kindness and good cheer. May the Holy Spirit work in my life to bring about the change I so much desire and now humbly request—cause me to more and more show generosity to family, friends, and even strangers. In so doing, enable me to glorify Christ. It's in his name I pray. Amen."

Remember, the Lord's help is vital to cultivating Christian character. Only his power can enable you to change. When you fail to show the character trait of generosity, confess it before God and ask for his forgiveness and help.

HARP Chart for Generosity

Definition: Generosity reflects an altruistic willingness to give time, money, or other resources to people or causes without expecting something in return.

Key verses: "One man gives freely, yet gains even more; another withholds unduly, but comes to poverty. A generous man will prosper; he who refreshes others will himself be refreshed" (Prov 11:24–25, NIV). "In a severe test of affliction, their abundance of joy and their extreme poverty have overflowed in a wealth of generosity on their part. For they gave according to their means, as I can testify, and beyond their means, of their own accord, begging us earnestly for the favor of taking part in the relief of the saints" (2 Cor 8:2–4).

Bible characters: Far from preserving wealth, Nabal's surly stinginess proved his untimely demise. Mephibosheth's lameness meant he could never repay David's kingly kindness.

How often do you show generosity in your life: 5 = nearly always, 4 = most of the time, 3 = about half the time, 2 = less than half the time, or 1 = hardly ever? Your response is ____.
In what ways, if any, has the Holy Spirit enabled you to show generosity?
In what ways, if any, have God and others shown you generosity?
In what ways, if any, has the Holy Spirit revealed to you a need to be more generous?
What petition related to generosity, if any, would you like to bring before the throne of grace?

Gentleness

Engage in one or more of these introductory activities:

1. Game Night—Play Jenga, Operation, or some other game requiring steady hands. For large groups, making two or more games available allows additional people to participate. Success depends on delicacy, while negative consequences ensue from heavy-handedness. To win, players must be very careful when removing blocks or performing surgery.

2. Movie Night—Watch "A Beautiful Day in the Neighborhood" (2019, PG) as a class or individually. This endearing film is about the soft-spoken, caring TV personality, Mr. Rogers, who befriends a cynical reporter named Lloyd. In just one word, how would you describe Mr. Rogers? In what specific instances was he gentle? What question did Mr. Rogers often ask his audience, and how did it show gentleness?

3. Nature Study—Learn about *Mimosa pudica* (aka sensitive briar) and share your findings through online photos, short video clips, or actual specimens in nearby woods. This fern-like, creeping plant grows in the southern United States and other tropical regions. When touched, its binate compound leaves recoil, folding inward very quickly and reopening several minutes later, which consumes a lot of the organism's energy. This "rapid plant movement" may be a defense mechanism that frightens away harmful insects. Just like treading gently around *Mimosa pudica*, believers should be sensitive to things that might cause others to shrivel up or withdraw.

These activities introduce the notion of interacting gently with others. Gentleness has much in common with humility; indeed, the two traits often can be found coexisting within the same individual. But gentleness relates to the disposition towards and treatment of others, while humility, which a later lesson covers, relates primarily to one's view of self. Indeed, humility might be considered a precursor to gentleness; few truly gentle believers lack humility. But what is this Christian character trait of gentleness? Here's one way to define it:

> Gentleness involves a mild temperament, soft speech, and tender acts.

God desires his children to be sensitive towards others and their needs, speaking and acting gently towards family members, friends, acquaintances, colleagues, and even strangers. From a biblical perspective, what does this character trait of gentleness look like, and how can Christians improve it? This lesson addresses these points under the headings of "God's Word to Mankind," "God's Work in Believers," and "God's Grace for Change."

God's Word to Mankind

Key Verses

"A gentle answer turns away wrath, but a harsh word stirs up anger" (Prov 15:1, NIV). This aphorism appraises polar responses—"a gentle answer" and "a harsh word"—under incendiary conditions. Sharp, contentious words provoke wrath, stirring up smoldering coals of anger into a blazing conflagration. Spewing harsh words at the agitated is like pouring gasoline on a hot surface. Recall how Rehoboam's discordant reply to the northern tribes split a nation (2 Chr 10:13–14). At the opposite extreme, a gentle response disarms the perturbed and distressed, defusing a high-octane state. A tender answer proceeds quietly and carefully, offering sympathy, respect, or a solution through conciliatory, inoffensive words. Abigail's soft answer soothed David's anger, preventing many needless deaths (1 Sam 25:23–35), and Gideon's calm reasoning assuaged the Ephraimites' fury, averting civil war (Judg 8:1–3).

"We were gentle among you, like a nursing mother taking care of her own children" (1 Thess 2:7). Paul, Silas, and Timothy did not lord their authority as "apostles of Christ" over the recently established Thessalonian church (1 Thess 2:6). Instead, the three ministers lovingly cherished this congregation, being sensitive to their needs as new believers. Much as mothers tenderly nourish newborn babies with their own milk, Paul and his companions gently nourished the Thessalonians with the spiritual

milk of God's Word. Moreover, they encouraged and comforted them in their Christian faith, urging them to "walk in a manner worthy of God" (1 Thess 2:12). Unlike some of Paul's other epistles that confronted difficult issues (e.g., 1 Cor and Gal), this one exudes warm, tender affection throughout.

Bible Characters

Caustic Companions (Job 1:1—2:13)

Job feared God and shunned evil. Yet, for his own purposes, God allowed Satan to strike Job, taking away his ten children, numerous livestock, and, eventually, his health. Though wretched and bewildered, Job accepted these losses as God's sovereign will. Even when his wife said to "curse God and die," Job would not sin. He continued "blameless and upright" in God's sight.

Three friends arrived to comfort Job in his misery. Perhaps, at first, their intentions were noble. But Job's expression of his intense sorrow and distress induced his companions to utter harsh, caustic words. Indeed, the first remarks of each lacked sympathy and set the tone for all that followed. Eliphaz began, "If one ventures a word with you, will you be impatient?" (Job 4:2). Bildad referred to Job's protests as a "great wind" (Job 8:2). And Zophar commenced, "Should . . . a man full of talk [Job] be judged right?" (Job 11:2). And so, they continued each time they spoke, becoming more and more abrasive. Rather than bringing gentle solace, the three friends frustrated and angered Job. Hear his pain-filled exclamations: "You whitewash with lies; worthless physicians are you all" (Job 13:4). "Miserable comforters are you all" (Job 16:2). "How long will you torment me and break me in pieces with words?" (Job 19:2). Does the tenor of these exchanges bring anything to mind? Doesn't it perfectly illustrate the truth of the key verse above? "A harsh word stirs up anger" (Prov 15:1).

Meek Master (John 8:3–11)

During his earthly ministry, Jesus dealt gently with those seeking truth or experiencing hurt. Once, Jewish leaders dragged a woman caught in adultery, a capital offense, before him. Caring little about her, they hoped Jesus might damage his reputation or entrap himself through a careless misstep. And so, they asked whether the woman should be stoned to death according to the Law. Sensitive to her dolorous state and grave danger, Jesus did not respond immediately. Instead, the Master knelt meekly and wrote on the ground with his finger. What exactly did Jesus write? No living mortal knows for sure. Some speculate he jotted down specific sins of the ringleaders, stinging their collective consciences. Be that as it may, they continued pressing him to answer.

At last, Jesus stood and spoke gentle words, disarming the angry mob. He agreed the execution could begin but stipulated a sinless person should cast the first stone. If a cricket resided nearby, its chirping must have become distinct. The perfect stillness might have reminded the disciples of when Jesus spoke three words to the howling winds, "Peace! Be still!" (Mark 4:39), and the raging, storm-tossed waters became a perfect slick. Similarly, in the temple court, the clamoring instantly stopped as Jesus, once more, knelt and wrote on the ground. What immense power emanates from the gentle voice of Jesus!

Review Questions

1. What is the Christian character trait of gentleness?

2. What words are missing from this verse? "A _____ answer turns away _____, but a _____ word stirs up _____" (Prov 15:1, NIV).

3. What words are missing from this verse? "We were _____ among you, like a nursing _____ taking care of her own _____" (1 Thess 2:7).

4. Why should Job's friends have spoken gently to him?

5. What harshness characterized each friend's opening words to Job?

6. How did Job react to his friends' words?

7. How did Jesus deal gently with the religious leaders who brought the adulteress before him?

8. How was Jesus gentle with the woman caught in adultery?

God's Work in Believers

Society often equates gentleness with weakness. In contrast, the Bible commonly attributes gentleness to powerful authority figures. The apostle Paul, for instance, was "gentle . . . like a nursing mother taking care of her own children" (1 Thess 2:7) and appealed to the saints through the "meekness and gentleness of Christ" (2 Cor 10:1). Indeed, as the quintessential example, Jesus was "gentle and lowly in heart" (Matt 11:29), especially to those hurting, like the woman caught in adultery, or those seeking truth. So, rather than weakness, gentleness in Scripture often cloaks tremendous power. To what degree does this quality exist in your life? Consider three aspects of true biblical gentleness—a mild temperament, soft speech, and tender acts.

Gentleness requires a mild temperament. Yet, believers cannot simply work hard to restrain rough or austere impulses, developing an inner gentleness through sheer effort. As with other Christian character traits, this is the Holy Spirit's work. Indeed, gentleness is one of the Spirit's nine fruits (Gal 5:22–23). Look for inward evidence—a calm quietness deep in your soul that, when well developed, persists undisturbed even when all around erupts in conflict and chaos. A mild temperament allows you to respond peaceably to combative or abusive words, react tenderly in difficult situations and towards abrasive people, and remain calm and composed no matter what, controlling or softening every word and deed. A mild temperament rests rather than frets. "A gentle and quiet spirit . . . in God's sight is very precious" (1 Pet 3:4).

Pray earnestly for this spiritual fruit that germinates deeply within the soul and distills quietly to the world through soft speech and tender acts. The apostle Paul admonished saints to display their inward gentleness outwardly. "Let your gentleness be evident to all" (Phil 4:5, NIV). "Clothe yourselves with . . . gentleness" (Col 3:12, NIV). Suggestions follow about being gentle with others through what you say and do, just as Paul instructed.

Always show gentleness to everyone. But be especially tender towards the weak, including the elderly, young, sick, injured, discouraged, or despondent. Don't emulate the indiscretions of Job's friends. Tread carefully around those rare individuals who criticize or judge themselves too harshly; they may be particularly vulnerable to even the least suggestion of wrongdoing. Also, be gentle with fragile people who suffer from past abuses and tend to shrink or pull back from perceived threats. Recall how the sensitive briar recoils quickly when mishandled.

Gentleness involves delicacy and diplomacy. Consider how your words or deeds might be interpreted or misconstrued. In touchy situations, think carefully before speaking or acting. "Let every person be quick to hear, slow to speak" (Jas 1:19). How important is it that you be right and voice it? In relatively small matters, is it better to express your opposing opinion or even correct someone, or is it preferable to remain quiet, maintaining and promoting harmony and goodwill? As the old adage teaches, silence is sometimes golden. Job's companions may have comforted him during their week-long silence (Job 2:12–13). But then, of course, any solace dissipated once their painful pontificating began; they assumed their opinions were correct and felt compelled to express them.

As much as possible, every word you speak should be gentle. But in each conversation—whether casual and light or purposeful and tense—your first words, especially, should convey respect and goodwill in a soft tone. Difficult topics might arise later in the same discourse, but beginning well increases the likelihood gentleness will prevail throughout. For example, when greeting a family member at breakfast, which beginning seems gentle? (a) "Did you finish preparing for that presentation? I hope you finally stopped procrastinating and got it done. You waste too much time." or (b) "How did you sleep? I hope your presentation goes well today. I'm praying for you." First words are so important, particularly when the discussion will involve awkward matters about which the parties may feel some anxiety and may, in fact, disagree.

Here's another example, involving three alternative ways to begin a business debriefing: (a) "Daniel! What happened to you yesterday? You dropped the ball! Why weren't you more prepared?" or (b) "Hey, Daniel, how are you? Please sit down. Coffee? . . . I want you to know how much I appreciate all the work you do, particularly since you've had extra demands on your time with Becky on maternity leave. . . . I wanted to talk with you briefly about the financial presentation yesterday. How do you think it went?" or (c) "Sit down, Daniel. I know you're going to get all bent out of shape about what I'm fixing to say, because you always do, but I'm going to say it anyway because it must be said. Yesterday's presentation was unacceptable." The (a) start to the debriefing seems insensitive and uncaring, but the (c) beginning is pure incendiarism; neither comes close to meeting any standard of gentleness. And likely, Daniel won't perceive anything that follows these harsh openings as gentle either. But the middle opening starts with pleasantries and recognizes that, recently, Daniel has had to do part of Becky's work. Also, it gives Daniel a chance to explain what happened before exploring what can be done differently next time.

On occasion, conversations become heated. Individuals imply or say hurtful things; emotions run high, and egos bruise. And, like James and John (aka the "Sons of Thunder" in Mark 3:17), people sometimes express over-the-top outrage for even small slights (Luke 9:54). When volatile words begin, remain tranquil. Be gentle, doing no harm, declining to enter acrid tit-for-tat exchanges. Eschew abrasive talk, listen calmly, and speak softly. Moreover, don't insist on having the last word. On hearing caustic insults and personal affronts, don't retaliate; meekly bear the hurt in silence. Remember, "a gentle answer turns away wrath" (Prov 15:1). Through God's power, your gentle response may disarm and soothe the wrathful, defusing conflict and rancor.

Speaking hard truth requires gentleness too. Stern words spoken brusquely, even if true, tend to close the heart. Thus, when explaining the good news to a lost sinner, speak softly and tenderly. "Always be . . . prepared to make a defense to anyone who asks you for a reason for the hope that is in you; yet do it with gentleness and respect" (1 Pet 3:15). Likewise, when a fellow believer drifts into sin or doctrinal error, "restore him in a spirit of gentleness" (Gal 6:1) or "correct . . . with gentleness" (2 Tim 2:25).

Consistent, day-in-and-day-out gentleness is a tall order. Occasionally, in the heat of the moment, you may respond harshly or act sternly to others. Perhaps you'll even rant and rave. What should you do after such outbursts or tirades? Well, you can't put toothpaste back in the tube, but you can apologize for squirting it on the bathroom ceiling and work to clean it up. Ask the Father's forgiveness and Holy Spirit's help, seek forgiveness from people you offended or hurt, restore whatever you may have damaged, and consider how you might do things differently going forward. Next time, when a discussion turns combative, calmly excuse yourself before losing your cool, walk away to a quiet place, reflect on the situation and your mounting anxiety, and pray. Then, return to resume the conversation with a renewed spirit of meekness.

In conclusion, desire the gentleness of Christ in your soul; pray earnestly for it. Ask the Holy Spirit to shine his light where you lack gentleness and then grant you more and more of his grace to change. The Holy Spirit's power can transform any saint's temperament, making it more and more gentle like that of Jesus.

God's Grace for Change

Before examining your heart, considering how you might improve, and seeking divine help, ponder one last point—Any success or prosperity you enjoy in this life flows directly from God's clemency and gentleness. "You have given me the shield of your salvation, and your right hand supported me, and your gentleness made me great" (Ps 18:35). Let this brief reminder about and appreciation for God's undeserved grace prepare and motivate you to develop more of this lesson's character trait in yourself.

Then, complete the "Heart Assessment, Reflection, and Petition" (HARP) chart, assessing your own gentleness. Reflect on times the Holy Spirit enabled or empowered you to be gentle in words or deeds as well as times God and others showed you gentleness. Consider whether the Spirit might be revealing a need for you to show gentleness more consistently. If you want God to increase your gentleness, put that desire in writing. This is a very important exercise that can help you respond to God's direction for your life. Pray over your completed chart once or twice this next week.

Finally, talk to the Lord, using the words that follow or incorporating the thoughts into your own prayer: "Dear Father, how loving and merciful you are to put up with my harshness and sternness towards others. Forgive me when I am abrasive and austere. Holy Spirit, develop within me a mild temperament so my speech becomes soft and my acts tender. Thank you for promising to sanctify me, making me more and more like the gentle Savior. May my spiritual growth glorify him. In his holy name, I pray. Amen."

Remember, the Lord's help is vital to cultivating Christian character. Only his power can enable you to change. When you fail to show the character trait of gentleness, confess it before God and ask for his forgiveness and help.

HARP Chart for Gentleness

Definition: Gentleness involves a mild temperament, soft speech, and tender acts.

Key verses: "A gentle answer turns away wrath, but a harsh word stirs up anger" (Prov 15:1, NIV). "We were gentle among you, like a nursing mother taking care of her own children" (1 Thess 2:7).

Bible characters: Job's caustic companions responded harshly to his misery. The meek Master spoke gentle words to disarm an angry mob intent on stoning an adulteress.

How often do you show gentleness in your life: 5 = nearly always, 4 = most of the time, 3 = about half the time, 2 = less than half the time, or 1 = hardly ever? Your response is ____.
In what ways, if any, has the Holy Spirit enabled you to show gentleness?
In what ways, if any, have God and others been gentle towards you?
In what ways, if any, has the Holy Spirit revealed to you a need to be gentler?
What petition related to gentleness, if any, would you like to bring before the throne of grace?

Humility

Engage in one or more of these introductory activities:

1. Brainstorm—Think of people in the Bible who showed themselves guilty of pride, giving reasons for your selections. You might mention how Adam and Eve ate the forbidden fruit because they coveted things belonging only to God (Gen 3:5) or Diotrephes caused dissension because he "like[d] to put himself first" (3 John 9). Next, name biblical characters showing genuine humility and, again, mention support. For instance, Joseph and Daniel humbly refused glory belonging rightfully to God (Gen 41:16 and Dan 2:27–28), and King David, reflecting on his successes, credited the Lord (2 Sam 7:18).

2. Intriguing Insights—The quotations below make observations about humility and, its opposite, pride. Explain each quotation's meaning or otherwise comment about it.

   > "A great man is always willing to be little."[1]

   > "Nothing is more deceitful . . . than the appearance of humility. It is often only carelessness of opinion, and sometimes an indirect boast."[2]

   > "Humility is the foundation of all other virtues."[3]

3. Nature Study—Learn about earthworms and share your findings through online photos or short video clips. Except perhaps for Richard Scarry's Lowly Worm,[4] these unpretentious creatures rarely get much press. Though a wide variety of animals enjoy them as

---

1. Emerson, *Works*, 43.
2. Mr. Darcy as cited in Austen, *Pride and Prejudice*, 41.
3. Saint Augustine as cited in Weniger, *Perfect Religious*, 53.
4. Scarry, *Lowly Worm Storybook*.

gustative delights (e.g., robins) while avid gardeners and anglers also appreciate their virtues, earthworms perform menial tasks that mostly go unnoticed. Nonetheless, their silent, plodding, subterranean journeys benefit all mankind as they aerate and enrich the soil and consume harmful nematodes.

These activities introduce defining aspects of humility such as appropriately attributing glory and humbly performing modest tasks. Humility has much in common with two character traits earlier lessons discuss—deference and gentleness. Simply put, humility involves a humble mindset, whereas deference involves yielding to others. Deference can be one result of humility. As to the second comparison, humility deals with how to view yourself, while gentleness involves how to treat others. As with deference, gentleness often is an outgrowth of humility. But what specifically is this Christian character trait of humility? Here's one way to define it:

> Humility entails a lowliness of mind freed from vain thoughts of self-importance.

God does not want his children to think too highly of themselves. From a biblical perspective, what does this character trait of humility look like, and how can Christians improve it? This lesson addresses these points under the headings of "God's Word to Mankind," "God's Work in Believers," and "God's Grace for Change."

God's Word to Mankind

Key Verses

"Do nothing from selfish ambition or conceit, but in humility count others more significant than yourselves. Let each of you look not only to his own interests, but also to the interests of others" (Phil 2:3–4). Those united with Christ should reflect his mind and love, letting a singular, unifying spirit control and dictate their behavior towards everyone (Phil 2:1–2). Therefore, they must not follow "selfish ambition or conceit," overvaluing their own opinions and contributions while under-esteeming those of others. They should not strive, trying to outshine everyone else while displaying their own superiority. Instead, mindful of their own frailties and failures, they must learn to recognize and appreciate different views and efforts,

often considering others better than themselves. Especially in the church, their purpose must include a deep, loving desire to preserve peace within the body of Christ. They must appropriately value the opinions, contributions, reputations, needs, desires, feelings, and "interests" of their spiritual brothers and sisters, resisting and rejecting the temptation to focus principally on self. This is true humility, like Jesus showed, that maintains and protects the precious unity of God's people.

"Clothe yourselves, all of you, with humility toward one another, for 'God opposes the proud but gives grace to the humble.' Humble yourselves, therefore, under the mighty hand of God so that at the proper time he may exalt you" (1 Pet 5:5–6). Adorn your attitude, speech, and behavior with the simple garment of true humility. God favors the humble, exalting or elevating them according to his own schedule. Whereas the apostle Paul urged humility for the sake of unity (Phil 2:1–4), the apostle Peter does so because "God opposes the proud." This should terrify! Scripture teaches that pride glorifies self, and God opposes self-glorification. Who can stand, much less succeed or prosper, when God opposes? Such warnings, of course, appear throughout Scripture. For example, "Everyone who is arrogant in heart is an abomination to the LORD; be assured, he will not go unpunished" (Prov 16:5). "The LORD abundantly repays the one who acts in pride" (Ps 31:23). "The haughty looks of man shall be brought low, and the lofty pride of men shall be humbled" (Isa 2:11).

Bible Characters

Herod's Hubris (Acts 12:19–23)

In Jerusalem, King Herod Agrippa executed the apostle James (John's brother) and saw that this unjust action pleased the Jews. Then, out of arrogant pride to further his popularity, Herod imprisoned the apostle Peter, intending cruelty to him as well (Acts 12:2–3). But God sent his angel to deliver Peter from the king's evil purpose (Acts 12:6–11).

Later, Herod left Jerusalem for the seaport of Caesarea, perhaps to attend public games honoring Claudius Caesar. While there, citizens of Tyre and Sidon (Phoenician cities further north) requested a meeting to resolve some undisclosed controversy. Apparently, these coastal people depended on Galilee (under Herod's rule) for their food supply, which quarreling now threatened. So, the Tyrians and Sidonians sought to smooth the matter over and had, through the king's chamberlain, secured a hearing in Caesarea.

When the day arrived, Herod entered with ostentatious pomp, full of hubris, and began to speak. As he addressed the assembly, men from Tyre and Sidon (and likely others) shouted in unabashed flattery, "The voice of a god, and not of a man!" Crediting God for neither his own abilities nor royal position, Herod swelled with pride on hearing such praise. However, his vaingloriousness proved short-lived when God's angel smote him with a disease that soon proved fatal.

Lord's Lowliness (Phil 2:5–8)

The apostle Paul admonishes all believers to show humility like Christ. Though in the "form of God," Jesus willingly left heaven's splendor, setting aside his majesty and glory. Born in a stable to unassuming parents, he took on "human form" to identify with sinful mankind.

Rather than coming to earth as a great king or warrior, Christ took the "form of a servant." Serving the miserable and hurting, he healed diseases, cast out demons, associated with sinners, helped the poor, and consoled the destitute. At the Last Supper, Jesus reminded his proud, squabbling disciples, "I am among you as the one who serves" (Luke 22:27). Indeed, washing their feet demonstrated the lowly attitude of God's divine servant (John 13:4–17).

And yet, Jesus humbled himself further. When arrested, he submitted to an unjust, rigged court proceeding. Falsely accused and convicted as the worst of criminals, he suffered shame and violence, ending in his painful death on a cruel Roman cross. From heaven's glory to a lowly manger birth to a humble servant's life to a disgraceful death, Christ epitomized humility.

Review Questions

1. What is the Christian character trait of humility?

2. According to 3 John 9, who loved promoting his own self-interest?

3. What words are missing from these verses? "Do nothing from selfish _____ or _____, but in _____ count others more

_____ than yourselves. Let each of you look not only to his
___ _____, but also to the interests of others" (Phil 2:3–4).

4. What words are missing from these verses? "_____ yourselves, all
of you, with _____ toward one another, for 'God _____ the
proud but gives _____ to the humble.' _____ yourselves, therefore,
under the mighty hand of God so that at the proper time he may
_____ you" (1 Pet 5:5–6).

5. In the preceding verses, why did the apostles Paul and Peter recommend humility to the saints?

6. Why did King Herod imprison the apostle Peter?

7. Why did God smite King Herod?

8. In John 13:4–17, how did Jesus demonstrate humility to his disciples?

9. In broad terms, how did Jesus show humility to mankind?

10. In Dan 4:29–33, how did King Nebuchadnezzar fail to show humility, and what were the consequences?

God's Work in Believers

Humility requires a humbleness of mind, emptied of sinful thoughts about one's own supposed importance. Its absence hamstrings the development of all other Christian character traits. The opposite of humility, of course, is pride, about which the Bible says much. For example, "haughty eyes and a proud heart, the lamp of the wicked, are sin" (Prov 21:4).

All saints struggle with some pride some of the time. So, even if you are mostly humble, pride might, nonetheless, reign in parts of your life. And, even if usually humble, you still might become vainglorious occasionally. Prayerfully ponder the questions below to identify areas where and times when you lack humility. Ask the Holy Spirit to shine his light on your attitudes and motives, giving you godly discernment and grace for change.

1. How do you respond when good things happen to others? Are you sincerely happy for them, or does secret pride make you wish the good things had happened instead to you? "Rejoice with those who rejoice" (Rom 12:15).

2. Do you perform good deeds publicly so others will see and think highly of you, or do you try to keep your good deeds private so only God knows? "Beware of practicing your righteousness before other people in order to be seen by them" (Matt 6:1).

3. Do you avoid the uneducated, poor, unknown, dull, or unattractive, gravitating mostly towards those who can help you achieve your own objectives? "Do not be haughty, but associate with the lowly. Never be wise in your own sight" (Rom 12:16).

4. Out of sinful pride, do you occasionally argue about things of little consequence or otherwise become involved in matters that don't concern you? "O LORD, my heart is not lifted up; my eyes are not raised too high; I do not occupy myself with things too great and too marvelous for me" (Ps 131:1). "It is an honor for a man to keep aloof from strife, but every fool will be quarreling" (Prov 20:3). "Whoever meddles in a quarrel not his own is like one who takes a passing dog by the ears" (Prov 26:17). Some are "puffed up with conceit . . . [and have] an unhealthy craving for controversy and for quarrels about words" (1 Tim 6:4).

5. Do you humbly accept criticism from others, consider their advice, and listen to their opinions or ideas? "Let a righteous man . . . rebuke [you]—it is oil for [your] head" (Ps 141:5). "By insolence comes nothing but strife, but with those who take advice is wisdom" (Prov 13:10). Everyone should be "quick to hear, slow to speak, slow to anger" (Jas 1:19).

6. When evaluating, advising, or instructing others, does pride cause you to forget or ignore your own frailties or past failures and, thus, speak too forcefully? "Show true humility toward all men. At one time [you] too were foolish" (Titus 3:2–3, NIV).

7. Do you draw undue attention to yourself and your accomplishments? "Let another praise you, and not your own mouth; a stranger, and not your own lips" (Prov 27:2). "Let not the wise man boast in his wisdom, let not the mighty man boast in his might, let not the rich man boast in his riches, but let him who boasts boast in this, that he understands and knows [the LORD]" (Jer 9:23–24). "What do you have that you did not receive? If then you received it, why do you boast as if you did not receive it?" (1 Cor 4:7).

8. When you set goals and try to meet them, do you consciously seek to glorify God, or is it all about you? "He must increase, but I must decrease" (John 3:30). "Whether you eat or drink, or whatever you do, do all to the glory of God" (1 Cor 10:31).

9. Do you proudly assert knowledge of things without good evidence or support? "Certain persons . . . have wandered away into vain discussion, desiring to be teachers of the law, without understanding either what they are saying or the things about which they make confident assertions" (1 Tim 1:6–7).

10. Does pride make it difficult to admit when you are wrong? "Whoever conceals his transgressions will not prosper, but he who confesses and forsakes them will obtain mercy" (Prov 28:13). "Confess your sins to one another" (Jas 5:16).

To be clear, humility does not preclude you from taking reasonable satisfaction in accomplishments. However, it's essential to understand who deserves credit and eschew the hubris of King Herod Agrippa. Recognize that God created and redeemed you for his own purpose, granting you skills and abilities to glorify him. Thus, if you received a prestigious award for some feat or achievement, would you think, "I'm really quite talented, and now everyone knows how great I am" or "God is great and gracious in giving me these abilities and blessing me with this honor"? The former oozes conceit, while the latter suggests humility.

Just as you should not think too highly of yourself, neither should you think too lowly; self-degradation can be carried too far. Saying "I'm a no-good, useless failure; I'll never amount to anything" ignores the fact that God made you in his own image just the way he intended. If redeemed, you are God's "workmanship, created in Christ Jesus for good works" (Eph 2:10). This high calling, when rightly understood, extinguishes thoughts of self-loathing or worthlessness. However, if you yet struggle with such negativity, seek God's help to think correctly about who you are and why you exist.

Sometimes, it's hard to distinguish between pride and humility since the former can masquerade as the latter (Col 2:18–23). "Pride perceiving humility honorable, often borrows her cloak"[5] and "apes humility."[6] Guard against false humility. Don't feign humbleness as a means of

---

5. Fuller, *Aphorisms of Wisdom*, 144.

6. Southey, "Devil's Walk," 207.

receiving praise or avoiding responsibilities. Repent of such motives, asking the Holy Spirit for genuine humility rather than its cheap counterfeit.

In conclusion, love the Lord with all your heart, soul, and mind and others as yourself (Matt 22:37–39). Pray fervently for the Holy Spirit to purge your soul of pride, replacing it with "humility, that low, sweet root, from which all heavenly virtues shoot."[7] In all you do, seek God's glory and the good of others. If these objectives become your constant focus, little time will be left to indulge self and its sinful pride.

God's Grace for Change

Before examining your heart, considering how you might improve, and seeking divine help, ponder one last point—Jesus left heaven's splendor and humbled himself to save you. "Behold, your king is coming to you; righteous and having salvation is he, humble and mounted on a donkey" (Zech 9:9). Let this brief reminder about and appreciation for God's undeserved grace prepare and motivate you to develop more of this lesson's character trait in yourself.

Then, complete the "Heart Assessment, Reflection, and Petition" (HARP) chart, assessing your own humility. Reflect on times the Holy Spirit enabled or empowered you to be humble as well as times Jesus showed humbleness during his earthly life. Consider whether the Spirit might be revealing a need for you to become humbler. If you want God to increase your humility, put that desire in writing. This is a very important exercise that can help you respond to God's direction for your life. Pray over your completed chart once or twice this next week.

Finally, talk to the Lord, using the words that follow or incorporating the thoughts into your own prayer: "God of all glory, splendor, and majesty, I praise you! My heart overflows with thankfulness for your redeeming grace. And yet, even as a new creature in Christ, I find selfish ambition and vain conceit lurking within my soul and wreaking havoc in my life. Forgive my sinful pride. Clothe me with the Lord's humility and give me a humble servant's heart like Jesus had. In his name, I pray. Amen."

Remember, the Lord's help is vital to cultivating Christian character. Only his power can enable you to change. When you fail to show the character trait of humility, confess it before God and ask for his forgiveness and help.

7. Moore, *Poetical Works*, 310.

HARP Chart for Humility

Definition: Humility entails a lowliness of mind freed from vain thoughts of self-importance.

Key verses: "Do nothing from selfish ambition or conceit, but in humility count others more significant than yourselves. Let each of you look not only to his own interests, but also to the interests of others" (Phil 2:3–4). "Clothe yourselves, all of you, with humility toward one another, for 'God opposes the proud but gives grace to the humble.' Humble yourselves, therefore, under the mighty hand of God so that at the proper time he may exalt you" (1 Pet 5:5–6).

Bible characters: Basking in praise rightfully belonging to God alone, Herod's hubris proved his undoing. Leaving heaven's splendor to be born in a manger, live as a humble servant, and suffer a disgraceful death, the lowly Lord Jesus epitomized humility.

How often do you show humility in your life: 5 = nearly always, 4 = most of the time, 3 = about half the time, 2 = less than half the time, or 1 = hardly ever? Your response is _____.
In what ways, if any, has the Holy Spirit enabled you to show humility?
How did Jesus model humility during his earthly life in ways benefiting you?
In what ways, if any, has the Holy Spirit revealed to you a need to be humbler?
What petition related to humility, if any, would you like to bring before the throne of grace?

Joyfulness

Engage in one or more of these introductory activities:

1. Hearth and Home—Do you have a family dog or friends with canine pets? What do you like about dogs? Why do pooches wag their tails? Many dogs, especially the enthusiastic tail swishers, personify unabashed joy. Search for a few humorous video clips of dogs excitedly swishing tails and allow everyone to share a heart-warming dog tale.

2. Hymn Sing—Find hymns about joy.[1] Possible selections include: "Jesus, Thou Joy of Loving Hearts," "Joy to the World! The Lord Is Come," "Rejoice, the Lord Is King," and "Rejoice, Ye Pure in Heart." Sing (or read aloud) one or more verses of two or more hymns. Alternatively, play online recordings of the hymns. What does each song say about the source of real joy?

The happiness dogs display through wagging tails resembles human joy, but many hymns correctly identify Christ as the fountainhead of true joy. What is this Christian character trait of joyfulness? Here's one way to define it:

> Joyfulness is an inward sense of divine blessing that encourages
> the soul regardless of outward circumstances.

God desires his children to be joyful through good times and bad. From a biblical perspective, what does this character trait of joyfulness look like, and how can Christians improve it? This lesson addresses these points under the headings of "God's Word to Mankind," "God's Work in Believers," and "God's Grace for Change."

---

1. The initial idea of using hymn sings to introduce the character trait of joyfulness came from Carden and Carden, *Christian Character Curriculum* 2, 55.

God's Word to Mankind

Key Verses

"When the cares of my heart are many, your consolations cheer my soul" *(Ps 94:19)*. The wicked distressed the psalmist. He wondered, "How long shall the wicked exult?" as they "pour[ed] out their arrogant words," "crush[ed]" and "afflict[ed]" the saints, "kill[ed] the widow and the so-journer," and "murder[ed] the fatherless" (Ps 94:3–6). Understandably, this saint's anxiety was great. But then, the Lord provided loving comfort, showing himself to be a spiritual fortress and refuge (Ps 94:18, 22). Such "consolations" brought joy to the psalmist's soul. Thus, amid perplexing fears, he reposed his troubled mind in the Lord, and an inward sense of divine favor calmed his anxiety, producing joy.

"Rejoice in the Lord always; again I will say, rejoice" *(Phil 4:4)*. God never wants his people to despair. Far from it, God desires, indeed commands, the opposite—rejoice! But being joyful only when outward circumstances elate is not full obedience. No, rejoice "always" in good times and bad, including seasons of great disappointment, distress, suffering, loneliness, and grief. Indeed, the apostle Paul wrote this verse from prison to a church experiencing much affliction (Phil 1:13, 29–30). For emphasis, he repeated the command, underscoring how vital it is for Christians to rejoice always.

Bible Characters

Melancholy Mouthpiece (Hab 3:16–19)

The prophet Habakkuk sorrowfully complained about wicked leaders in Judah who oppressed the poor, perverting justice (Hab 1:1–4). The Lord replied he would send the cruel Babylonians to punish Judah (Hab 1:5–11). This answer really distressed the prophet, so he questioned why the Lord would send a nation even more despicable than Judah to execute judgment (Hab 1:12—2:1). In other words, why not discipline through other means? Notwithstanding the prophet's demur, the Lord assured Habakkuk the Babylonians would come, and Judah's punishment would be just (Hab 2:2–20).

Certain now of Judah's impending doom, God's melancholy mouthpiece reflected on all he had heard, and his "body tremble[d]," his "lips quiver[ed]," his bones seemed to "rot," and his "legs tremble[d]." Yet even though the Lord would use Babylon to bring a "day of trouble" when the crops and livestock would fail, Habakkuk resolved to "rejoice in the LORD" and "take joy in the God of [his] salvation." How could he rejoice amid such overwhelming dread and gloom? Well, the sovereign Lord who rules all nations in perfect justice gave him joyfulness, enabling him, like a deer, to scale the heights.

Afflicted Apostle (2 Cor 4:7–9, 6:4–10, 7:4–7, 11:23–29)

The apostle Paul experienced many grave afflictions as God's servant. He suffered from hunger, thirst, sleeplessness, exposure, shipwrecks, slanders, imprisonments, beatings, floggings, and even a stoning. These hardships would have broken most individuals; they would have plunged many into despair.

Amid these frequent, severe trials, what did Paul say? He was "perplexed, but not driven to despair," "sorrowful, yet always rejoicing." Not only did he always rejoice, but his joyfulness abounded. "I am filled with comfort. In all our affliction, I am overflowing with joy. . . . I rejoiced still more." Such deep, heartfelt joyfulness comes only from God, and, like one Old Testament saint, the apostle Paul found this "joy of the LORD [was his] strength" (Neh 8:10).

Review Questions

1. What is the Christian character trait of joyfulness?

2. What words are missing from this verse? "When the _____ of my heart are many, your consolations _____ my ____" (Ps 94:19).

3. In Ps 94, who or what distressed the writer?

4. In Ps 94, from where did the writer's joyfulness come?

5. What words are missing from this verse? "_____ in the Lord _____; _____ I will say, rejoice" (Phil 4:4).

6. Where was Paul when he wrote to the Philippian church?

7. In Hab 1:1–4, who or what distressed the writer?

8. After Habakkuk learned God would use the Babylonians to punish Judah, what distressed the prophet?

9. Even though Judah's livestock and crops would fail when the Babylonians attacked, what did Habakkuk say he would do?

God's Work in Believers

Joyfulness often happens in response to good news or happy events such as when God miraculously freed his people from Babylonian captivity and returned them to Judah. "Our mouths were filled with laughter, our tongues with songs of joy. . . . The LORD has done great things for us, and we are filled with joy" (Ps 126:2–3, NIV). Joyfulness also may occur amid times of great sorrow or distressing events; prime examples appeared earlier in the anxious psalmist, melancholy mouthpiece named Habakkuk, and afflicted apostle Paul. Thus, inward joy does not depend on outward circumstances, and this facet distinguishes happiness from biblical joy. Happiness occurs in response to positive, outward stimuli or events that delight, uplift, or cheer. In contrast, joy occurs without regard to outward circumstances, arising instead from the Holy Spirit's inward work. Thus, a Christian can be happy and joyful at the same time or, in response to outward difficulties, sad and joyful.

Joy should be normal for believers. Don't be content with infrequent or weak joy; instead, crave perpetual, overwhelming joy. Repeatedly, God commands his people to rejoice. "Rejoice in the LORD, O you righteous" (Ps 97:12). "Make a joyful noise to the LORD, all the earth! Serve the LORD with gladness! Come into his presence with singing!" (Ps 100:1–2). "This is the day that the LORD has made; let us rejoice and be glad in it" (Ps 118:24). "Rejoice in hope" (Rom 12:12). "Rejoice with those who rejoice" (Rom 12:15). "Rejoice in the Lord always; again I will say, rejoice" (Phil 4:4). "Rejoice always" (1 Thess 5:16).

Though God commands joyfulness, you can't simply jump-start it, when downcast, through self-exertion. Since a "fruit of the Spirit" (Gal 5:22), biblical joy occurs only as the divine will directs. So, that presents a dilemma—though commanded to rejoice greatly and always, joyfulness depends entirely on the Holy Spirit. If you lack joy, what can you do? The simple answer is that when you trust and obey God, joyfulness follows. "To pursue it [joy] is to lose it. The only way to get it is to follow steadily the path of duty, without thinking of joy, and then, like sleep, it comes most surely unsought, and we 'being in the way,' the angel of God, bright-haired Joy, is sure to meet us."[2] Like the grand old hymn teaches, "Trust and obey, for there's no other way to be happy [or joyful] in Jesus but to trust and obey."[3] As to trust, "you believe in him and rejoice with joy that is inexpressible and filled with glory" (1 Pet 1:8). As to obedience, the psalmist marvels, "I rejoice in following your statutes as one rejoices in great riches" (Ps 119:14, NIV).

Finally, spend much time learning about and praying to the only true and living God whom you have the privilege to trust and obey. Meditate on his steadfast love, great faithfulness, abundant mercy, unlimited power, inexhaustible wisdom, and eternal goodness. God chose, redeemed, called, regenerated, justified, and adopted you. Throughout this earthly life, he will sanctify you, and, when leaving this earthly life, he will glorify you. God keeps his "everlasting arms" directly beneath you (Deut 33:27) and promises you an eternal dwelling place (Ps 23:6), a glorious heritage (Ps 16:6). As you reflect on these things, how can you not rejoice? Is it reasonable that lapses exist in your joyfulness? Certainly not—rejoice always!

God's Grace for Change

Before examining your heart, considering how you might improve, and seeking divine help, ponder one last point—When you obey God's commandments, you abide in his love, and Jesus gives you abundant joy. "These things I have spoken to you, that my joy may be in you, and that your joy may be full" (John 15:11). Let this brief reminder about and appreciation for God's undeserved grace prepare and motivate you to develop more of this lesson's character trait in yourself.

Then, complete the "Heart Assessment, Reflection, and Petition" (HARP) chart, assessing your own joyfulness. Reflect on times the Holy Spirit enabled or empowered you to be joyful in bright and difficult times as well as times Jesus rejoiced during his earthly life. Consider whether the Spirit might be revealing a need for you to be more joyful. If you want God to increase your joyfulness, put that desire in writing. This is a very important exercise that can help you respond to God's direction for your life. Pray over your completed chart once or twice this next week.

2. Maclaren, *Music for the Soul*, 80.
3. Sammis, "Trust and Obey," 9.

Finally, talk to the Lord, using the words that follow or incorporating the thoughts into your own prayer: "My Father, with great joy I come into your holy presence. In this life, I will be happy at times and discouraged at others. Sometimes, my happiness will be blissful; sometimes, my sadness will be overwhelming. Holy Spirit, cause me to rejoice in the good times as well as the bad. Teach me to trust and obey you in every aspect of my life, remembering how wonderful you are and the great salvation you give to me, your precious child. Teach me to remember and believe your promises, jubilantly resting in them. Thank you for assuring me of your everlasting arms and giving me a beautiful inheritance. Let me greatly rejoice in you now, always, and forever. In Jesus' name, amen."

Remember, the Lord's help is vital to cultivating Christian character. Only his power can enable you to change. When you fail to show the character trait of joyfulness, confess it before God and ask for his forgiveness and help.

HARP Chart for Joyfulness

Definition: Joyfulness is an inward sense of divine blessing that encourages the soul regardless of outward circumstances.

Key verses: "When the cares of my heart are many, your consolations cheer my soul" (Ps 94:19). "Rejoice in the Lord always; again I will say, rejoice" (Phil 4:4).

Bible characters: Though the cruel Babylonians would punish Judah, Habakkuk, God's melancholy mouthpiece, said he would rejoice in the Lord his Savior. Though severely afflicted and often sorrowful, the apostle Paul always rejoiced greatly.

How often do you show joyfulness in your life: 5 = nearly always, 4 = most of the time, 3 = about half the time, 2 = less than half the time, or 1 = hardly ever? Your response is _____.
In what ways, if any, has the Holy Spirit enabled you to rejoice, especially in difficult times?
How did Jesus model joyfulness during his earthly life in ways benefiting you?
In what ways, if any, has the Holy Spirit revealed to you a need to be more joyful?
What petition related to joyfulness, if any, would you like to bring before the throne of grace?

Patience

Engage in one or more of these introductory activities:

1. Brainstorm—Think of people in the Bible who showed themselves patient, giving reasons for your selections. You might mention Noah bearing ridicule while building an enormous ark on dry land (Gen 6:9–22); Jacob working seven years to wed Laban's youngest daughter, Rachel (Gen 29:20); or David ignoring Shimei's stinging taunts as he fled Jerusalem to escape Absalom (2 Sam 16:5–13). Next, consider biblical characters who were impatient and, again, mention support. For instance, King Saul made offerings contrary to the law and Samuel's command because he became impatient when the prophet did not arrive on time (1 Sam 10:8, 13:5–14), and the apostles James and John lost patience with the Samaritan villagers who did not welcome Jesus (Luke 9:52–55).

2. Intriguing Insights—The quotations below make observations about patience or its lack. Explain each quotation's meaning or otherwise comment about it.

   > "PATIENCE, *n.* A minor form of despair, disguised as a virtue."[1]

   > "Beware the fury of a patient man."[2]

   > "A patient Christian, like the anvil, bears all strokes invincibly; thus the martyrs overcame their enemies by patience."[3]

   > "All commend patience, but none can endure to suffer."[4]

1. Bierce, *Devil's Dictionary*, 248.
2. Dryden, *Poems*, 101.
3. Watson, *Body of Practical Divinity*, 395.
4. Fuller, *Aphorisms of Wisdom*, 18.

3. Movie Night—Watch "42" (2013, PG-13) as a class or individually. Based on the true story, Jackie Robinson becomes the first black major league baseball player, signing with the Brooklyn Dodgers in 1947. The team's owner, Branch Rickey, wants to break professional baseball's racial barrier. However, he knows Robinson will face hostile prejudice in the process and, thus, must exercise extraordinary self-control and patience to succeed. At what times did Robinson show self-control, courage, and patience? Which people encouraged Robinson, and how might things have been different if Robinson had "struck out" against his antagonists? If time is short, just play the film clip in which Rickey asks Robinson whether he can absorb the abuse without fighting back.

As these activities emphasize, life presents constant opportunities to demonstrate patience. This lesson differs from the earlier one about endurance. As defined, endurance demands persistence through difficulties, while patience calls for placidity or composure during difficulties. Of course, the dividing line between these two traits is not always distinct, and many experiences demand patient endurance (or enduring patience). Be that as it may, what is this Christian character trait of patience? Here's one way to define it:

> Patience requires calm waiting or restraint when dealing with painful suffering, trying people, agonizing losses, daily irritants, or unfulfilled dreams.

God desires his children to develop and demonstrate patience in the many experiences of their daily lives. From a biblical perspective, what does this character trait of patience look like, and how can Christians improve it? This lesson addresses these points under the headings of "God's Word to Mankind," "God's Work in Believers," and "God's Grace for Change."

God's Word to Mankind

Key Verses

"A hot-tempered man stirs up dissension, but a patient man calms a quarrel" (Prov 15:18, NIV). A longsuffering person who is not easily provoked, through patience, precludes many quarrels. But, even after a quarrel

begins, conciliatory patience can douse contentious flames, preempting a full-fledged conflagration. How blessed are families, churches, businesses, communities, and nations that include patient saints whom God has equipped and positioned to prevent and squelch harmful quarrels.

"*With patience, bear . . . with one another in love*" *(Eph 4:2)*. People differ in their temperaments, habits, idiosyncrasies, and opinions, and these differences can occasion many irritations or annoyances. Even among believers, impatience occurs often. Knowing this, the apostle Paul admonishes Christians to be patient, forbearing with the foibles, infirmities, faults, inexperience, foolishness, and, yes, even the provocations of their brothers and sisters in the faith. How can this be done? The short answer is "in love." Love and patience are inseparably intertwined. If one languishes, so does the other; where one abounds, so does the other. "Love is patient" (1 Cor 13:4).

Bible Characters

Conflicted Couple
(Gen 12:1–7; 13:14–17; 15:1–6; 16:1–5; 17:1–8, 15–19; 21:1–7)

When God promised to make Abram into a great nation, he was seventy-five, and his wife, Sarai, was sixty-five. They also were childless. Yet, God pledged their offspring would become numerous like the dust of the earth and stars in the heavens. So, Abram, the great man of faith, waited on God to fulfill his promise day after day, year after year. He clung to God's promise even as he and Sarai continued to grow older, getting further and further from the time of normal childbearing. Humanly speaking, they would never have their own child. But then, at age one hundred, "having patiently waited, [Abraham] obtained the promise" (Heb 6:15) when Sarah bore a son named Isaac. Sixty years later, Isaac's wife bore twin sons, Esau and Jacob, and Abraham lived until his two grandsons turned fifteen. In due course, Jacob fathered twelve sons whose descendants became twelve tribes, the great nation of Israel God had promised.

Yet, Abram and Sarai did not show perfect patience all the time. After waiting ten years on God's promise for offspring, they began having thoughts such as, "Will God still do as he promised? Maybe we misunderstood, or maybe God needs a little help." In short, the couple grew anxious waiting and became conflicted. On the one hand, they trusted God's word and power; but, on the other hand, their patience waned.

That's when Sarai suggested her eighty-five-year-old husband bear them a child through her Egyptian handmaiden, Hagar. Using this method, Sarai reasoned, God's promise of offspring could be accomplished. Abram agreed, and Hagar birthed a son named Ishmael. However, Isaac, not Ishmael, would be the son of promise (Gal 4:22–23). Having a son through Hagar substituted Abram and Sarai's reckless self-reliance for what should have been their calm, unwavering dependence on God. Further, their impatience kindled painful jealousies and family discord that lasted many years.

Bewildered Believer (Job 1:1—4:6)

Though righteous, Job suffered greatly when God allowed Satan to take away his ten children and numerous livestock. Early on, Job's patience shined through: "The LORD gave, and the LORD has taken away; blessed be the name of the LORD" (Job 1:21). Even when painful sores erupted all over Job's body and his wife goaded him to curse God, he "did not sin with his lips" (Job 2:10). And yet, Job showed impatience too, for example, in lamenting his birth (Job 3:1–26). Though his three friends can be faulted for much they said and how they said it, some of their words rang true. Consider Eliphaz's initial rebuke to Job's cursing the day of his birth: "If one ventures a word with you, will you be impatient? . . . But now [trouble] has come to you, and you are impatient; it touches you, and you are dismayed" (Job 4:2, 5). In short, Eliphaz said Job's outburst of discouragement and dismay did not comport with the patience of saints.

How Job responded to prolonged hardship might be characterized more as endurance than patience. But surely, his sudden loss of family and property, painful rebukes from friends, and bewilderment over God's purpose required daily patience. Later, according to the Lord's schedule, prosperity returned to Job's life—God gave him ten more children and twice his prior livestock (Job 42:10–17). The New Testament writer sums up the miserable ordeal and its aftermath this way: "You have heard of the steadfastness [and patience] of Job, and you have seen the purpose of the Lord" (Jas 5:11).

Review Questions

1. What is the Christian character trait of patience?

2. What words are missing from this verse? "A hot-_____ man stirs up _____, but a _____ man calms a _____" (Prov 15:18, NIV).

3. What words are missing from this verse? "With _____, ____ . . . with one another in ____" (Eph 4:2).

4. What words are missing from this verse? "____ is _____" (1 Cor 13:4).

5. What did God promise Abram?

6. Who was Abram's son of promise?

7. How many years did Abram and Sarai wait for God to fulfill his promise?

8. Abraham patiently waited for God's promise. Do you agree or disagree?

9. Job patiently waited for God's deliverance. Do you agree or disagree?

10. When Christians calmly wait on the Lord as they deal with painful suffering, trying people, agonizing losses, daily irritants, or unfulfilled dreams, God rewards them like he did Job. Do you agree or disagree?

God's Work in Believers

Many believers experience painful suffering, trying people, agonizing losses, daily irritants, or unfulfilled dreams frequently as a normal part of life. Painful suffering may proceed from an illness, injury, or fear. Trying people can include family members, close friends, church members, classmates, work colleagues, or complete strangers who disappoint, complain, gossip, nag, bore, disrespect, insult, abuse, or provoke. Agonizing losses might be physical, social, or financial in nature. Daily irritants could include the texting driver who fails to see a traffic light change, long grocery checkout lines, inattentive or uncaring retail clerks, boisterous library patrons, tyrannical or incompetent people in authority, misbehaving children, or delayed departures. Unfulfilled dreams may be career or family goals that seem ever elusive such as Abram and Sarai's intense desire for a child in their old age. In these and many similar difficulties, eschew hasty, knee-jerk reactions like giving up, behaving rashly, or murmuring. Instead, plead for the Holy Spirit's aid to remain calm, exercising godly restraint. "Be still before the LORD and wait patiently for him" (Ps 37:7).

Yet, impatience is the all-too-common human response to life's many problems and hardships. How can you be patient when trouble intrudes uninvited from so many quarters? First, understand that all difficulties proceed from God's hand. Really, really grasp that fundamental truth and then grapple with its clear implication—every affliction, without exception, is his express will for you. "Patience is a submission to [God's] sovereignty. . . . To be patient because we cannot avoid or resist it, is a violent, not a loyal patience."[5] Second, understand impatience as a token of unbelief. It evidences some distrust in God's wisdom, goodness, timing, justice, or power. Therefore, submit to God's sovereign will amid every difficulty, remaining patient, remembering that "for those who love God all things work together for good" (Rom 8:28).

Even with these two understandings, you still will be tempted occasionally, just like Abram and Job, to respond impatiently. But, at those times, let quietness be your first defense. "Whoever restrains his words has knowledge" (Prov 17:27). When the first small sparks of annoyance flare within you, resist the impulsive urge to blurt out words that can only stoke your soul's restive tinder and, perhaps, combust into anger. Instead, silently pray that you do not complain, display annoyance, or lose your temper. In every difficulty, respond first with quiet patience. "A patient man has great understanding" (Prov 14:29, NIV). "Be quick to hear, slow to speak, slow to anger" (Jas 1:19). Yet, silence alone is not true patience; the quietness must be rooted in a deep dependence on the Almighty. Biblical patience waits trustingly on God to enlighten, strengthen, guide, content, deliver, or console. "In quietness and in trust shall be your strength" (Isa 30:15).

Just as the ancient city of Rome wasn't built in a day, neither should you expect that, overnight, calm waiting or restraint will become your normal response to life's difficulties. Learning patience requires much practice, persistence, and prayer. You might even say developing patience takes patience. Don't be discouraged that you might show impatience

---

5. Stephen Charnock as cited in Plumer, *Vital Godliness*, 483.

ten times more often than you manifest a calm, trusting restraint. While thanking the Lord for every victory, repent over each failure, asking the Holy Spirit to grant you more and more patience day by day. "Put on then, as God's chosen ones, holy and beloved, . . . patience" (Col 3:12).

God's Grace for Change

Before examining your heart, considering how you might improve, and seeking divine help, ponder one last point—While still a sinner, God patiently drew you to himself. "Do you presume on the riches of his kindness and forbearance and patience, not knowing that God's kindness [led] you to repentance?" (Rom 2:4). Let this brief reminder about and appreciation for God's undeserved grace prepare and motivate you to develop more of this lesson's character trait in yourself.

Then, complete the "Heart Assessment, Reflection, and Petition" (HARP) chart, assessing your own patience. Reflect on times the Holy Spirit enabled or empowered you to be patient as well as times God and others showed you patience. Consider whether the Spirit might be revealing a need for you to become more consistently patient. If you want God to increase your patience, put that desire in writing. This is a very important exercise that can help you respond to God's direction for your life. Pray over your completed chart once or twice this next week.

Finally, talk to the Lord, using the words that follow or incorporating the thoughts into your own prayer: "My Father, merciful, compassionate, and slow to anger, you are worthy of all praise, adoration, and glory. My sins are many and great, but you patiently bear with my frailties and faults, forgiving me again and again. From a thankful heart, I marvel that Jesus, the Lamb of God, loved me so much that he was willing to be broken for such a helpless, hopeless sinner. As Jesus bore so much for me, help me to bear patiently and lovingly with other people. When difficulties arise in my life, when I must eat the bread of adversity or drink the water of affliction, teach me to wait calmly on you; restrain my sinful inclinations and wayward tendencies. Holy Spirit, teach me to trust quietly in the all-wise, all-powerful Father, knowing he desires my eternal good. In Jesus' name, I pray. Amen."

Remember, the Lord's help is vital to cultivating Christian character. Only his power can enable you to change. When you fail to show the character trait of patience, confess it before God and ask for his forgiveness and help.

HARP Chart for Patience

Definition: Patience requires calm waiting or restraint when dealing with painful suffering, trying people, agonizing losses, daily irritants, or unfulfilled dreams.

Key verses: "A hot-tempered man stirs up dissension, but a patient man calms a quarrel" (Prov 15:18, NIV). "With patience, bear . . . with one another in love" (Eph 4:2).

Bible characters: Except in the matter of Hagar, Abram and Sarai patiently trusted God 25 years to provide the offspring he had promised. With some lapses, Job patiently hoped in God through the sudden loss of family and property, painful rebukes from friends, and bewilderment over God's purpose.

How often do you show patience in your life: 5 = nearly always, 4 = most of the time, 3 = about half the time, 2 = less than half the time, or 1 = hardly ever? Your response is _____.
In what ways, if any, has the Holy Spirit enabled you to show patience?
In what ways, if any, have God and others shown patience to you?
In what ways, if any, has the Holy Spirit revealed to you a need to be more patient?
What petition related to patience, if any, would you like to bring before the throne of grace?

Purity

Engage in one or more of these introductory activities:

1. Brainstorm—Think of people in the Bible who promoted or practiced sexual purity, giving reasons for your selections. You might mention how Joseph fled from the seduction of Potiphar's wife (Gen 39:6–12); Phinehas, Aaron's grandson, killed the Israelite man and Midianite woman who indulged in sexual immorality within the camp (Num 25:6–13); and Job covenanted with his eyes not to look lustfully at other women (Job 31:1). Next, name biblical characters committing sexual immorality. For instance, Sodomites demanded homosexual relations with Lot's visitors (Gen 19:1–5); Lot's daughters intoxicated their father so that he impregnated them (Gen 19:30–36); Shechem the Hivite raped Jacob's daughter, Dinah (Gen 34:1–2); Judah committed fornication with his daughter-in-law, Tamar (Gen 38:12–18); Benjamites sought sexual relations with a Levite but, failing that, raped the man's concubine (Judg 19:16–28); King David committed adultery with Uriah's wife, Bathsheba (2 Sam 11:2–5); and a member of the Corinthian church committed incest with his father's wife (1 Cor 5:1–5). The Bible often raises questions of sexual purity.

2. Nature Study—Learn about peacocks and share your findings through online photos or short video clips. Three species of peacocks exist within the pheasant family: blue peacocks reside in India and Sri Lanka, green peacocks live in Southeast Asia from Myanmar (aka Burma) to the island of Java in Indonesia, and Congo peacocks dwell in the Congo Basin rainforests. Technically, only males are peacocks; females are peahens, and males and females together are peafowl. During courtship, peacocks attract two to five peahens into their harems with loud, exotic calls. The more intricate the male's call, the more agreeable to females. But peacocks have a second way

to allure peahens. They sport nearly two hundred long, iridescent tail feathers, comprising 60 percent of their body's length, which they elevate and spread behind them when courting. The colorful, flamboyant plumage includes many concentric eyespots, which some believe peahens find particularly appealing. To attract females further, peacocks vibrate their tail feathers, producing a shimmering effect and rustling sound. Believers, like peafowl, can see and hear things that ignite or inflame sexual thoughts and actions.

These activities warn God's people about the devastating effects of sexual immorality and the role visual and audial stimuli play. But what is this Christian character trait of purity? Here's one way to define it:

> Purity is freedom from sexual immorality whether in attitudes, thoughts, speech, or actions.

God desires his children to eschew sexual temptations and transgressions. From a biblical perspective, what does this character trait of purity look like, and how can Christians improve it? This lesson addresses these points under the headings of "God's Word to Mankind," "God's Work in Believers," and "God's Grace for Change."

God's Word to Mankind

Key Verses

"Flee from sexual immorality. Every other sin a person commits is outside the body, but the sexually immoral person sins against his own body" (1 Cor 6:18). Believers' physical bodies are "members of Christ" and "temple[s] of the Holy Spirit" (1 Cor 6:15, 19). As such, their bodies are "not meant for sexual immorality" (1 Cor 6:13). It dishonors Christ when someone united to him then unites with a prostitute (1 Cor 6:16–17). Thus, the apostle Paul says to "flee from sexual immorality," underscoring the serious nature of these temptations. Other sins like rebellion, murder, theft, deceit, and covetousness do not directly harm the transgressor's body, but sexual immorality defiles the body (which belongs to God) and, in addition, may lead to sexually transmitted diseases that impair or ravage physical health.

"This is the will of God, your sanctification: that you abstain from sexual immorality; that each one of you know how to control his own body in holiness and honor, not in the passion of lust like the Gentiles . . . . For

God has not called us for impurity, but in holiness" (1 Thess 4:3–7). God desires and commands that his people be sanctified or holy, a prominent element of which involves sexual purity. Indeed, its opposite—sexual immorality—includes a hodgepodge of vile, perilous sins that blight the soul and defile the body. In New Testament times, many unbelieving Gentiles did not view lasciviousness and unchasteness as immoral but as socially acceptable or, at worse, only slightly objectionable. In contrast, the apostle Paul says saints should control all sexual urges outside biblical marriage, keeping to God's path of purity and holiness.

Bible Characters

Respectful Redeemer (Ruth 3:7–14)

Due to famine, Naomi, her husband, and two sons left Bethlehem of Judah to dwell in Moab. While away, her husband died, her sons married, and then both sons died. Bereaved, Naomi returned to Bethlehem after a ten-year absence with one daughter-in-law, Ruth the Moabitess.

To provide for their sustenance, Ruth picked up small amounts of barley that harvesters left behind. The Judean fields where she gleaned belonged to a prosperous, honorable man named Boaz, who was a near relative of Naomi's deceased husband. Boaz showed much kindness to Ruth as she gleaned. His benevolence prompted Naomi to devise a plan when she knew Boaz would be staying overnight on the threshing floor. Naomi instructed her daughter-in-law to wait until Boaz slept and then uncover his feet and lay down there, and Ruth complied. When Boaz awoke and discovered Ruth, she asked for his protection as a kinsman-redeemer.

What happened next reveals Boaz as a respectful redeemer, one who scrupulously avoided impurity or even its appearance. First, he instructed Ruth to remain at his feet; Boaz did not summon her to his side for sexual intimacy. Second, he called her a "worthy woman" and took pains to assure idle, misguided gossip did not damage her good reputation. Third, after determining a nearer kinsman did not wish to redeem Ruth, Boaz married her and, only afterwards, engaged with her sexually (Ruth 4:13).

Lustful Leader (2 Sam 11:1–5)

A man after God's own heart, David loved the Lord with all his heart, soul, and mind (1 Sam 13:14). From this intense love, he sought to obey all God's commandments consistently and faithfully. But, just like other saints, David experienced many temptations and sometimes yielded. Devastating consequences followed when David yielded to a particular sexual allurement, allowing a lustful desire to spark, flicker, and flame into an iniquitous inferno.

While King David's army fought the Ammonites beyond the Jordan River, he remained in Jerusalem. One night, maybe unable to sleep, the king arose from his bed and walked along the palace roof. Seeing a beautiful woman bathing on a lower roof or, perhaps, in a courtyard, he lusted after her. That is, Israel's leader committed sexual immorality in his mind. Then, things went from bad to worse. David learned her name—Bathsheba—and that she was married to Uriah, one of his greatest warriors (1 Chr 11:41). Knowing Uriah was engaged in the military campaign, David brought Bathsheba to his palace where he slept with and impregnated her. So, what began as an impure thought, which was bad enough, developed into a sexually immoral act. Later, trying to conceal his adultery, David deceived Uriah and, later still, gave orders resulting in his murder. Killing Uriah caused collateral casualties to other innocent combatants (2 Sam 11:6–17). Though David eventually repented of these heinous sins, they brought great harm to his family over many years (2 Sam 12:11).

Review Questions

1. What is the Christian character trait of purity?

2. What words are missing from this verse? "_____ from sexual _____. Every other sin a person commits is _____ the body, but the _____ immoral person sins against his own ____" (1 Cor 6:18).

3. In 1 Cor 6, what are the physical bodies of believers called?

4. What words are missing from this verse? "The body is not meant for _____ _____" (1 Cor 6:13).

5. In what sense does the believer committing sexual immorality sin "against his [or her] own body" (1 Cor 6:18)?

6. What words are missing from these verses? "This is the _____ of God, your _____: that you abstain from sexual _____; that each one of you know how to control his own _____ in holiness and honor, not in the passion of _____ like the Gentiles . . . . For God has not called us for _____, but in _____" (1 Thess 4:3–7).

7. How did Boaz show concern for his and Ruth's purity?

8. What might David have done differently to avoid sexual immorality with Bathsheba?

9. What sins followed David's sexual immorality?

God's Work in Believers

Sexual immorality typified the religious rituals of several nations near ancient Israel. For instance, the Canaanites worshiped a fertility goddess called Asherah (aka Ashtoreth), which many posit involved sensual rites and ceremonial prostitution. Sadly, like the pagan nations around them, Israel often pursued Asherah (e.g., see Judg 2:13; 1 Kgs 11:5, 18:19; 2 Kgs 23:4–7). The license to practice sexual immorality, no doubt, played some role in Israel's persistent entanglement with this false deity.

Perhaps, not much has changed. Today, it's common for people to pursue idols of pleasure, particularly as to sexual practice. The prevailing thought runs something like this: It is proper and good to seek erotic pleasure so long as it doesn't restrict someone else's pleasure or infringe on someone else's rights. A prominent corollary is that, except as just noted, any moral criticism or restriction of sexual pleasure is wrong and, thus, should be attacked and condemned. Since the desire for sinful pleasure often proves insatiable, many unbelievers hate the Bible's language that warns against sexual immorality.

Society's widespread pursuit of sexual pleasure takes several forms and goes by many names: love affair, consensual non-monogamy, swinging, relationship anarchy, polyamory, common law marriage, co-habitation, civil partnership, same sex marriage, open relationship, friend with benefits, one-night stand, casual hookup, tryst, romantic encounter, sexual rendezvous, sleeping around, booty call, and recreational sex. But these euphemisms just put lipstick on a pig; each term describes iniquitous mutations of age-old wickedness that defiles body and soul. Lost on today's culture are the broad scriptural descriptors of these collective sins—adultery and fornication (both defined below)—and the haven that biblical marriage offers.

Marriage is a life-long commitment, union, or covenant between one biological male and one biological female. God sanctions sex within marriage. "A man shall leave his father and his mother and hold fast to his wife, and they shall become one flesh" (Gen 2:24). "Let marriage be held in honor among all, and let the marriage bed be undefiled" (Heb 13:4). Conversely, God forbids sex outside marriage. Sexual immorality includes (a) fornication, which is an unmarried person's consensual sex, (b) adultery, which is a married person's consensual sex with someone other than his or her spouse, and (c) rape, which involves someone's non-consensual sex forced on an innocent party. Purity requires abstention from fornication, adultery, and rape in attitude, thought, speech, and action.

Yielding to sensual temptations can inflict physical, mental, and spiritual harm. Impure activities may lead to sexually transmitted diseases, pollute perspectives and expectations about marriage, and bring down God's chastisement or punishment. But the damage often extends beyond those intimately involved. As King David discovered after his affair with Bathsheba, sexual immorality can lead to other sins, and the collateral fallout often affects many innocent people over numerous years (2 Sam 11:17, 12:11). For example, fornication resulting in pregnancy may tempt the mother to consider abortion; in effect, sexual immorality sometimes leads to the further sin of killing an innocent, unborn child. Also, the faultless husband or wife usually pays a heavy price for an unfaithful spouse's adultery, as do their children.

Sexual immorality's pervasiveness and severe consequences pose clear and present dangers for believers. So, how can you stay or become pure? Stated differently, how can you resist or overcome sexual immorality with all its tantalizing, worldly allurements? The simple answer, of course, is you cannot prevail in your own strength. Indeed, you may feel powerless against the relentless, daily onslaught of impure words and images that tempt you to sin. However, Christians can resist or overcome sexual immorality through God's strength. "The weapons of our warfare are not of the flesh but have divine power to destroy strongholds" (2 Cor 10:4). "Be strong in the Lord and in the strength of his might" (Eph 6:10). In addition to the Lord's great power working within you, he promises to moderate your temptations and provide escape routes. "God is faithful, and he will not let you be tempted beyond your ability, but with the temptation he will also provide the way of escape, that you may be able to endure it" (1 Cor 10:13). Thus, God delivers you through his (not your) power, protects from allurements stronger than you can handle, and provides means for resisting temptations you do face.

Since God promises to provide "the way of escape" (1 Cor 10:13), he expects you to follow that course in resisting sensual temptations and overcoming sexual immorality. To illustrate, consider four prudent steps you might take if a highly contagious plague broke out and you wanted to do everything possible to survive. First, you could eat healthily and exercise regularly to build up your body's natural resistance to infection. Second, you could minimize chances the disease enters your home or invades other areas you frequent through infected food, water, or carriers. Third, you could withdraw quickly if you stumbled, by accident, into quarantined areas. Fourth, you could seek immediate medical treatment if symptoms of the disease appeared. Here's the point: God, as the first cause, would be the one who protects you, but he still would expect you to use whatever good sense and reasonable measures he provides to survive the outbreak.

Your soul's health is much more important than your body's (Mark 8:37; 1 Tim 4:8). So, take even greater precautions to guard against the spiritual plague of sexual immorality. The four steps below (parallel to the ones above) might be viewed as God's "way of escape" for resisting sensual temptations and overcoming such sins.

1. Pursue all means of grace to strengthen your soul against sexual immorality. "Put on the whole armor of God, that you may be able to stand against the schemes of the devil" (Eph 6:11). The means of grace and spiritual armor include the Word of God and prayer. Meditate on the Scriptures and listen attentively to solid Bible instruction. "Watch and pray that you may not enter into temptation. The spirit indeed is willing, but the flesh is weak" (Matt 26:41). Pray as the Lord taught, "Lead [me] not into temptation, but deliver [me] from evil" (Matt 6:13). Though pursuing the means of grace and putting on spiritual armor do not guarantee purity, they inoculate you against easily yielding to sensual lusts; they bolster your defenses and weaken temptation's power. Therefore, "put on the Lord Jesus Christ, and make no provision for the flesh, to gratify its desires" (Rom 13:14). "Walk by the Spirit, and you will not gratify the desires of the flesh" (Gal 5:16). Walk daily in close communion with the God of all grace, building up your spiritual strength and immunity so you can become more and more pure.

2. Avoid language, music, pictures, video, places, people, and other sensual triggers that tempt you to be sexually immoral, focusing on three areas. First, make your home a haven, removing things that might catalyze or incite impure attitudes, thoughts, speech, or actions. Second, consider your electronic devices, your consumption of their content, and their impact on your spiritual life. Salacious content can pose real sexual dangers to your soul, so evaluate your usage and prayerfully consider what changes to make. As preventative or remedial measures, consider: (a) switching to an internet service provider with potent settings that filter out most objectionable content, (b) selecting a default browser with settings that further remove sensual material, (c) unsubscribing to entertainment that tempts you to sin, (d) installing an effective ad blocker to prevent unsolicited offers, especially sexually charged ones, (e) eschewing otherwise safe internet pages (e.g., news sites) that too often feature tantalizing, clickable links that too easily lead to risqué materials, (f) turning off electronic devices late at night or other times when weariness or boredom tempts you to access impure content, (g) changing your e-mail account if your current one gets bombarded with salacious messages, and (h) asking a mature saint or Christian organization for help with any of the preceding points and, if necessary, counseling for sexual addiction. Third, structure daily activities to avoid provocative people and unsavory places that might lead to impurity. "Keep your way far from [temptation], and do not go near the door of her house" (Prov 5:8).

3. Flee sexual temptations that appear in your life unexpectedly. While pursuing means of grace and avoiding sensual triggers promote and facilitate purity, they will not remove every unchaste allurement from your life. Despite all precautions, Satan and your old sin nature still will place sexual stumbling blocks in your way, sometimes with very little warning. Unlike many other sins, the mind or will often proves unreliable or even useless against the temptation of sexual lust. So, when these unforeseen enticements first arise, flee as opposed to all other alternatives. Don't depend on your own internal strength or supposed virtue to protect you. Don't inwardly debate the situation, pause to consider a middle course, or otherwise dawdle. Instead, discern the extreme, perilous danger and scram, skedaddle, vamoose! Flee like righteous Joseph from the unholy seduction of Potiphar's wife: "She caught him by his garment, saying,

'Lie with me.' But he left his garment in her hand and fled and got out of the house" (Gen 39:12). Like the godly patriarch, remember the one word from holy Scripture that encapsulates your only safe response to sensual temptation and flee (1 Cor 6:18). After doing so, don't glance back to consider what you may have missed but, instead, contemplate what you have kept—your purity—and thank the Lord for his safe deliverance.

4. Confess and repent of all sexual immorality and do so quickly before your heart hardens, leading you further astray. Recall how King David did not acknowledge his sin and reconcile with God after committing adultery, which led to further iniquity and much heartache for him and others (2 Sam 11:6—18:33). So, when you sin, run quickly to the throne of grace, confessing every impure attitude, thought, word, or deed as disobedience to God's moral law. "If we confess our sins, he is faithful and just to forgive us our sins and to cleanse us from all unrighteousness" (1 John 1:9). In godly sorrow, turn away from sin and towards God, putting off sexual immorality and putting on righteous behavior in its place. "Let not sin therefore reign in your mortal body, to make you obey its passions. Do not present your members to sin as instruments for unrighteousness, but present yourselves to God as those who have been brought from death to life, and your members to God as instruments for righteousness" (Rom 6:12–13). "Just as you once presented your members as slaves to impurity and to lawlessness leading to more lawlessness, so now present your members as slaves to righteousness leading to sanctification" (Rom 6:19). "Flee youthful passions and pursue righteousness, faith, love, and peace, along with those who call on the Lord from a pure heart" (2 Tim 2:22). In short, rather than uniting with immorality, unite with the Lord (1 Cor 6:15–20).

Sexual sins are among the most difficult to resist and the most destructive when not withstood. "Do not desire [another's] beauty in your heart, and do not let [that person] capture you with [his or] her eyelashes; for the price of a [sexually immoral person] is only a loaf of bread, but [an adulterer] hunts down a precious life. Can [anyone] carry fire next to his [or her] chest and his [or her] clothes not be burned?" (Prov 6:25–27). "I find something more bitter than death: the woman [or man] whose heart is snares and nets, and whose hands are fetters" (Eccl 7:26). "Desire when it has conceived gives birth to sin, and sin when it is fully grown brings forth death" (Jas 1:15). "My will the enemy [Satan] held, and thence had made a chain for me, and bound me. For of a forward [irreverent] will, was a lust made; and a lust served [indulged], became custom [habit]; and custom not resisted, became necessity. By which links, as it were, joined together (whence I called it a chain) a hard bondage held me enthralled [captive]."[1] Therefore, pursue all means of grace to strengthen your soul against sexual immorality, avoid or remove all sensual triggers, flee from unchaste allurements that still arise, and confess and repent of improper sexual attitudes, thoughts, speech, or actions. May God's great power give you victory over sexual sins and keep you pure.

God's Grace for Change

Complete the "Heart Assessment, Reflection, and Petition" (HARP) chart, assessing your own purity. Reflect on times the Holy Spirit enabled or empowered you to be sexually pure. Then, consider whether the Spirit might be revealing a need for you to become more consistently pure. If you want God to increase your purity, put that desire in writing. This is a very important exercise that can help you respond to God's direction for your life. Pray over your completed chart once or twice this next week.

Finally, talk to the Lord, using the words that follow or incorporating the thoughts into your own prayer: "Great Father, Redeemer, and Comforter, glorious is your name! How thankful I am that you have clothed me in the righteousness of Christ and called me to holiness. And yet, my attitude, thoughts, speech, and actions often lack purity. In mercy, forgive these sins. Lead me not into temptation but deliver me from evil. Cause me to avoid and flee from sexual immorality. Give me single-mindedness, filling me with true, noble, right, pure, lovely, admirable, excellent, and praiseworthy thoughts. May my words and deeds always be pure, full of grace, and seasoned with spiritual salt. Grant me clean hands and a pure heart so I can reflect your image through my daily life, glorifying you. In the name of Jesus my Savior, I bring these petitions. Amen."

Remember, the Lord's help is vital to cultivating Christian character. Only his power can enable you to change. When you fail to show the character trait of purity, confess it before God and ask for his forgiveness and help.

---

1. Augustine, *Confessions*, 177.

HARP Chart for Purity

Definition: Purity is freedom from sexual immorality whether in attitudes, thoughts, speech, or actions.

Key verses: "Flee from sexual immorality. Every other sin a person commits is outside the body, but the sexually immoral person sins against his own body" (1 Cor 6:18). "This is the will of God, your sanctification: that you abstain from sexual immorality; that each one of you know how to control his own body in holiness and honor, not in the passion of lust like the Gentiles . . . . For God has not called us for impurity, but in holiness" (1 Thess 4:3–7).

Bible characters: Boaz, the respectful redeemer, protected his own and Ruth's purity. King David lusted after another man's wife, which led to an adulterous act and other sins.

How often do you show purity in your life: 5 = nearly always, 4 = most of the time, 3 = about half the time, 2 = less than half the time, or 1 = hardly ever? Your response is ____.
In what ways, if any, has the Holy Spirit enabled you to be pure?
In what ways, if any, has the Holy Spirit revealed to you a need for more purity?
What petition related to purity, if any, would you like to bring before the throne of grace?

Repentance

Engage in one or more of these introductory activities:

1. Hymn Sing—Find hymns about repentance. Possible selections include: "Come, Ye Sinners, Poor and Wretched," "God, Be Merciful to Me," "In Thy Wrath and Hot Displeasure," "Kind and Merciful God, We Have Sinned," "Lord, Like the Publican I Stand," "No, Not Despairingly Come I to Thee," and "O Thou That Hear'st When Sinners Cry." Sing (or read aloud) one or more verses of two or more hymns. Alternatively, play online recordings of the hymns. What does each song teach about human repentance and God's response?

2. Intriguing Insights—The quotations below make observations about repentance. Display each entry one at a time. Explain each quotation's meaning or otherwise comment about it.

   > "Repentance is . . . the fair daughter of a foul mother, i.e. sin."[1]

   > "Repentance is faith's twin brother, and is born at the same time."[2]

   > "There is one death bed repentance recorded in Scripture, that none may despair; there is only one, that none may presume."[3]

   > "There is no repentance where a man can talk lightly of sin, much less where he can speak tenderly and lovingly of it."[4]

---

1. Trapp, *Commentary*, 438.
2. Spurgeon, "Forgiveness and Fear," 5.
3. Matthew Henry as cited in "Reviews of Recent Literature," 488.
4. Spurgeon, "Christ's First and Last," 4.

"Repentance is the inseparable companion of saving faith in Christ."[5]

"True believers repent to their dying day—they are always repenting!"[6]

"Many mourn for their sins that do not truly repent of them, weep bitterly for them, and yet continue in love and league with them."[7]

"There is no true gospel fruit, without faith and repentance."[8]

"Oh, how blessed it is to know where these two lines meet, the stripping of repentance, and the clothing of faith! The repentance that ejects sin as an evil tenant, and the faith that admits Christ to be the sole Master of the heart."[9]

"It is the greatest and dearest blessing that ever God gave to men, that they may repent; and therefore to deny or to delay it is to refuse health brought by the skill of the Physician; it is to refuse liberty indulged to us by our gracious Lord."[10]

"Many think they repent, when it is not the offense, but the penalty that troubles them; not the treason, but the bloody axe."[11]

"Repentance is the relinquishment of any practice from the conviction that it has offended God."[12]

These activities highlight various facets of biblical repentance, which is related to two character traits in prior lessons—faith and forgiveness.

5. Ryle, *Expository Thoughts*, 29.

6. Spurgeon, "The Pierced One," 6.

7. Henry, *Exposition*, 411.

8. Owen, *The Works*, 447.

9. Spurgeon, "Faith and Repentance," 4.

10. Jeremy Taylor as cited in Cooksey, *Doctrine and Duty*, 36.

11. Watson, *Discourses*, 354.

12. Johnson, *Life and Writings*, 50.

Repentance and faith are gifts from God, without which salvation is impossible; they always exist together. As to forgiveness, repentance is its mirror image; ideally, the offending individual repents, and the offended person forgives, resulting in reconciliation. But what is this Christian character trait of repentance? Here's one way to define it:

> Repentance involves sorrowing for sin and turning from it to God.

God desires his children, each time they sin, to mourn their wrongdoing and resolve to follow righteousness. From a biblical perspective, what does this character trait of repentance look like, and how can Christians improve it? This lesson addresses these points under the headings of "God's Word to Mankind," "God's Work in Believers," and "God's Grace for Change."

God's Word to Mankind

Key Verses

"If my people who are called by my name humble themselves, and pray and seek my face and turn from their wicked ways, then I will hear from heaven and will forgive their sin and heal their land" (2 Chr 7:14). Through prayer and sacrifice, King Solomon dedicated the majestic temple he had built, and the Lord's glory filled it (2 Chr 7:1). Later, God warned he might withhold rain, send locust, or allow a plague if Israel sinned (2 Chr 7:13). However, he promised to hear prayers from those with repentant hearts, "forgive their sin[,] and heal their land." Genuine repentance requires people to "humble themselves," sorrowing for sin, as well as "turn from their wicked ways" and "seek [God's] face."

"You were grieved into repenting. For you felt a godly grief.... Godly grief produces a repentance that leads to salvation without regret, whereas worldly grief produces death" (2 Cor 7:9–10). Grief or sorrow comes in two forms—worldly and godly. The distinction lies in sorrow's origin and end. Worldly grief begins with a sad sense of having lost something earthly (e.g., reputation or wealth) and ends pining away over its loss. In contrast, godly sorrow begins with contriteness at having offended the Lord and ends restoring the broken relationship through a course reversal or change in direction. In essence, true repentance involves (a) godly grief and (b) turning from sin to God. Unlike its fake counterpart, godly

sorrow targets the root cause of sadness—namely, sin—and provides an effective solution—namely, turning around. This becomes a way of life for believers. Repentance doesn't just arise when the elect first come to Christ; it also recurs repeatedly as the Holy Spirit sanctifies them. No believer ever regrets the outcome of true repentance, which is reconciliation and communion with God.

Bible Characters

Sorrowful Sovereign (2 Sam 12:1–14; Ps 51:1–17)

King David committed adultery with Bathsheba and then killed her husband as a coverup (2 Sam 11). To make matters worse, months passed without the king repenting of these egregious crimes. Perhaps he thought the passage of time would lessen his wickedness and, thus, ignored it. Or maybe he hoped marrying Bathsheba and becoming a good husband would offset his wrongdoing. Or possibly he assumed his sovereign kingship shielded him from punishment, presuming on God's grace. But repentance is the sole remedy for human sin. So, God rebuked David through Nathan the prophet, using an allegory about a poor man's little ewe lamb. The parable confronted the king about his immense guilt, which led him to repent.

David's repentance provides an exemplary model for other believers. First, he "felt a godly grief" or sorrow (2 Cor 7:9). Through a "broken and contrite heart," the king confessed his offense—"I know my transgressions, and my sin is ever before me. Against you, you only, have I sinned and done what is evil in your sight." Second, David turned from his sin to the Lord—"Hide your face from my sins, and blot out all my iniquities. Create in me a clean heart, O God, and renew a right spirit within me. . . . Restore to me the joy of your salvation." After the king's repentance, Nathan said, "The LORD also has put away your sin."

Wayward Wizard (Acts 8:1–24)

A sorcerer named Simon lived in Samaria, the middle region between Galilee in the north and Judah in the south. His black magic amazed the citizenry, and his blatant self-promotion led people to call him "the power of God that is called Great." But then, Philip the evangelist, one of the original deacons (Acts 6:5), left Jerusalem during the church's early persecution, preached the gospel in Samaria, and performed numerous miracles. As a result, many professed faith in Jesus and received Baptism, including Simon.

From the beginning, the preacher's miracles intrigued the sorcerer. Unlike Simon's own trickery, Philip's exorcisms and healings were real. But then, the apostles Peter and John arrived from Jerusalem with a new wonder. Laying their hands on recent converts, the Holy Spirit filled the new believers. This phenomenon astonished Simon, who immediately offered the apostles money for the ability to wield such power through his own hands. That's when Peter stingingly rebuked Simon: "Your heart is not right before God. . . . I see that you are in the gall of bitterness and in the bond of iniquity."

Some say Simon never really trusted Christ but had become a mere pretender, while others think Simon did genuinely believe in Jesus but committed, on this occasion, a grievous wrong. For the discussion here, it really doesn't matter which is true. The point is that Simon sinned, and Peter urged Simon to "repent of this wickedness." Whether the wayward wizard was (a) still unconverted and needed to repent of all his sins and be born again through faith in Jesus or (b) a true saint but needed to repent of this particular sin, it doesn't change the remedy. Simon needed to repent, sorrowing for sin and turning from wickedness, including his desire to "obtain the gift of God with money."

Review Questions

1. What is the Christian character trait of repentance?

2. What words are missing from this verse? "If __ people who are called by my ____ _____ themselves, and pray and ____ my face and ____ from their wicked ways, then I will ____ from heaven and will _____ their sin and heal their land" (2 Chr 7:14).

3. What words are missing from these verses? "You were _____ into _____. For you felt a ____ grief . . . . Godly grief produces a _____ that leads to salvation without regret, whereas _____ grief produces death" (2 Cor 7:9–10).

4. What's the difference between worldly and godly grief or sorrow?

5. Some believers associate repentance only with their initial trusting in Christ (i.e., regeneration and justification). Is this correct?

6. What sins did King David commit?

7. Why didn't David repent soon after committing these sins?

8. Whom did God use to help David repent?

9. When David finally repented, what did God do?

10. What sin did Simon commit before his profession of faith in Christ?

11. What sin did Simon commit after his profession of faith in Christ?

12. What solution did the apostle Peter propose for Simon's sin?

God's Work in Believers

The new birth comes to God's elect only through the complementary traits of repentance unto life and biblical faith. As the apostle Paul often declared, "[You] must turn to God in repentance and have faith in our Lord Jesus" (Acts 20:21, NIV). "Can true repentance exist without faith? By no means."[13] Godly repentance and genuine faith reside side by side within someone, or the person has neither characteristic; one trait cannot exist if the other is absent. Have you repented unto eternal life—sorrowing for your sins and turning from them to God—and placed your faith in Jesus as Savior and Lord? If not, cry out to him for the saving graces of repentance and faith.

But, as a Christian character trait, repentance is so much more than a one-time sorrow and turning from sin at the moment you believe in Jesus. Nor is it "a thing of days or weeks, a temporary penance to be [gotten] over as fast as possible!"[14] Instead, repentance is a daily way of life for faithful saints, persisting and developing in tune with God's moral law. "It is the grace of a lifetime, like faith itself. God's little children repent, and so do the young men and fathers. Repentance is the inseparable companion of faith."[15]

Therefore, learn to keep short accounts with God as well as those you offend or wrong, repenting of your sins every day. Recall how King David

13. Calvin, *Institutes*, 499.
14. Spurgeon, "Repentance Must Go," n.p.
15. Spurgeon, "Repentance Must Go," n.p.

refused or neglected to repent, resulting in much heartache and family troubles over many years; learn from his mistake and follow a different path. Though you may not recall every transgression, confess and repent of every known or remembered sin without delay, seeking to reconcile with God and your fellow man. Don't allow unconfessed sin to fester and putrefy, hardening and desensitizing your soul. "If thou hast sinned, lie not down without repentance; for the want [lack] of repentance, after one has sinned, makes the heart yet harder and harder."[16] "Whoever conceals his transgressions will not prosper, but he who confesses and forsakes them will obtain mercy" (Prov 28:13).

Possessing the character trait of repentance also lays the groundwork for much comfort and peace when difficulties arise, especially when nearing death. "He who hath constantly exercised himself in [repentance] in his health and vigor, will do it with less pain in his sickness and weakness; and he who hath practiced [repentance] all his life, will do it with more ease and less perplexity in the hour of his death."[17] "Every day by repentance pull out the sting of some sin, that so when death comes, [you] may have nothing to do but to die. To die well is the action of the whole life."[18]

Many saints neglect to repent consistently or well, finding it hard to humble themselves and admit fault before God or others. Some might feel self-remorse or attempt self-reform, mistaking these for genuine repentance. However, feeling remorse for negative consequences (e.g., being caught in a lie), without more, is not godly sorrow for offending God or a fellow human being. Similarly, trying to reform past behavior, without acknowledging wrong, is not the same as confessing sin and turning from it to God. The ability to change does not lie in self-reform but in the Holy Spirit's power and sanctifying work. Feeling only remorse and attempting to reform through personal efforts, without more, fail to remove sin's guilt, produce lasting change, or bring real satisfaction. In contrast, much joy accompanies true repentance, especially when the offended person forgives and reconciles. God, of course, always forgives and reconciles with sinners who genuinely repent. As the Lord declared, "Return to me, and I will return to you" (Mal 3:7). Whether people will forgive, however, is less certain. To reach the heart of someone you have

16. Bunyan, *Entire Works*, 447.

17. Samuel Johnson as cited in Edwards, *Dictionary of Thoughts*, 484.

18. Sibbes, *Complete Works*, 350.

hurt and make it easier for them to reconcile, include these elements as part of your apology:

1. Confess your wrong clearly, fully, and honestly; don't minimize it, rationalize it, or attempt to shift or share its blame. Even if your fault amounts to only 1 percent of the total wrongdoing, focus on that 1 percent and state that you erred. For instance, the person to whom you are apologizing might have done or said egregious things to you over an extended period, and you only vented your anger after enduring the prolonged abuse. Nonetheless, apologize for your 1 percent—such as the angry outburst. Don't even hint at or allude to the other person's part of the blame for now, leaving that between them and God or, possibly, as a separate issue to address later. If they bear some guilt but don't repent for their role in the conflict, follow the prescripts in the earlier lesson on forgiveness.

2. After admitting fault, say you are sorry for what you did and the harm it caused. That is, put into words your heart's godly sorrow. Then, tell them you will try, with the Lord's help, not to hurt them like that again, verbalizing your heart's desire to turn from sin to God. Such expressions show "fruit in keeping with repentance" (Matt 3:8).

3. If possible and as appropriate, try to repair any harm or restore anything lost. For example, if you damaged someone's reputation, communicate with those who witnessed your slander or libel, correcting wrong impressions you gave them. If you destroyed someone's property, even accidentally, replace it with a new version.

4. Humbly and sincerely ask the offended person to forgive and reconcile with you. If the individual cannot or will not, don't let that refusal surprise or anger you. It's entirely up to that other person to forgive; you can't force them, nor should you try. Calmly drop the matter for now, seek the Holy Spirit's counsel, and, perhaps, return later to repeat afresh your expression of confession and repentance, offer of restoration, and desire for reconciliation.

In most cases, formulating your apology according to the suggestions above should lead to reconciliation. But, to increase the likelihood of success, avoid negative miens and dodgy expressions when seeking forgiveness:

1. Don't say, "I'm sorry" through clenched teeth, in a harsh tone, with an eye roll, or as though the apology had to be dragged from you. Demeanor and tone matter a great deal if the goal is to reconcile.

2. Never say, "I'm sorry you felt hurt by my words or behavior" since it sounds like the wrong lies in the other individual's unstable emotions or personality disorder rather than your own impropriety. It might even be interpreted as, "I'm sorry my reasonable words or behavior triggered something crazy inside you" or "I'm sorry you're such an emotional mess." Even if somewhat true, using such words is like extinguishing a small fire with lighter fluid. Instead, focus your apology on what you said or did that was wrong.

3. Don't say, "Please forgive me for any wrong I *might* have done" or "*If I was out of line, please forgive me.*" Such requests sound phony, as though you don't really believe you've done anything wrong. They lack confession of guilt and, thus, seem disassociated with genuine sorrow and a changed heart. In effect, these statements signal you don't find the other person's complaint legitimate and you're not really accepting responsibility for the issue. If you honestly aren't sure what you did wrong, gently ask the offended person to help you understand.

4. Avoid asking for reconciliation in a way that sounds like an order or command. "I need you to forgive me" suggests the so-called "apology" is more about reestablishing your inner comfort than restoring harmony with the other person.

Finally, understand that true repentance is a saving grace, a gift from God to Christians. Ask the Holy Spirit to develop this character trait within you, teaching you to repent every day. Pray for a soft heart that regularly sorrows for sin and constantly turns from it to God.

God's Grace for Change

Complete the "Heart Assessment, Reflection, and Petition" (HARP) chart, assessing your own repentance. Reflect on times the Holy Spirit enabled or empowered you to repent. Then, consider whether the Spirit might be revealing a need for you to repent more consistently or effectively. If you want God to increase your repentance, put that desire in writing. This is a very important exercise that can help you respond to God's direction for your life. Pray over your completed chart once or twice this next week.

Finally, talk to the Lord, using the words that follow or incorporating the thoughts into your own prayer: "Dear Father, my sins are many and great. Yet, I rejoice because, in your tender mercy, you gave me the saving grace of repentance. Holy Spirit, teach me to sorrow in a godly way and turn from evil. Cleanse and refresh my soul through repentance every day, keeping me in close fellowship with you. As I repent, blot out my iniquity, purify my heart, renew a steadfast spirit within me, and restore the joy of my salvation. Should my heart ever become stubborn or hard and I stop confessing my sin, lovingly draw me back to repentance. Help me to become holy like you are holy. In the name of Jesus my Savior, amen."

Remember, the Lord's help is vital to cultivating Christian character. Only his power can enable you to change. When you fail to show the character trait of repentance, confess it before God and ask for his forgiveness and help.

HARP Chart for Repentance

Definition: Repentance involves sorrowing for sin and turning from it to God.

Key verses: "If my people who are called by my name humble themselves, and pray and seek my face and turn from their wicked ways, then I will hear from heaven and will forgive their sin and heal their land" (2 Chr 7:14). "You were grieved into repenting. For you felt a godly grief . . . . Godly grief produces a repentance that leads to salvation without regret, whereas worldly grief produces death" (2 Cor 7:9–10).

Bible characters: When King David repented of his sin from a broken and contrite heart, God blotted out his iniquity, purified his heart, renewed a steadfast spirit within him, and restored the joy of his salvation. Simon, the wayward wizard who loved prestige and power, needed to repent for his sinful desire to buy God's gift with money.

How often do you show repentance in your life: 5 = nearly always, 4 = most of the time, 3 = about half the time, 2 = less than half the time, or 1 = hardly ever? Your response is ____.
In what ways, if any, has the Holy Spirit enabled you to repent?
In what ways, if any, has the Holy Spirit revealed to you a need for more repentance?
What petition related to repentance, if any, would you like to bring before the throne of grace?

Respectfulness

Engage in one or more of these introductory activities:

1. Intriguing Insights—The quotations below make observations about respectfulness. Explain each quotation's meaning or otherwise comment about it.

   > "There is no respect for others without humility in one's self."[1]

   > "Show respect to all people [but] grovel to none."[2]

   > "Men are respectable only as they respect."[3]

2. Movie Night—Watch "Searching for Bobby Fischer" (1993, PG) as a class or individually. The film focuses on Josh Waitzkin, a young chess prodigy, and his struggle for identity amid conflicting signals from those who care about him. How did (a) Josh respect others, (b) Josh's parents respect or disrespect others, (c) Vinnie, the chess hustler, respect or disrespect Josh, and (d) Bruce Pandolfini, the chess coach, show respect or disrespect. Also, how did Josh receive the advice to show contempt for his opponents?

3. Name that Person—Name people whom you respect. Likely, family members, friends, teachers, coaches, church members, Bible characters, or celebrities will come to mind. Explain what you respect about these people or how you show respect to them. Is your respect based on their accomplishments or authority? The Christian character trait of respectfulness is broader than these two criteria.

---

1. Henri Frederic Amiel as cited in Wood, *Dictionary of Quotations*, 474.
2. Chief Tecumseh as cited in *Congressional Record 108th Congress*, 6435.
3. Ralph Waldo Emerson as cited in Wood, *Dictionary of Quotations*, 274.

Believers also should give due regard for those with few accomplishments who are not in positions of authority.

These activities touch on the Christian character trait of respectfulness. Two earlier lessons addressed tangential topics. The one about attentiveness discussed how careful use of our physical senses can facilitate respectfulness. The other lesson about deference involved volitionally yielding to others. Somewhat different, the present subject of respectfulness views other people honorably and charitably, which makes it easier, in appropriate circumstances, to show deference. You might say attentiveness expedites respectfulness, which, in turn, enables deference. So, what is this Christian character trait of respectfulness? Here's one way to define it:

> Respectfulness is a gracious regard for the feelings, opinions, rights, accomplishments, or authority of others.

God desires his children to show proper respect to everyone. From a biblical perspective, what does this character trait of respectfulness look like, and how can Christians improve it? This lesson addresses these points under the headings of "God's Word to Mankind," "God's Work in Believers," and "God's Grace for Change."

God's Word to Mankind

Key Verses

"We ask you, brothers, to respect those who labor among you and are over you in the Lord and admonish you, and to esteem them very highly in love because of their work" (1 Thess 5:12–13). Pastors and elders "labor among" and "admonish" the "brothers," ruling over them "in the Lord." Believers should highly regard God's representatives for their ecclesiastical toil—biblical preaching, teaching, admonishing, exhorting, reproving, and counseling, whether through public sermon, classroom instruction, small group discussion, or private discourse. They should "esteem" pastors and elders "very highly in love because of" their vital and arduous labor caring for the Lord's flock and tending to eternal souls.

   "Show proper respect to everyone" (1 Pet 2:17, NIV). Since God created each human being in his own image, aspire to honor everyone. Because the touchstone is "proper" respect, however, some people warrant

more honor than others. The respect due a revered authority figure, for instance, exceeds that due someone who recklessly scorns sound wisdom and instruction.

Bible Characters

Obeisant Outcast (1 Sam 24:1–22; 26:1–25)

As a loyal subject, David faithfully served King Saul and Israel, playing his harp to calm the king's tormented spirit (1 Sam 16:14–23), slaying the giant who defied Israel and God (1 Sam 17:1–58), and, indeed, performing all the king's bidding (1 Sam 18:5). However, Saul became jealous when the citizenry praised David's accomplishments more than his own (1 Sam 18:6–9). He became so angry that he tried to kill David several times. Saul threw a spear at David (1 Sam 18:10–11); sent him on a dangerous military mission, hoping he'd receive a fatal wound (1 Sam 18:17–27); instructed his royal attendants to kill David (1 Sam 19:1–2); made a second attempt with his spear (1 Sam 19:9–10); dispatched an assassination team to David's home (1 Sam 19:11–17); and sent men to arrest David, which, no doubt, would have led to his execution (1 Sam 19:18–24).

After surviving all these attempts, David fled from Saul's presence into the wilderness. Yet, Saul doggedly pursued him with three thousand of his best warriors, seeking his whereabouts from the priests at Nob (1 Sam 22:11–19), the residents of Keilah (1 Sam 23:7–13), the Ziphites (1 Sam 23:19), and other informants (1 Sam 24:1). In each instance, Saul sought David's life without justification. Many would not have blamed David for fighting back against such unprovoked, undeserved attacks.

During the king's pursuits, David had two chances to take Saul's life. However, he refused to strike the king both times. His reason for restraint was telling: "Who can put out his hand against the Lord's anointed and be guiltless?" Despite all the evil directed against David, he recognized Saul as the leader God placed over Israel and, thus, respected the king as God's authority. Rather than taking vengeance on Saul, ridding himself of a mortal enemy, David submitted to God's choice and rule. Though Saul raged, the outcast showed obeisance.

Elihu's Elders (Job 32:1–12)

God blessed Job with a large family, numerous servants, much livestock, and good health. But then, God permitted Satan to take all these things from him. In Job's misery, four friends visited him, one younger than the others. The older friends wrongly assumed Job's misfortunes resulted from unconfessed sin. Without evidence, they repeatedly called Job a hypocrite and urged him to repent.

The younger friend, Elihu, waited for Job's three older friends to finish, respecting his elders, allowing them to express their counsel first. Though talking much, they never pointed out Job's sin nor addressed Job's point that God sometimes allows bad (good) things to happen to good (bad) people. When Elihu finally spoke, his counsel proved superior. Yet, he respected his elders and kept silent until they had spoken first.

Review Questions

1. What is the Christian character trait of respectfulness?

2. What words are missing from these verses? "We ask you, brothers, to _____ those who _____ among you and are ____ you in the Lord and _____ you, and to _____ them very highly in ____ because of their work" (1 Thess 5:12–13).

3. What language in 1 Thess 5:12–13 identifies the recipients of respect to be pastors and elders?

4. What words are missing from this verse? "Show proper _____ to _____" (1 Pet 2:17, NIV).

5. Why does everyone deserve respect?

6. Do some people deserve more respect than others?

7. For what two reasons did David owe Saul respect?

8. How did David show respect for Saul?

9. How did the three friends who initially spoke disrespect Job?

10. How did Elihu show respect to Job's other three friends?

God's Work in Believers

Depending fully on the Holy Spirit's power and wisdom, "show proper respect to everyone" (1 Pet 2:17, NIV). The Lord commands you to regard those he created graciously, each of whom bears his image. Respecting the feelings, opinions, rights, accomplishments, and authority of others, in effect, respects your Creator and theirs. Even if you occasionally take issue with them over opinions or behaviors, you still can respect them as fellow humans. So, "outdo one another in showing honor" (Rom 12:10). "Submit . . . to one another out of reverence for Christ" (Eph 5:21). Indeed, how is it possible to respect God while disrespecting his image bearers? "Whoever mocks [disrespects] the poor insults his Maker" (Prov 17:5). "With [the tongue] we bless our Lord and Father, and with it we curse [disrespect] people who are made in the likeness of God. From the same mouth come blessing and cursing. My brothers, these things ought not to be so" (Jas 3:9–10). Strive to be charitable and dutiful to all, while resolving to treat no one with indifference, incivility, intolerance, or disdain. Treating others respectfully often requires humility. Humbly apprehending your own weaknesses keeps you from magnifying someone else's, which, in turn, promotes respectfulness.

Through God's grace, respect all people without regard to their abundance or paucity of fame, power, intelligence, skill, or wealth and regardless of their personality, appearance, popularity, ethnicity, nationality, age, gender, or religion. Showing favoritism towards one person (or class or group) to another's detriment disrespects the latter. "You shall not be partial to the poor or defer to the great, but in righteousness shall you judge your neighbor" (Lev 19:15). "To show partiality is not good" (Prov 28:21). "My brothers, show no partiality . . . . If you show partiality, you are committing sin and are convicted by the law as transgressors" (Jas 2:1, 9). Here's one way to apply this call to impartiality. When speaking face-to-face with someone, resist the temptation to answer a phone call or respond to a text. Answering or responding suggests the person calling or texting is more important than the person in your immediate presence; it shows favoritism to the former. If genuinely urgent, apologize for the interruption, respond to the call or text as quickly as possible, and then return to your original conversation, perhaps apologizing again.

Though the Bible says to respect everyone and avoid favoritism, it does not mandate equal honor to everyone on every occasion. Indeed, those living recklessly are due less respect. "Like snow in summer or rain in harvest, so honor is not fitting for a fool. . . . Like one who binds the stone in the sling is one who gives honor to a fool" (Prov 26:1, 8). Too much honor given to the irresponsible, heedless, or foolish can be inappropriate or even harmful. At the other extreme, some people are due more respect because of familial, generational, organizational, or contractual relationships, as the following paragraphs discuss.

Always respect your parents, grandparents, great-grandparents, or other guardians. "Honor your father and your mother, that your days may be long in the land that the LORD your God is giving you" (Exod 20:12). Teens and children have further duties to obey (not just respect) those caring for them. "Children, obey your parents in the Lord, for this is right" (Eph 6:1). At the same time, parents and guardians should lovingly respect their teens and children as individuals created in God's image for whom they have solemn responsibilities. "Fathers, [mothers, and guardians,] do not provoke your children to anger, but bring them up in the discipline and instruction of the Lord" (Eph 6:4). "Fathers, [mothers, and guardians,] do not provoke your children, lest they become discouraged" (Col 3:21). These two verses do not mean it's necessarily a parent's or guardian's fault every time children become exasperated or embittered. Rather, they mean parents and guardians should be neither overbearing nor overindulgent in their responsibilities; they should be careful to instruct and discipline children respectfully and lovingly, praying often for God's wisdom.

God's grace enables Christian spouses to respect each other. "Husbands, live with your wives in an understanding way, showing honor to the woman as the weaker vessel, since they are heirs with you of the grace of life, so that your prayers may not be hindered" (1 Pet 3:7). Similarly, wives must respect their husbands (Eph 5:33). As part of this respect, wives should submit to their husbands' leadership. "Wives, submit to your own husbands, as to the Lord. For the husband is the head of the wife even as Christ is the head of the church, his body, and is himself its Savior. Now as the church submits to Christ, so also wives should submit in everything to their husbands" (Eph 5:22–24). "For this is how the holy women who hoped in God used to adorn themselves, by submitting to their own husbands, as Sarah obeyed Abraham, calling him lord" (1 Pet 3:5). In turn, as part of their respect, husbands should love their wives sacrificially while, at the same time, providing godly leadership. "Husbands, love your wives, as Christ loved the church and gave himself up for her . . . . Husbands should love their wives as their own bodies. He who loves his wife loves himself. For no one ever hated his own flesh, but nourishes and cherishes it, just as Christ does the church, because we are members of his body. . . . Let each [husband] love his wife as himself" (Eph 5:25–26, 28–30, 33). "Husbands, love your wives, and do not be harsh with them" (Col 3:19).

People from different generations occasionally struggle to understand each other. Pray for wisdom to apprehend the views of those much younger and older than you. Disparate cultural references, educational experiences, worldviews, and values combine to make any meeting of the minds, at times, difficult. Nonetheless, younger believers, like Elihu, should respect their elders, listening to their opinions, seeking their wisdom, and handling any disagreements graciously. "You shall stand up before the gray head and honor the face of an old man" (Lev 19:32). "Do not rebuke an older man but encourage him as you would a father, . . . older women as mothers" (1 Tim 5:1–2). Likewise, older saints should give due respect to the younger generation, especially those in the church. Treat "younger men as brothers, . . . younger women as sisters, in all purity" (1 Tim 5:2).

Respect your pastors, ministers, elders, teachers, and deacons who serve faithfully. "Obey your leaders and submit to them, for they are keeping watch over your souls, as those who will have to give an account. Let them do this with joy and not with groaning, for that would be of no advantage to you" (Heb 13:17). "Let the elders who rule well be considered worthy of double honor, especially those who labor in preaching and teaching" (1 Tim 5:17). "Esteem them very highly in love because of their work" (1 Thess 5:13). At the same time, church leaders should not exercise their authority in domineering, pompous, dismissive, abusive, or negligent ways. Instead, they should gently and lovingly shepherd the local flock, treating each member with due respect as created in God's image and born again to a living hope. Pray for mutual respect between church leaders and individual members.

Ask the Holy Spirit to give you respect for government authorities as instruments for promoting social justice. "Let every person be subject to the governing authorities. For there is no authority except from God, and those that exist have been instituted by God. Therefore whoever resists the authorities resists what God has appointed, and those who resist will incur judgment" (Rom 13:1–2). Remember "to be submissive to rulers and authorities, to be obedient, to be ready for every good work" (Titus 3:1). "Be subject for the Lord's sake to every human institution, whether it be to the emperor as supreme, or to governors as sent by him to punish those who do evil and to praise those who do good" (1 Pet 2:13–14). Of course, you should not obey government edicts that promote evil (e.g., laws forbidding worship or facilitating suicides). On their parts, government leaders should respect and guard the natural and legal rights of each citizen and ask for God's wisdom to do so properly.

Pray for grace to respect those who compensate you for services rendered. Regarding such contractual relationships, one caveat bears mentioning at the start—slavery and all forms of human trafficking are reprehensible evils that wrongfully strip individuals of their natural and legal rights. In contrast, the reference to "slaves" in some Bible versions likely refers to those voluntarily becoming bond or indentured servants, whose compensation often involved removal or satisfaction of their legal debts. Thus, in significant ways, bond or indentured servants were more similar in today's parlance to employees and independent contractors. Consistently, "masters" would refer to employers. With those clarifications in mind, consider the respect due employers. "Bondservants, obey your earthly masters with fear and trembling, with a sincere heart, as you would Christ, not by the way of eye-service, as people-pleasers, but as bondservants of Christ, doing the will of God from the heart, rendering service with a good will as to the Lord and not to man, knowing that whatever good anyone does, this he will receive back from the Lord, whether he is a bondservant or is free" (Eph 6:5–8). "Bondservants, obey in everything those who are your earthly masters, not by way of eye-service, as people-pleasers, but with sincerity of heart, fearing the Lord" (Col 3:22). "Let all who are under a yoke as bondservants regard their own masters as worthy of all honor, so that the name of God and the teaching may not be reviled. Those who have believing masters must not be disrespectful on the ground that they are brothers; rather they must serve all the better since those who benefit by their good service are believers and beloved. Teach and urge these things" (1 Tim 6:1–2). "Servants, be subject to your masters with all respect, not only to the good and gentle but also to the unjust" (1 Pet 2:18). Through the Holy Spirit's wisdom and guidance, employers also should respect those they hire, treating them with dignity and compensating them fairly. "Masters, do the same to [your bondservants], and stop your threatening, knowing that he who is both their Master and yours is in heaven, and that there is no partiality with him" (Eph 6:9). "Masters, treat your bondservants justly and fairly, knowing that you also have a Master in heaven" (Col 4:1).

Only a few key points about respectfulness remain:

1. The Bible commands respectfulness even if you receive no respect in return or, harder yet, disrespect.[4] As the Lord instructed, "As you wish that others would do to you, do so to them" (Luke 6:31). Follow the Golden Rule without stipulating any preconditions about other people's attitudes or behaviors towards you; treat them like you want to be treated, period. As just one example, wives should submit to husbands even if the latter do not always love sacrificially in return. Similarly, husbands should love wives sacrificially even if the latter do not always submit. None should refuse to submit (or love sacrificially) because the spouse does not love sacrificially (or submit). Where both spouses follow these gracious precepts, the marriage tends to be more satisfying and successful.

2. Always respect people's time. Don't be late for meetings and appointments and, in important matters, think through what you intend to say and hope to accomplish in advance. Especially when someone seems busy, don't waste time with excessive chitchat, but get straight to the point. Even in more casual exchanges with friends and acquaintances, be sensitive to their schedules and interests. Don't prolong conversations past the time of their demise lest the idiom proves true—familiarity breeds contempt. King Solomon put it more bluntly: "Let your foot be seldom in your neighbor's house, lest he have his fill of you and hate you" (Prov 25:17). To be clear, it's a good thing to interact socially with others, and, in many cases, long discussions can be very satisfying, profitable, or edifying to all parties. In contrast, the caution here is against unduly extending meetings and visits without showing a respectful concern for another person's time.

3. Respect people's privacy also. Don't eavesdrop on their conversations nor read their correspondence when it doesn't concern you. Nosiness that discovers what others desire to keep private is usually an improper, disrespectful invasion. Thus, if a person with whom you are speaking receives an important telephone call that interrupts your tête-à-tête, occupy yourself with another task during the

---

4. Serious abuse, on the other hand, requires biblical responses not covered here.

call or politely excuse yourself, leaving the immediate area until the phone conversation ends. Notwithstanding the above, parents and guardians, consistent with their responsibilities before God, generally should monitor their teen's and children's activities (e.g., overseeing their internet usage and establishing curfews).

4. Have you ever noticed how often dogs look raptly into your face as you speak? That's what respectfulness looks like. Listen carefully whenever people talk to you, looking them in the eye if possible (though not so intently as to cause them discomfort). Cease competing activities, even if your communication is via phone, so that nothing unessential impedes or distracts your attention. Through your countenance and demeanor, let them sense you hear and care. Let them perceive you respect their thoughts, ideas, opinions, and anxieties. Show genuine concern if they mention troubles or worries yet avoid the temptation to talk too much in return. Guard against launching into your own griefs or proffering unwanted advice as misguided ways to show you understand or care.

God's Grace for Change

Complete the "Heart Assessment, Reflection, and Petition" (HARP) chart, assessing your own respectfulness. Reflect on times the Holy Spirit enabled or empowered you to show respect. Then, consider whether the Spirit might be revealing a need for you to be more respectful. If you want God to increase your respectfulness, put that desire in writing. This is a very important exercise that can help you respond to God's direction for your life. Pray over your completed chart once or twice this next week.

Finally, talk to the Lord, using the words that follow or incorporating the thoughts into your own prayer: "Our Father, you alone are worthy of all glory, honor, and worship. With a thankful heart, I praise you for family, friends, brothers and sisters in Christ, teachers, co-workers, and other people you bring into my life. Yet, I often have disrespected those whom you created and, at times, even those whom you redeemed. In your great mercy, forgive me these sins of disrespect. May the Holy Spirit give me a gracious, proper regard for the feelings, opinions, rights, accomplishments, and authority of others. Consistent with the Golden Rule, enable me to respect even those who disrespect me. Forgive me when I show partiality or favoritism. Teach me to listen respectfully, giving my full attention to others. Remind me to respect the time and privacy of everyone too. In all these things, conform me increasingly to the perfect image of Christ Jesus the Lord. Amen."

Remember, the Lord's help is vital to cultivating Christian character. Only his power can enable you to change. When you fail to show the character trait of respectfulness, confess it before God and ask for his forgiveness and help.

HARP Chart for Respectfulness

Definition: Respectfulness is a gracious regard for the feelings, opinions, rights, accomplishments, or authority of others.

Key verses: "We ask you, brothers, to respect those who labor among you and are over you in the Lord and admonish you, and to esteem them very highly in love because of their work" (1 Thess 5:12–13). "Show proper respect to everyone" (1 Pet 2:17, NIV).

Bible characters: Though King Saul tried to kill David several times, the obeisant outcast spared the Lord's anointed twice. Elihu respected his elders by letting them speak first to Job.

How often do you show respectfulness in your life: 5 = nearly always, 4 = most of the time, 3 = about half the time, 2 = less than half the time, or 1 = hardly ever? Your response is _____.
In what ways, if any, has the Holy Spirit enabled you to show respect to others?
In what ways, if any, has the Holy Spirit revealed to you a need to become more respectful?
What petition related to respectfulness, if any, would you like to bring before the throne of grace?

Responsibility

Engage in one or more of these introductory activities:

1. Movie Night—Watch "Roughing It" (2002, NR) as a class or individually. The film presents a rollicking tale within a tale in which Mark Twain (aka Samuel Clemens) reluctantly delivers the keynote address at his daughter's graduation ceremony. Twain tells his young audience how he found his calling in life. Along the way, of course, he had numerous adventures, which, as expected, may have become exaggerated in the retelling. Be that as it may, the movie focuses on his youthful irresponsibility before finally settling down to a steady profession. How did Sam and others show irresponsibility? How did some characters (e.g., Sam's brother, Orion) prove dependable and trustworthy?

2. Neglect and Consequences—How important is the character trait of responsibility? When people neglect their responsibilities, what consequences follow? What would happen if:

> Everyone stopped learning (or, alternatively, working)?
>
> Drivers started ignoring traffic laws?
>
> Businesses quit paying bills?
>
> Grocers decided to sell only junk food?
>
> Teachers (or bosses) stopped coming to school (or work)?
>
> People decided to ignore everyone else and stop talking?
>
> Adults gave up trying to floss and brush their teeth?
>
> Parents no longer told their children what to do?

You stopped going to church, reading your Bible,
and praying?

These activities emphasize the importance of doing your best, making careful decisions, and accepting responsibility. Diligence, covered in an earlier lesson, plays a key role in developing responsibility. But what is this Christian character trait of responsibility? Here's one way to define it:

> Responsibility requires conscientious performance of duties, principled decision-making, and full acceptance of any negative consequences from performance or decisions.

God desires his children to show and accept responsibility. From a biblical perspective, what does this character trait of responsibility look like, and how can Christians improve it? This lesson addresses these points under the headings of "God's Word to Mankind," "God's Work in Believers," and "God's Grace for Change."

God's Word to Mankind

Key Verses

"The Levites are to be responsible for the care of the tabernacle of the Testimony" (Num 1:53, NIV). The patriarch Jacob (aka Israel) had twelve sons, one of whom he named Levi. Thus, the Levites were one of the twelve tribes comprising the nation of Israel. Moses and Aaron, who later led this nation out of Egyptian bondage, descended from Levi. After the exodus, God assigned this tribe responsibility to care for the tabernacle. The tabernacle was a portable tent where God dwelt among the Israelites before King Solomon, centuries later, built the Jerusalem temple as a more permanent structure. The tabernacle (and later the temple) housed the candlestick, shewbread table, altar of incense, and Ark of the Covenant. The Ark contained two stone tablets summarizing the moral law, aka the Ten Commandments or God's "Testimony." The Lord gave Levites sacred responsibility for the tabernacle's care, including dismantling and packing it up, transporting it, unpacking and setting it up, and tending to its furnishings, vessels, and instruments. The Levites' also guarded the tabernacle from any given to profane curiosity or unwise presumption, encamping around it to protect Israel's other tribes from God's wrath (Num 1:50–53). Later instructions divided the tabernacle's overall duties

(and those of its courtyard) according to families or bloodlines within the tribe of Levi (e.g., see Num 3:25–31).

"Brothers, pick out from among you seven men [deacons] of good re-pute, full of the Spirit and of wisdom, whom we [the twelve apostles] will appoint to this duty" (Acts 6:3). The daily task was great and the need immediate—to fairly distribute food (or maybe alms) among the church's poor widows. The apostles could not perform this work because preaching demanded all their time and energy. So, the early church chose men "full of the Spirit and of wisdom" for the task. Being full of the Spirit implied piety, compassion, and goodness. Being full of wisdom implied prudence, discretion, sound judgment, fairness, and managerial aptitude. In short, the Spirit had instilled certain men with a keen sense of responsibility. The church chose seven men who it believed would be conscientious in performing duties and principled in making decisions.

Bible Characters

Culpable Couple (Gen 3:1–13)

God created Adam and Eve as rationale beings, responsible for their choices. Living in a garden paradise, they enjoyed its beauty and bounty every day. God imposed only one restriction—they must not eat from a certain tree; its fruit was off limits. But one day, Satan took the form of a serpent and slithered into the garden. He tempted Eve through doubts, lies, and innuendoes. Instead of trusting what God said, Eve listened to Satan and wavered. Thinking the fruit would taste good and prove nutritious to her body, observing its aesthetic form and color, and believing Satan's assertion that, somehow, the fruit would make her as wise as God, Eve plucked the forbidden fruit and ate. In doing so, she failed to trust and obey God and neglected her responsibility to Adam, thinking only about what she desired. After sinning, she gave some fruit to Adam, and he ate also. Just like Eve, he failed to trust and obey God. But he also failed to consider his unique responsibility as federal head to the entire human race. With a single bite, he passed the curse of original sin to every mortal who would ever live.

When God asked Adam, the first man, about his deed, he should have manned up and accepted full responsibility. From a broken and contrite heart, he should have said, "I did eat the fruit. For disobeying you, I'm very sorry. I deserve punishment, but I ask for mercy. Please forgive me." But, in contrast, his dodgy answer partially implicated God, who had put Eve in the garden, and partially blamed Eve, who had plucked the forbidden fruit. In short, Adam accepted very little responsibility in the matter. His answer might even be paraphrased like this: "You gave me this woman, she gave me this fruit, and fruit is made to eat, which I did. Why are you blaming me?" Following this shameful, self-absolving response, God asked Eve about her actions. Since Adam pointed the finger at her, she attempted to blame the serpent. Thus, the culpable couple neglected their duty to obey God, made sinful decisions, and tried to avoid much or all the responsibility.

Pusillanimous Pilate (John 18:28—19:16)

It was Passover week, and many thousands of Jewish pilgrims (some estimate two million or more) packed Jerusalem. As the Roman governor over Judea, Pilate knew he must manage this religious event carefully. His soldiers could control small skirmishes, but large riots were another matter, and, if word that he couldn't handle affairs got back to Caesar, Pilate might lose his prestigious post. He felt a strong motivation to keep the peace. So, when the Sanhedrin officials and an angry rabble dragged a man named Jesus before him, demanding his execution, the governor found himself in a serious quandary. Finding no evidence of guilt, Pilate wanted to release Jesus, thrice saying, "I find no guilt in him." But then, the Jewish leaders and crowd turned things up a notch: "If you release this man, you are not Caesar's friend." Of course, only Pilate could order an execution, so the responsibility for justice rested squarely on his shoulders. He loathed the Jewish leaders and their hypocrisy, but he feared the tumultuous crowd more.

In the end, Pilate caved to the Jews' pressure, shirking his responsibility; he went along to get along and sentenced an innocent man to a painful death by crucifixion. "When Pilate saw that he was gaining nothing, but rather that a riot was beginning, he took water and washed his hands before the crowd, saying, 'I am innocent of [Jesus'] blood; see to it yourselves'" (Matt 27:24). The symbolic washing of hands meant nothing. The pusillanimous governor bore the responsibility but failed to show it as a character trait through his (a) neglect of civic duty to administer justice evenhandedly, (b) unprincipled, cowardly decision to appease the masses, and (c) absurd, craven attempt to shift the blame.

Review Questions

1. What is the Christian character trait of responsibility?

2. What words are missing from this verse? "The Levites are to be _____ for the care of the _____ of the _____" (Num 1:53, NIV).

3. Who were the Levites?

4. What was the tabernacle?

5. What was the Testimony?

6. What words are missing from this verse? "Brothers, pick out from among you _____ men of good repute, full of the _____ and of _____, whom we will appoint to this ____" (Acts 6:3).

7. What office did the seven men hold whom the early church put in charge of the daily distribution?

8. According to Acts 6:3, with what two things should the first deacons be filled?

9. What duties were the first deacons assigned?

10. How did Eve show irresponsibility?

11. How did Adam show irresponsibility?

12. "All that is in the world—the desires of the flesh and the desires of the eyes and pride of life—is not from the Father but is from the world" (1 John 2:16). What parallels, if any, do you see between Eve's rationale for sinning and the threefold roots of sin in 1 John 2:16?

13. How did Pilate show irresponsibility?

God's Work in Believers

Having responsibility differs from showing responsibility. The former obligates you to perform duties of God's moral law as summarized in the Ten Commandments and clarified throughout Scripture, making righteous decisions consistent with that moral law. The obligation encompasses duties to God (Commandments One through Four) and duties to others (Commandments Five through Ten). As discussed in the lesson about respectfulness, duties to others include relational obligations between parents (or legal guardians) and children, husbands and wives, older and younger people, church leaders and members, teachers and students, civic authorities and citizens, and employers and employees. Fulfilling these obligations *shows* responsibility.

To illustrate, consider a teenage son whose mother asks him to wash dishes, but he fails to do so or does so carelessly. His obligation exists as a moral duty because of the parent-child relationship, but he does not fulfill it; he had a responsibility but did not show himself responsible. Similarly, in the key verses presented earlier, Israel's Levites and the early church's deacons received obligatory responsibilities related to God's people. If a particular Levite or deacon faithfully and carefully carried out his duties, he showed the character trait of responsibility. In addition to relational obligations, responsibilities can proceed from God's overarching commandment to love others. For instance, suppose a woman cannot care for her children overnight because of an unexpected medical emergency. In desperation, she asks a neighbor to keep her children until the next day. If the neighbor agrees but then neglects to provide adequate or good care, she fails to show responsibility in a duty for which the commandment to love others morally binds her.

To repeat, having responsibility differs from showing responsibility. The latter, on which this lesson focuses, requires three things—conscientious performance of duties, principled decision-making, and full acceptance of any negative consequences from performance or decisions. Each requires God's grace. The remaining paragraphs discuss these three aspects in turn.

Conscientiously performing a duty requires diligence, defined in an earlier lesson as the "persistent, steadfast pursuit of a worthwhile objective or purpose." Be diligent whether the duty involves a work-related project, school assignment, family chore, civic obligation, voluntary commitment, or gratuitous act. "Whatever you do, work heartily, as for the Lord and not for men" (Col 3:23). In your diligence, don't shortchange small tasks. "One who is faithful in a very little is also faithful in much, and one who is dishonest in a very little is also dishonest in much" (Luke 16:10). Helen Keller expressed the principle well: "I long to accomplish a great and noble task, but it is my chief duty to accomplish small tasks as if they were great and noble."[1] Part of conscientious performance involves timely arrival at meetings and appointments. Be punctual; arriving late

---

1. Keller, *Practice of Optimism*, 12.

disrespects the time of other people and betrays irresponsibility. Also, to complete your work as scheduled, don't procrastinate. As Abraham Lincoln once said, "You cannot escape the responsibility of tomorrow by evading it today."[2] The secret to finishing on time involves starting on time and then being steadfast in your work. Habitual procrastination and stalwart responsibility are rarely found to coexist comfortably within the same person. Ask the Holy Spirit for a conscientious attitude about every duty.

Principled decision-making, the second aspect of showing responsibility, requires a grounding in biblical truth combined with a determination to do right. When faced with difficult choices, start by checking your motives. What self-interest do you have in the outcome that might influence your decision in a wrong direction? If, after examining your motives, you find them suspect, check (or hand over) your motives at God's cloakroom, consigning them like a top hat to his safekeeping. That is, set aside your own biased, self-centered motives for God's desires, revisiting the decision solely in the light of biblical standards. This can be hard since, sometimes, a morally right choice forgoes personal opportunities and might even result in personal detriment. When it does, rest assured the righteous decision pleases and glorifies God more than an unprincipled one. Pray for his divine strength to do what's right. Recall that neither Adam and Eve nor Pilate made principled decisions. Though Adam and Eve chose what they thought would benefit them, they ended up losing their garden paradise and plunging all mankind into sin and misery. Though Pilate chose what he thought would best preserve his prestigious position as Roman governor, he ended up sentencing the Son of God to death and bearing that guilt. Decisions have consequences.

The third aspect of showing responsibility, fully accepting any negative consequences from performance or decisions, requires courageous accountability for personal fault. The temptation, of course, is to shift some or all blame to something or someone else much like Adam, Eve, and Pilate did. In the short-term, blame-shifting might make you feel safer or better, but its long-term effects often prove disastrous. Moreover, wrongfully blaming other things or people hinders you from developing the Christian character trait of responsibility. Seek God's help to accept full responsibility for negative outcomes attributable to your performance and decisions.

2. Abraham Lincoln as cited in *Congressional Record 98th Congress*, 4537.

God's Grace for Change

Before examining your heart, considering how you might improve, and seeking divine help, ponder one last point—Jesus conscientiously performed every task the Father gave him to do, securing your eternal salvation. "For I have come down from heaven, not to do my own will but the will of him who sent me" (John 6:38). Let this brief reminder about and appreciation for God's undeserved grace prepare and motivate you to develop more of this lesson's character trait in yourself.

Then, complete the "Heart Assessment, Reflection, and Petition" (HARP) chart, assessing your own tendency to be responsible. Reflect on times the Holy Spirit enabled or empowered you to show responsibility as well as times Jesus showed himself to be responsible during his earthly life. Consider whether the Spirit might be revealing a need for you to show more of this character trait. If you want God to increase your responsible attitudes and behaviors, put that desire in writing. This is a very important exercise that can help you respond to God's direction for your life. Pray over your completed chart once or twice this next week.

Finally, talk to the Lord, using the words that follow or incorporating the thoughts into your own prayer: "Holy Father, Holy Redeemer, Holy Comforter, I fear and praise your thrice holy name. Though my sins are immense and many, your great love and rich grace encourage me to approach you in prayer. Despite often being unreliable and irresponsible myself, you always, in contrast, prove truthful and faithful. Forgive my sins, especially when I neglect or ignore duties to you, Christian brothers and sisters, and unbelievers. Forgive choices I have made that depart from your Word in misguided efforts to protect or benefit myself. Forgive failures to accept full responsibility for my performance and decisions, blaming circumstances and people for my own shortcomings, mistakes, and sins. Holy Spirit, cause me to become more responsible in my life. Make me, each day, more and more holy, conforming me to the image of Christ. Thank you for the great promise that, as a believer, you will sanctify me. Cheer and invigorate me now with that certainty. In Jesus' name, amen."

Remember, the Lord's help is vital to cultivating Christian character. Only his power can enable you to change. When you fail to show the character trait of responsibility, confess it before God and ask for his forgiveness and help.

HARP Chart for Responsibility

Definition: Responsibility requires conscientious performance of duties, principled decision-making, and full acceptance of any negative consequences from performance or decisions.

Key verses: "The Levites are to be responsible for the care of the tabernacle of the Testimony" (Num 1:53, NIV). "Brothers, pick out from among you seven men of good repute, full of the Spirit and of wisdom, whom we will appoint to this duty" (Acts 6:3).

Bible characters: Adam and Eve, the culpable couple, neglected their duty to obey God, made sinful decisions, and tried to avoid much or all their responsibility. Pilate, the pusillanimous governor, neglected his civic duty to administer justice evenhandedly, reached an unprincipled decision to appease the masses, and attempted to shift his blame to the Jewish leaders.

How often do you show responsibility in your life: 5 = nearly always, 4 = most of the time, 3 = about half the time, 2 = less than half the time, or 1 = hardly ever? Your response is ____.
In what ways, if any, has the Holy Spirit enabled you to show responsibility?
How did Jesus model responsibility during his earthly life in ways benefiting you?
In what ways, if any, has the Holy Spirit revealed to you a need to be more responsible?
What petition related to responsibility, if any, would you like to bring before the throne of grace?

Thankfulness

Engage in one or more of these introductory activities:

1. Hymn Sing—Find hymns about thanksgiving. Possible selections include: "Come, Ye Thankful People, Come," "For All the Blessings of the Year," "Let All Things Now Living," "Now Thank We All Our God," "O Bless the Lord, O My Soul," "Sing to the Lord of Harvest," "Thanks to God," "We Plow the Fields," and "When All Your Mercies, O My God." Sing (or read aloud) one or more verses of two or more hymns. Alternatively, play online recordings of the hymns. What does each song say about thankfulness?

2. Intriguing Insights—The quotations below make observations about thankfulness or gratitude. Explain each quotation's meaning or otherwise comment about it.

   > "Gratitude is the least of the virtues, but ingratitude is the worst of vices."[1]

   > "I would maintain that thanks are the highest form of thought; and that gratitude is happiness doubled by wonder."[2]

   > "Some people are always grumbling because roses have thorns. I am thankful that thorns have roses."[3]

   > "From David, learn to give thanks for everything. Every furrow in the book of Psalms is sown with the seeds of thanksgiving."[4]

1. Fuller, *Aphorisms of Wisdom*, 61.
2. Chesterton, *Short History*, 59.
3. Jean-Baptiste Alphonse Karr as cited in "Question Drawer," 49.
4. Jeremy Taylor as cited in Edwards, *Light for the Day*, 60.

"Gratitude is the mother of the virtues."[5]

These activities remind everyone about the importance of thankful hearts for blessings large and small. But what is this Christian character trait of thankfulness? Here's one way to define it:

Thankfulness is gratitude to God for the multitude of his blessings.

God desires his children to show appreciation to himself and others. From a biblical perspective, what does this character trait of thankfulness look like, and how can Christians improve it? This lesson addresses these points under the headings of "God's Word to Mankind," "God's Work in Believers," and "God's Grace for Change."

God's Word to Mankind

Key Verses

"Give thanks in all circumstances; for this is the will of God in Christ Jesus for you" (1 Thess 5:18). Paul does not say to be thankful *for* all situations but *in* all situations. In prosperity and comfort, believers should be grateful for God's marvelous bounty and goodness. Moreover, in scarcity and hardship, they can be grateful for the Lord's abiding presence and sure promises, despite present circumstances. God desires those "in Christ Jesus" to express their thankfulness all the time *in* every situation, whether easy or difficult.

"Let us be grateful for receiving a kingdom that cannot be shaken" (Heb 12:28). The nation of Israel had been shaken many times. Civil strife split the realm between northern and southern kingdoms (932 BC), the Assyrians exiled the Northern Kingdom (722 BC), the Babylonians exiled the Southern Kingdom (586 BC), and the Romans subjugated Judea (63 BC). In stark contrast, believers belong to the unshakable kingdom of grace through faith in Christ; in this realm, the Almighty reigns supreme on the throne of human hearts. Moreover, at Christ's second coming, resurrected saints will enter the unshakable kingdom of glory. Neither Satan nor any other power can or ever will overthrow either kingdom; both will triumph and prevail against all opposition; both are unshakable. Be

---

5. Cicero as cited in Brady, *Beacon Search-Lights*, 181.

thankful for belonging to the kingdom of grace and the certain hope of entering the future kingdom of glory.

Bible Characters

Appreciative Assembly (1 Chr 15:1–3, 16:1–36)

Israel's Ark of the Covenant had come through turbulent times. During the Battle of Aphek, the Philistines captured the ark but later returned it after God sent plagues among them (1 Sam 4—6). On its return, Israel kept the ark in Kiriath Jearim for twenty years before trying to move it to Jerusalem. Unfortunately, they ignored God's instructions for carrying the ark, and Uzzah died as a result. Fearful of moving the ark any further, Israel suspended the journey for three months, leaving it temporarily in Obed-Edom (2 Sam 6:1–15).

The ark represented God's presence among his people, so great celebration accompanied its eventual arrival in Jerusalem. For the occasion, King David delivered a liturgical psalm of thanksgiving to Asaph, the musician. Presumably, a Levitical ensemble sang it before the appreciative assembly. The psalm began, "Oh give thanks to the LORD; call upon his name; make known his deeds among the peoples!" This was thanksgiving for past blessings, especially the Lord's great faithfulness and wondrous deeds. God had remembered and kept his covenantal promises to Israel, making them a great people and giving them the land of Canaan. The psalm ended, "Oh give thanks to the LORD, for he is good; for his steadfast love endures forever!" This was thanksgiving for God's personal attributes, specifically, his essential goodness and persistent, unfailing love.

Lone Leper (Luke 17:11–19)

In the New Testament, Israel consisted of separate provinces, including Galilee in the north, Judea in the south (with Jerusalem as capital), and Samaria in between. Most Galileans (as well as Jews in Judea) detested the Samaritans as a mixed race of people with a syncretic culture and religion. As a result, Galileans traveling to Jerusalem for holy feasts often avoided the most direct route. Instead, they skirted Samaria's northern border eastward to the Jordan River, crossed over into Perea before turning south, re-crossed the Jordan River just before it reached the Dead Sea, and then traveled westward through Judea to Jerusalem. It was a lengthy detour, illustrating how deeply Galileans despised Samaritans and, thus, avoided their territory.

Ten lepers lived near the well-traveled route along the common border between Samaria and Galilee. One leper was a Samaritan; presumably, the other nine were Galileans. Outcasts from society, their debilitating disease forced them to practice extreme social distancing (Lev 13:45–46; Num 5:2–4). So, they cried to Jesus from afar, begging for mercy. Under the law, a priest had to examine anyone recovered from leprosy (Lev 13:2). Resolved to cure them, Jesus sent all ten lepers to the local priest, and the healing occurred in route. However, only one lone leper, the Samaritan, returned to thank the Great Physician.

Review Questions

1. What is the Christian character trait of thankfulness?

2. What words are missing from this verse? "Give _____ in ___ circumstances; for this is the _____ of God in Christ Jesus for you" (1 Thess 5:18).

3. In 1 Thess 5:18, what does it mean to "give thanks in all circumstances"?

4. What words are missing from this verse? "Let us be _____ for receiving a _____ that cannot be _____" (Heb 12:28).

5. Historically, in what ways had the nation of Israel been "shaken"?

6. In Heb 12:28, what kingdom do believers receive "that cannot be shaken"?

7. How did the lone leper show gratitude to Jesus?

God's Work in Believers

"Giv[e] thanks always and for everything to God the Father" (Eph 5:20). This verse provides succinct answers to three essential questions, which are: (a) When should believers give thanks? (b) To whom should believers give thanks? (c) For what should believers give thanks? The following paragraphs address each question.

For Christians, thanksgiving should be more than an annual event structured around family and feasting; it should be something they do "always." This doesn't mean believers must express gratitude continuously, every second of every day, but it does mean they should develop appreciative attitudes that gladly and regularly erupt in thanksgiving. To cultivate grateful hearts, ask the Holy Spirit to teach you thankfulness: (a) before rolling out of bed each morning, (b) after crawling into bed each night, (c) before partaking of each meal, (d) after God answers prayer, meets a need, or otherwise blesses, (e) before presenting petitions when praying, (f) during alone times, and, indeed, (g) amid every situation. As one of the key verses says, "Give thanks in all circumstances; for this is the will of God in Christ Jesus for you" (1 Thess 5:18). Make thanksgiving a frequent habit throughout each day rather than just a holiday; always give thanks.

To whom should believers give thanks? People sometimes feel grateful *for* good things in life without being grateful *to* someone. Stated differently, they genuinely feel fortunate for their blessings but don't attribute them to anyone beyond themselves and, thus, see no need to thank anyone. Such gratitude, without recognizing God as the divine giver, is not biblical thankfulness. Beseech the Holy Spirit to direct your thankfulness to the source of all blessings. Of course, the Lord often uses human beings to confer benefits, and you should be thankful to them also. Appreciate family members, friends, teachers, church leaders, government officials, and other people who meet your daily needs, offer you well-meaning advice, help you with tasks or through difficult circumstances, give you gifts, transact business with you, answer your questions, or bless you in other ways, large and small. Furthermore, speak your thanks. Not verbalizing your gratitude is indistinguishable from rank ingratitude. At the same time, don't neglect to thank God for the people through whom he blesses you.

For what should believers give thanks? "Let them thank the LORD for his steadfast love, for his wonderous works to the children of man!" (Ps 107:21). In broad terms, be grateful in every circumstance for two things: God's person and his works. The person of God refers to the essential substance of who he is. The works of God include those of creation, salvation, and providence. Entreat the Holy Spirit to grant you a thankful heart for these things.

Thankfulness for God's *person* goes well beyond a formal listing and staid understanding of his attributes. Indeed, it advances from knowing the Lord to appreciating the wondrous benefits proceeding from that knowledge. Meditate on God's "infinite, eternal, and unchangeable ... wisdom, power, holiness, justice, goodness, and truth."[6] Don't quickly pass over these traits where Scripture mentions them but ponder what they reveal about God and what they mean for you. Why should such ruminations make you thankful? By way of example, consider just two of those attributes—truth and power. God's absolute truthfulness assures you he will keep all his promises, and God's omnipotence assures you he has the strength and ability to accomplish everything he pledges. When Jesus promises, "whoever believes in the Son has eternal life" (John 3:36), the saints can rest easy about their souls, knowing God never lies and has the power to save. Furthermore, since the Holy Spirit, through the apostle Paul, vows "for those who love God all things work together for good" (Rom 8:28), Christians can trust the Lord through good times and bad, knowing he will orchestrate all events to bring good into their lives. Thus, meditating on God's faithfulness to keep promises and his power to accomplish everything promised can relieve your anxieties, dissolve your worries, conquer your fears, and give you restful peace; many careworn, haggard souls would give all they possess to experience such benefits. If you regularly contemplate God's person and the blessings his attributes bestow, you will feel grateful that you know the only great, good, and glorious God and will delight to express your thankfulness to him exuberantly every day. "Enter his gates with thanksgiving, and his courts with praise! Give thanks to him; bless his name! For the LORD is good; his steadfast love endures forever, and his faithfulness to all generations" (Ps 100:4–5).

Believers also should give thanks for God's *works*, beginning with creation, the things he spoke into existence *ex nihilo* (Heb 11:3). What mortal mind can fully embrace the enormity of the universe with its vast distances measured in light years and seemingly endless galaxies of stars, planets, and space? At the opposite extreme, who can completely understand the microscopic world of cells, molecules, atoms, and sub-atomic particles? What human brain can comprehend the myriad species of fauna and flora as well as the multitudinous forms of inorganic matter? Who can explain the mysteries of the human body, mind, and spirit? Reflecting on the great diversity, complexity, harmony, and grandeur of everything God made staggers and overwhelms the imagination and

6. Westminster Assembly, *Shorter Catechism*, Q&A #4.

senses. Thank him for your many opportunities to explore, discover, and enjoy creation's wonders and beauty.

Thank the Lord for his work of salvation, which freed you from sin and misery, uniting you with Christ. Remember, again and again, Jesus purchased your redemption through his sacrificial death on Calvary. "A broken form upon the cross and souls set free. Thy anguish there has paid the penalty—Sin's awful price in riven flesh and pain and blood—Redemption's cost, the broken Lamb of God."[7] "He was pierced for [y]our transgressions; he was crushed for [y]our iniquities; upon him was the chastisement that brought [you] peace, and with his wounds [you] are healed. . . . Like sheep [you] have gone astray; [you] have turned—every one—to [your] own way; and the LORD has laid on him [your] iniquity" (Isa 53:5–6). Remember, again and again, your election before the world began, effectual calling to salvation, receipt of faith and repentance as free gifts, regeneration unto eternal life, justification or declaration as righteous, adoption into the Father's family, sanctification unto holiness, assurance of God's love, peace of conscience, joy in the Holy Ghost, increase of grace, perseverance to the end, and future glorification of soul and body. What a great salvation brought you into God's earthly kingdom of grace and will lead you into his eternal kingdom of glory! "Be grateful for receiving a kingdom that cannot be shaken" (Heb 12:28).

Finally, be thankful for God's work of providence, which refers to his sovereign control over everything that happens. In providence, he wisely and lovingly nurtures, sustains, protects, delivers, comforts, and supports his people. "No good thing does he withhold from those who walk uprightly" (Ps 84:11). Without providence, all events and outcomes would occur entirely through random chance. But the good things in your life are no accident; they come through God's divine will and direct guidance. Therefore, express your gratitude to the Lord for every blessing he sends, whether food, shelter, clothing, health, medical care, freedom, education, employment, family, or friends. Thank God for his presence in your life, daily mercies, deliverance from temptations, victories over sin, Christian fellowship, and all the means of grace that help you become more like Jesus. Through his work of providence, "God will supply every need of yours according to his riches in glory in Christ Jesus" (Phil 4:19). With such a promise from such a store, how can you not be always thankful to God for everything?

7. Jones, Jr., "Broken Things," n.p.

God's Grace for Change

Before examining your heart, considering how you might improve, and seeking divine help, ponder one last point—Jesus thanked the Father for the assurance of being heard. "Jesus lifted up his eyes and said, 'Father, I thank you that you have heard me'" (John 11:41). Similarly, the Creator and Sustainer of the universe, the Author of your eternal salvation, the one who keeps covenant with you every day, this awesome, magnificent God hears you when you pray. Let this brief reminder about and appreciation for God's undeserved grace prepare and motivate you to develop more of this lesson's character trait in yourself.

Then, complete the "Heart Assessment, Reflection, and Petition" (HARP) chart, assessing your own thankfulness. Reflect on times the Holy Spirit enabled or empowered you to be thankful as well as times Jesus showed thankfulness during his earthly life. Consider whether the Spirit might be revealing a need for you to be more consistently thankful. If you want God to increase your thankfulness, put that desire in writing. This is a very important exercise that can help you respond to God's direction for your life. Pray over your completed chart once or twice this next week.

Finally, talk to the Lord, using the words that follow or incorporating the thoughts into your own prayer: "Great Father of grace and glory, my heart overflows in gratitude and appreciation for who you are and what you have done, your person and your works. How thankful I am for your infinite, eternal, and immutable wisdom, power, holiness, justice, goodness, truth, and love. What an awesome God I serve! Thank you for such an awe-inspiring, beautiful creation to explore, discover, and enjoy. Thank you for the good people in my life—family, friends, and others—who teach, guide, encourage, and help me. How deep is my indebtedness for your great salvation, for choosing, calling, regenerating, justifying, adopting, sanctifying, and, some day, glorifying me. Thank you, Jesus, for purchasing my redemption through much agony with your own blood. Thank you, Holy Spirit, for giving me faith and repentance and uniting me with Christ for all eternity. Thank you, Triune God, for daily assurance, peace, joy, and grace as well as the promise that I will persevere to the end. I am profoundly grateful for your marvelous work of providence in nurturing, sustaining, protecting, delivering, comforting, and supporting me each day. In every situation, teach me to be grateful to you from whom all blessings flow. Like the lone leper, let me not take any blessing for granted, whether large or small, but remember to offer sacrifices of thanksgiving continuously. Amen."

Remember, the Lord's help is vital to cultivating Christian character. Only his power can enable you to change. When you fail to show the character trait of thankfulness, confess it before God and ask for his forgiveness and help.

HARP Chart for Thankfulness

Definition: Thankfulness is gratitude to God for the multitude of his blessings.

Key verses: "Give thanks in all circumstances; for this is the will of God in Christ Jesus for you" (1 Thess 5:18). "Let us be grateful for receiving a kingdom that cannot be shaken" (Heb 12:28).

Bible characters: As the ark arrived in Jerusalem, David's liturgical psalm assisted Israel's appreciative assembly to express gratitude to God for his person and works. Only one lone leper, a Samaritan, returned to thank Jesus for healing him.

How often do you show thankfulness in your life: 5 = nearly always, 4 = most of the time, 3 = about half the time, 2 = less than half the time, or 1 = hardly ever? Your response is ____.
In what ways, if any, has the Holy Spirit enabled you to be thankful?
How did Jesus model thankfulness during his earthly life in ways benefiting you?
In what ways, if any, has the Holy Spirit revealed to you a need to be more thankful?
What petition related to thankfulness, if any, would you like to bring before the throne of grace?

Truthfulness

Engage in one or more of these introductory activities:

1. Game Night—Ahead of time, select three people to settle on a true-life event that happened to one of them about which others in the class are likely unfamiliar. These three people must decide on a fictional name to adopt since to use any of their actual names before friends and acquaintances would disclose too much. Unless all three are male or all three are females, choose a first name that could be either gender such as Lee or Terry. Alternatively, select a humorous, made-up name like Snapdoodle Hollywart. The person to whom the real-life event happened is the real [fictional name] while the other two are "imposters." Then, review several online clips of the once-popular television program, "To Tell the Truth," to understand how the game works.[1] The three individuals should rehearse the game at least once (especially how imposters should respond confidently when they don't know the answer). In class, briefly explain the game's rules to everyone else before the three individuals enter and say, "My name is [fictional name]." Someone plays host and provides a short synopsis of the event about which all three people claim firsthand knowledge. Everyone else acts as the "panel," asking questions about the event and trying to discern which one of the three lived or experienced it. The real [fictional name] must tell the truth while the two imposters must try to sound truthful when they don't know the correct answer. After all questions, let the class vote on who they think experienced the event firsthand before you say, "Will the real [fictional name], please stand up." As frequently occurred on the actual game show, one or both imposters might start to stand without doing so before the real [fictional name] does

---

1. The initial idea of associating this game show with the character trait of truthfulness came from Carden and Carden, *Christian Character Curriculum* 1, 37.

stand. To wrap up, ask those in the class how they decided who was telling the truth, calling attention to any telltale signs that helped them decide (e.g., the imposters might have stammered, hesitated, or glanced to one side when they didn't know the answer). Also, ask the two imposters which questions they found most difficult to answer and why. To modify the procedures outlined above, bring three unknown people to the class, where one experienced an event that would be particularly interesting to the group.

2. Intriguing Insights—The quotations below make observations about truthfulness and its opposite, falsehood. Explain each quotation's meaning or otherwise comment about it.

> "A willful falsehood told is a cripple, not able to
>   stand by itself without another to support
>   it.—It is easy to tell a lie, but hard to tell only
>   one lie."[2]

> "It is well said in the old proverb, 'A lie will go round
>   the world while truth is pulling its boots on.'"[3]

> "Falsehoods not only disagree with truths but
>   usually quarrel among themselves."[4]

> "A charitable untruth, an uncharitable truth, and an
>   unwise managing of truth or love, are all to be
>   carefully avoided of him that would go with a
>   right foot in the narrow way."[5]

> "The worse men are, the less they are bound by
>   oaths; the better they are, the less there is need
>   for them."[6]

> "A lie is like a snowball, the longer one rolls it the
>   larger it grows."[7]

2. Thomas Fuller as cited in Edwards, *Dictionary of Thoughts*, 298.

3. Spurgeon, "Joseph Attacked," 5.

4. Webster, *Writings and Speeches*, 102.

5. Hall, *Selection from the Writings*, 148.

6. Henry, *Matthew Henry's Concise*, 2373.

7. Luther, *Table Talk*, 40.

> "You can fool some of the people all of the time, and
> all of the people some of the time; but you
> cannot fool all of the people all of the time."[8]

> "Truth is the most valuable thing we have. Let us
> economize it."[9]

> "Those who think it permissible to tell white lies
> soon grow color-blind."[10]

> "Honesty pays, but it don't seem t' pay enough t' suit
> a lot o' people."[11]

3. Marketing Malarkey—Find advertisements that are either truthful or misleading.[12] How do they show truthfulness or its lack? Suggest various synonyms for these opposing traits that might be more descriptive (e.g., candor or integrity for truth and artifice or hogwash for falsity). Many advertisements slant the truth, omit important facts, or otherwise promote narratives that distort purchase decisions or understanding. Indeed, advertisements often exaggerate benefits while burying relevant caveats in inconspicuous, small-font footnotes of indecipherable legalese.

These activities highlight difficulties in discerning truth, the pervasiveness of dishonesty in society, problems associated with lying, and reasons to tell the truth. But what is this Christian character trait of truthfulness? Here's one way to define it:

> Truthfulness means honesty in word and deed, taking care not
> to deceive or mislead.

God desires his children to tell the truth through their speech, written communication, and actions. From a biblical perspective, what does this character trait of truthfulness look like, and how can Christians improve it? This lesson addresses these points under the headings of "God's Word to Mankind," "God's Work in Believers," and "God's Grace for Change."

---

8. Lincoln, *Lincoln Year Book*, n.p.

9. Paine, *Moments with Mark Twain*, 273.

10. O'Malley, *Keystones of Thought*, 107.

11. Hubbard, *Abe Martin*, 117.

12. The initial idea of associating advertisements with the character trait of truthfulness came from Carden and Carden, *Christian Character Curriculum* 1, 37.

God's Word to Mankind

Key Verses

"A man who bears false witness against his neighbor is like a war club, or a sword, or a sharp arrow" (Prov 25:18). "False witness" encompasses perjurious statements in court as well as libel, slander, or other untruths through public or private communications. "Neighbors" include everyone, not simply friends living nearby (Luke 10:25–37). With these clarifications, bearing false witness harms others just like beating them with a club, thrusting them through with a sword, or piercing them from afar causes physical injury. Wrongful damage to reputations can hurt as much as weapons of war designed to kill, sometimes more so. Evil, malicious words have great power to destroy.

"Having put away falsehood, let each of you speak the truth with his neighbor, for we are members one of another" (Eph 4:25). Sometimes called the put-off, put-on principle, the apostle Paul admonishes saints to put off (or away) falsity and put on truthfulness; they should remove deceitful tendencies, practicing openness and honesty instead. In this verse, the rationale for truthfulness relates to Christians being "members one of another." The Father adopted them into one spiritual family, making them Jesus' brothers and sisters and uniting them as one church. Thus, any member's dishonesty with an outsider reflects negatively on the entire body, heaping disrepute on God and his people. Moreover, when believers deceive each other, it destroys trust and unity within the church, which dishonors God as well.

Bible Characters

Dissembling Disciple (Mark 14:27–31, 66–72)

After Thursday's Passover meal, Jesus told eleven apostles they would fall away or scatter as his death neared. Peter asserted, "Even though they all fall away, I will not." Jesus explained what would soon come to pass: "Before the rooster crows twice, you will deny me three times." Nonetheless, Peter was sure of himself: "If I must die with you, I will not deny you." What high-sounding loyalty and courage! Soon after, Judas betrayed Jesus, and soldiers led the Lord away. Then, the Sanhedrin held a middle-of-the-night kangaroo court to fast-track Jesus' execution.

Before sunrise on Friday, Peter entered the Sanhedrin courtyard and warmed himself incognito by a fire. Though pledging his life to Jesus only hours before, a lowly servant girl proved the beginning of his undoing. She accused him of knowing Jesus. Peter denied the charge and, feigning ignorance, walked out to the courtyard's entrance where someone, maybe the same maiden, charged him a second time. Fearing for his safety, the disciple lied about knowing Jesus again. By that time, perhaps Peter recalled how Jesus foretold three denials and resolved not to repeat his dissemblance. Yet, a short while later, those nearby accused Peter once more. Panicking and cursing this time, he blurted out, "I do not know this man of whom you speak," and the rooster crowed the second time. (Whether the first crow occurred much earlier or shortly before this third denial is uncertain.) Under threatening circumstances, Peter proved untruthful and denied knowing him to whom, in prior days, he had declared, "You are the Christ, the Son of the living God" (Matt 16:16). On this gloomy Friday when Jesus would be crucified, the disciple's dissembling denials cast a dark shadow over his prior good confession.

Perjurious Parishioners (Acts 5:1–11)

After Pentecost, the early church grew rapidly (Acts 2:41, 47; 4:4). However, many lacked necessities, possibly due to Jewish persecution against believers. In response and out of love for one another, church members willingly sold their own properties to help those in need (Acts 2:45; 4:32–35). For instance, Barnabas sold a field and donated money for the apostles to distribute as coin or food (Acts 4:36–37). Later, the apostles would turn such administrative duties over to deacons (Acts 6:1–6).

A married couple, Ananias and Sapphira, sold property and gave *part* of the proceeds to help the poor. However, they conspired between themselves to say they were giving the *entire* proceeds, hoping to appear more generous than they were. In effect, they lied to the apostles, the church, and, worst of all, the Holy Spirit. Lying in this manner prompted God's swift punishment. The perjurious parishioners paid with their lives.

Review Questions

1. What is the Christian character trait of truthfulness?

2. What words are missing from this verse? "A man who bears _____ witness against his _____ is like a war club, or a _____, or a sharp _____" (Prov 25:18).

3. How is false testimony like a club, sword, or arrow?

4. "Sticks and stones may break my bones, but words will never hurt me." Do you agree or disagree and why?

5. What words are missing from this verse? "Having put away _____, let each of you speak the _____ with his neighbor, for we are _____ one of another" (Eph 4:25).

6. In Eph 4:25, what principle does the apostle Paul mention in relation to truthfulness, and what does the principle say?

7. In Eph 4:25, what rationale does Paul give for being truthful?

8. What did the apostle Peter promise shortly before Jesus' trial and crucifixion?

9. How did Peter break his promise to Jesus and, thus, prove untruthful?

10. In addition to breaking his promise, how else did Peter prove untruthful?

11. Peter wept bitterly after denying Jesus three times. If he could have turned back the clock and done it all over again, how do you think Peter might have replied to those who accused him of knowing Jesus?

12. How did Ananias and Sapphira try to deceive?

13. Whom did Ananias and Sapphira attempt to deceive?

God's Work in Believers

A key element for all forms of lying is willfulness or, at least, carelessness. Unintentional errors due to genuinely honest mistakes or poor memories, even when they mislead and, thus, require an apology or even restitution, are not lies. Lying entails deliberate or negligent deceit; it's a spiritual defect, not a cerebral one. In contrast, truthfulness involves honesty in word and deed, taking care not to deceive or mislead. Always being honest is hard since temptations to deceive and mislead arise for so many reasons and in so many settings. Though examining these reasons and settings can enlighten, remember that veracity requires the Holy Spirit's power.

Common reasons to deceive or mislead fall into three broad categories—obtaining benefits, avoiding difficulties, and inflicting harm:

1. Falsehoods often arise from desires to obtain (or keep) benefits such as money, admiration, and power. Examples are nearly endless. Misstating your age in a restaurant procures a discount. Overstating hours worked increases pay. Cheating on a tax return lessens the liability. As to admiration, exaggerating abilities, accomplishments, or virtues enhances reputation and impresses people. Presumably, Ananias and Sapphira thought exaggerating their generosity would win them respect or praise. Inflating a resume or embellishing a dating profile might secure a job or relationship. As to power, lying might help prove a point, control a decision, win an argument, manipulate someone, or gain sympathy. Have you ever stretched the truth or outright lied to obtain money, admiration, or power?

2. Avoiding difficulties is another reason people deceive or mislead. Again, examples abound. Someone may lie to escape embarrassment, conflict, responsibilities, or punishment. The apostle Peter dissembled in the courtyard to avoid detection and its unpleasant consequences. A teenager might concoct a family emergency to wriggle out of a school assignment. People also may lie to protect co-workers, friends, or family members. A father, for instance, might mislead a store manager to protect his culpable son from a shoplifting charge. Still others tell seemingly inconsequential untruths to sidestep distasteful tasks, boring conversations, or disapproval. Have you ever deceived or misled someone to avoid trouble?

3. Whether due to thoughtlessness, cruelty, or vengefulness, people often assassinate the character of others. Lies that carelessly or deliberately harm bear labels such as gossip, backbiting, vindictiveness, and hatred. These dangerous weapons inflict serious injuries. When used covertly, malicious words may not hurt victims' feelings at once, but such words hurt their reputations instantly and, perhaps, their feelings later. Lies told over lunch in Boston, for example, can destroy a reputation in Seattle. In some sense, lying about people *in absentia* hurts them more than telling the lie in their presence; the

former provides no opportunity for rebuttal and, thus, can spread unchecked like a raging wildfire. "A man who bears false witness against his neighbor is like a war club, or a sword, or a sharp arrow" (Prov 25:18). Have you ever spoken or written untrue words that harmed someone?

With these broad reasons in mind, consider five diverse settings—familial, educational, vocational, political, and religious—in which someone might speak, write, or act mendaciously:

1. Within families, consistent honesty cultivates trust. But untruthfulness can take root and spread like noxious weeds, sowing dysfunctional seeds of distrust, disharmony, and disunity. Strive against this happening; practice truthfulness and lovingly emphasize its importance to other family members. Aspire to an atmosphere that promotes open and honest dialog in all situations. Neither adults, teens, nor children should deceive or mislead to assert independence; keep secrets or suppress the truth; rebel against authority; or control, modify, or manipulate someone's behavior. When dishonesty does occur, repentance, forgiveness, and reconciliation should follow.

2. Obtaining an education involves exchanges. In exchange for grades, students complete assignments and take tests. In doing so, they should submit only work reflecting their personal abilities and efforts, resisting any temptations to cheat. Teachers, instructors, and professors also must be truthful, following standards of fairness and abiding by any contractual terms (e.g., in syllabi) when assigning grades. Untruthfulness from either side fosters distrust, impedes learning, and displeases God.

3. A person's vocation provides numerous, almost daily opportunities to choose between truthfulness and falsehood. Consider the latter, starting with job applications and resumes—some exaggerate qualifications or contain fabricated entries such as college degrees never earned. At work, employees, contractors, managers, and executives may hide mistakes or wrongdoing to the detriment of customers, clients, colleagues, or companies. Society often cannot assume veracity in business dealings. Even small transactions require written contracts because of widespread distrust, relegating simple handshakes to a bygone era. Against this backdrop, set a godly example

for others to follow. Be honest in all aspects of your job, trade, profession, or career, showing others what biblical truthfulness looks like.

4. How do you know when a politician is lying? His (or her) lips are moving. It's an old joke, but many running for office assume they cannot be elected without stretching the truth or vowing things they can't or won't deliver. As with education, an exchange is proffered—"Elect (or reelect) me, and I'll do such and such!" Making promises obtains votes and increases political prowess. Failing to do as promised, however, is rank dishonesty. Once elected, the pledges, too often, lie broken. Better not to promise than to promise and not do. The fact that many other politicians speak falsely is no excuse. Neither does the end (election) justify the means (lying).

5. Christians are not a loosely confederated group of independent people; they are "fellow citizens with the saints and members of the household of God" (Eph 2:19) through Jesus' atonement, the Spirit's regeneration, and the Father's adoption. Untruthfulness within this sacred family causes great damage. Lies release a spiritual toxin into the church's bloodstream that flows through the entire body of Christ. Gossip and backbiting destroy bonds of trust and dismantle unity, turning believers against believers though they sit but a few pews apart. Even more damaging, perhaps, are untrustworthy, weak, or self-willed church leaders who mislead or deceive the flock (see the lesson about watchfulness).

Before continuing, juxtapose the five settings immediately above with the earlier three reasons why people mislead or deceive others. For each setting, can you identify common motivations for untruthfulness? Are they to obtain benefits, avoid difficulties, or inflict harm?

As implied earlier, honesty (or its lack) doesn't just relate to the past or present. People frequently commit to performing future tasks. Later, doing as promised shows truthfulness; failing to follow through reveals untruthfulness. Don't make promises you can't or won't keep. Breaking a promise is wrong. Occasionally, unforeseen circumstances may prevent you from fulfilling a promise, but those times should be rare occurrences, not the norm. If you find yourself habitually quick to promise and then slow or unable to fulfill, stop promising. Perhaps tell people you'd like to help but can't commit in advance; better not to promise than to commit and not fulfill. If you can't keep obligations, don't cavalierly make promises since doing so deceives or misleads those depending on you. Examine and understand yourself, learning responsibility as well as veracity. If unreliable, don't add untruthfulness to your faults. Instead, seek the Holy Spirit's help to become more responsible.

Another issue involves deceiving or misleading others for their own or society's good. Lying is not an acceptable means of getting people to eat healthier, learn more, fulfill duties, exercise regularly, attend church, or otherwise improve their lives or discharge their responsibilities. Sometimes, an elitist presumption—"I know better than you do what's best"—leads to manipulation of or influence over people through half-truths or outright falsehoods. Even when a person does know better, deceiving or misleading others, no matter how well-intentioned, breaks the moral law. Such can become a slippery slope, tempting a person to justify every falsehood in an I-know-best fashion. Though contexts vary, this control issue sometimes arises between (a) parents, guardians, or other adults and (b) children or adolescents. True, adults usually know what is best and should guide minors under their care, not leaving all decisions to them. But that doesn't make manipulating them through misleading statements or other deceptions an acceptable means of guidance. To avoid conflict, a mother might tell little Johnny that she doesn't have money to buy a treat or time to visit the arcade when the real reason involves something entirely different. The lie is wrong in the present and potentially damaging in the future. Deceiving or misleading young people can become a habit and, potentially, continue past childhood. In this manner, parents can destroy their own credibility and may occasion rebellion, causing their offspring to distrust authority figures, doing much unforeseen harm.

One more issue begs addressing, and it's one many have disagreed about and wrestled over for centuries. Is deceiving or misleading someone always wrong?[13] Some Christians say it is never right for any purpose. After all, "lying lips are an abomination to the Lord" (Prov 12:22). Others insist misleading someone is acceptable in certain narrow circumstances, arguing that all deception is not lying and, thus, not sinful. However, these individuals don't always agree on what these narrow circumstances are. This short lesson, regrettably, won't resolve the matter. However, being aware of the question and thinking through it now might better prepare you for handling moral dilemmas of this nature as they arise.

13. The author struggled with whether to mention this issue but, in the end, perceiving it as the proverbial elephant in the room, thought raising it trumped ignoring it.

With that in mind, three areas where people often have argued it's okay to deceive or mislead follow.

First, the rules for many sports and games tacitly permit deception. Consider baseball, for example, in which the pitcher seeks to deceive players on the opposing team. He intermingles his fastball, slider, change-up, and curve, disguising the delivery of each. He is not required to alert the batter, "The next pitch will be a slider," nor inform the runner on second, "Here comes my pickoff move." Neither must the batter declare his plan to bunt or, on a 3-0 pitch, swing away. Indeed, deception is part of the sport, and the same can be said for basketball, football, hockey, and soccer. Or think about chess. Neither player must explain the strategy behind each move such as "I'm beginning a five-step strategy to checkmate, hoping this first move misleads you." And the long-running game show, "To Tell the Truth," presupposes two imposters who will utter blatant untruths. Based on the popularity of these and other sports and games, most people find nothing wrong with instances of "understood deception." Some good-natured, practical jokes involving "temporary deception" might be viewed similarly. However, desiring to be truthful and keep consciences clear, other Christians frown on practical jokes and gravitate towards games and sports involving little, if any, deception like Trivial Pursuit, Scrabble, track and field, horseshoes, and fishing (though some may question this last entry).

Second, what about white lies that supposedly (a) harm no one due to their triviality, (b) spare feelings, or (c) provide comfort to another? Here are several examples. A passing acquaintance asks how you are, and you reply "fine" even though your life seems tumultuous. You mislead a friend, inviting her to your house for a quiet dinner where, instead, a surprise birthday or retirement party awaits. When asked directly about a meal, you commend your dinner host with "Yes, this is delicious," even though he undercooked the meat, oversalted the veggies, and scorched the dinner rolls. After a wedding or sporting event, you praise someone on her appearance or performance even though you don't really consider it noteworthy. You comfort the distraught father of a teen daughter killed in a tragic accident by saying, "I'm sure she died instantly," even though you don't really know. Your elderly mother, once more, forgets your father passed away years ago, becomes agitated, and repeatedly asks if he will get home soon. To calm her, you say, "Oh, it shouldn't be long now." Do you think it's okay to tell white lies in some or all these situations? Why or why not? What, if anything, distinguishes acceptable white lies from sinful deceptions? Is telling a white lie wrong only if you obtain a benefit, avoid a difficulty, or inflict harm? In an attempt not to lie, suppose you equivocate. Do evasive responses that deceive or mislead differ from straightforward lies? To avoid untruthfulness, is it possible to avoid awkward situations like these entirely? If not, yet you think prevaricating is wrong, could straight-up truthful responses sometimes be harmful or unloving to the hearer? For many Christians, these are hard questions.

Third, should you ever deceive or mislead to safeguard the innocent? Is lying to anyone ever acceptable to prevent a much greater sin against someone else? What do you do when the Sixth Commandment about protecting life seemingly conflicts in its application with the Ninth Commandment about truthfulness? Consider two instances from Scripture: (a) The midwives lied to Pharaoh to keep newborns from being slaughtered (Exod 1:15–22) and (b) Rahab lied to protect two spies serving Israel and God (Josh 2:1–24, 6:17–25; Heb 11:31). What would you have done in these situations? When faced with difficult choices between "two evils," should you speak deceitful words to deliver the guiltless or truthful words that may enable the wicked? Though the biblical text does not explicitly excuse or condemn the midwives and Rahab for their lies, God did protect them. But would truthfulness have been the better choice, relying on the Almighty to protect both babies and spies? Ponder a more contemporary example. During World War II, the entire Huguenot community of Le Chambon-sur-Lignon in southern France sheltered as many as five thousand Jews, mostly children, and helped them escape German forces and the collaborative Vichy police. The villagers repeatedly deceived the authorities, feigning ignorance of Jews living among them, hiding them in nearby forests during raids, forging identification papers, and smuggling innocents nearly two hundred miles to safety in neutral Switzerland. Clearly, the French villagers had altruistic, rather than self-interested or malicious, motives for these deceptions since, in protecting others, they placed their own lives at risk. Their courageous, heroic efforts presumably allowed many Jews to avoid the Nazi death camps and survive the Holocaust, but were their untruths sinful? What would you have done under similar circumstances? Is lying okay in times of war? Closer to home, would you lie to (or even shoot) an armed intruder to protect your family? Some theologians believe deception in rare cases like these for a righteous purpose might be the best moral choice, but, if true, identifying those instances calls for much introspection and prayer. Others believe Scripture requires nothing less than complete truth, after which, the consequences must be left in the capable hands of the God who controls all things. When such quandaries arise in your life, may the Holy Spirit help you apply Scripture correctly.

Notwithstanding possible disagreements in these three areas, practice truthfulness in your daily life. Remember, the devil "is a liar and the father of lies" (John 8:44). In contrast, Jesus is filled with truth and, indeed, is the embodiment of all truth (John 1:14, 14:6). Flee from Satan. Follow Jesus. "Blessed is the man . . . in whose spirit there is no deceit" (Ps 32:2). "What man is there who desires life and loves many days, that he may see good? Keep your tongue from evil and your lips from speaking deceit" (Ps 34:12–13). Pray for the Holy Spirit's guidance and strength to be truthful.

God's Grace for Change

Before examining your heart, considering how you might improve, and seeking divine help, ponder one last point—God is the only one who never lies, never misleads, never deceives; all his words are wholly true all the time. "By two unchangeable things, in which it is impossible for God to lie, we who have fled for refuge might have strong encouragement to hold fast to the hope set before us" (Heb 6:18). "All the promises of God find their Yes in him" (2 Cor 1:20). Let this brief reminder about and appreciation for God's undeserved grace prepare and motivate you to develop more of this lesson's character trait in yourself.

Then, complete the "Heart Assessment, Reflection, and Petition" (HARP) chart, assessing your own truthfulness. Reflect on times the Holy Spirit enabled or empowered you to be truthful as well as times God and others were truthful with you. Consider whether the Spirit might be revealing a need for you to be more truthful. If you want God to increase your truthfulness, put that desire in writing. This is a very important exercise that can help you respond to God's direction for your life. Pray over your completed chart once or twice this next week.

Finally, talk to the Lord, using the words that follow or incorporating the thoughts into your own prayer: "God of all truth, teach me to be truthful in all my words and deeds. Forgive me for testifying falsely against my neighbors, especially fellow believers. Forgive me for sinfully deceiving and misleading others. Enable me to put off lying and put on truthfulness in future days. Teach me to keep promises and commitments.

Help me, Holy Spirit, to become more and more like Jesus who was the embodiment of perfect truth. In his name, I pray in faith, believing that you can surely accomplish these things in my life. Amen."

Remember, the Lord's help is vital to cultivating Christian character. Only his power can enable you to change. When you fail to show the character trait of truthfulness, confess it before God and ask for his forgiveness and help.

HARP Chart for Truthfulness

Definition: Truthfulness means honesty in word and deed, taking care not to deceive or mislead.

Key verses: "A man who bears false witness against his neighbor is like a war club, or a sword, or a sharp arrow" (Prov 25:18). "Having put away falsehood, let each of you speak the truth with his neighbor, for we are members one of another" (Eph 4:25).

Bible characters: The disciple's dissembling denial of Jesus cast a dark shadow over Peter's prior declaration. Ananias and Sapphira, the perjurious parishioners, pursued praise for part of the proceeds.

How often do you show truthfulness in your life: 5 = nearly always, 4 = most of the time, 3 = about half the time, 2 = less than half the time, or 1 = hardly ever? Your response is ____.
In what ways, if any, has the Holy Spirit enabled you to be truthful?
In what ways, if any, have God and others been truthful with you?
In what ways, if any, has the Holy Spirit revealed to you a need to be more truthful?
What petition related to truthfulness, if any, would you like to bring before the throne of grace?

Watchfulness

Engage in one or more of these introductory activities:

1. Name that Danger—Involve others in a discussion about dangerous things. Carefully steer away from unnecessarily frightening or inappropriate subjects. Is anything inside your home dangerous? Are there dangerous things in schools or at work? Can you think of anything in the great outdoors that is dangerous? Shifting the focus, what does God say is dangerous?

2. Nature Study—Learn about the colorful ring-necked pheasant and share your findings through online photos or short audio or video clips. The bird stays alert to approaching danger through its keen sense of sight and hearing. If foxes, raccoons, or coyotes draw near, the pheasant runs away to escape, dodging back and forth beneath dense underbrush. When predators get too close, the bird launches vertically and flies to new ground cover.

3. Talking and Walking—Engage others in a discussion about mobile phones. Have you ever seen someone talking on a cell phone while walking in public? Likely, everyone has seen this. Have you ever seen someone placing themselves in danger because they are walking while on the phone? People on mobile phones have walked into glass doors, outdoor fountains, and oncoming traffic. They become inattentive to surrounding dangers.

Yes, some things in life can cause harm, and it's important to stay alert. However, the most dangerous things are not those affecting body and mind, which an earlier lesson about caution addressed, but those imperiling the soul when Christians aren't watchful. What is this Christian character trait of watchfulness? Here's one way to define it:

> Watchfulness is alertness to and wariness of spiritual dangers.

God desires his children to watch for anything threatening their spiritual well-being and growth. From a biblical perspective, what does this character trait of watchfulness look like, and how can Christians improve it? This lesson addresses these points under the headings of "God's Word to Mankind," "God's Work in Believers," and "God's Grace for Change."

God's Word to Mankind

Key Verses

"Beware of false prophets, who come to you in sheep's clothing but inwardly are ravenous wolves" (Matt 7:15). "Beware" means watch out, remain on high alert. As the devil's emissaries, "false prophets" teach things contrary to Scripture. Such deceivers include church leaders who do not believe fundamental Bible doctrines like the deity of Christ and Jesus' resurrection and, thus, deny and contradict the truth through their words and deeds. False prophets also include politicians, entertainers, athletes, teachers, and others who promote or endorse ungodly views or sinful behaviors that lead others astray. Saints must stay alert to worldviews opposing or denying God's Word, keeping "ravenous wolves" away from their souls.

"Be sober-minded; be watchful. Your adversary the devil prowls around like a roaring lion, seeking someone to devour" (1 Pet 5:8). Satan is behind all false teaching and temptations in the world. The Christian's struggle is not "against flesh and blood, but against the rulers, against the authorities, against the cosmic powers over this present darkness, against the spiritual forces of evil in the heavenly places" (Eph 6:12). Remember that Jesus taught his disciples to pray, "Lead us not into temptation, but deliver us from the evil one" (Matt 6:13, NIV). Satan is a formidable foe who, deceptively appearing at times as an angel of light, tirelessly works to destroy believers. Throughout life, the devil lays out many stumbling blocks and pitfalls to ambush and harass the saints. Sometimes, God's people walk too near these obstacles, tripping over or plunging into them. Satan is the great enemy who desires to wreak spiritual havoc in the Christian's life. Be aware of his ploys; remain watchful.

Bible Characters

Heedful Hebrew (Gen 39:1–12)

Joseph became a slave for an Egyptian official named Potiphar. God helped Joseph succeed in everything he tried. So, Potiphar put Joseph in charge of his entire household and all his belongings. But since Joseph was strong and handsome, Potiphar's wife tried seducing him. Wanting to glorify God and not wishing to betray his master, Joseph refused her advances time after time.

But one day, when no one else was around, Potiphar's wife tried once more, grabbing Joseph by his cloak. Fortunately, Joseph was alert to her wiles and ran from the house, leaving his cloak behind. Though Joseph suffered wrongly for this encounter, his watchfulness for the devil's schemes and the woman's seductive ways allowed him to escape temptation and continue pleasing God.

Drowsy Disciples (Mark 14:27–72)

After the Last Supper, Jesus told his eleven disciples they soon would scatter from him. (Judas was away, betraying Jesus to the chief priests.) Peter protested he would remain with the Lord even if everyone else fled. Jesus corrected him, saying Peter would not only run away but deny knowing him three times. Like Peter, the eleven disciples objected to what Jesus had said, insisting they would never disown their Lord.

Then, Jesus took them to the Garden of Gethsemane for a prayer meeting. Greatly distressed about the struggle to come, Jesus admonished the eleven to watch and pray so they would be alert to spiritual danger. But instead of remaining vigilant, they slept. Awakened just before Judas arrived with the temple guards who arrested Jesus, all eleven disciples soon fled. A short time later, Peter denied knowing Jesus three times just as foretold.

Review Questions

1. What is the Christian character trait of watchfulness?

2. What words are missing from this verse? "Beware of _____ _____, who come to you in _____ clothing but inwardly are ravenous _____" (Matt 7:15).

3. What words are missing from this verse? "Be sober-minded; be _____. Your adversary the _____ prowls around like a roaring ____, seeking someone to devour" (1 Pet 5:8).

4. In Matt 7:15 and 1 Pet 5:8, for what two things should Christians be watchful?

5. In Matt 7:15 and 1 Pet 5:8, to what two animals are false prophets and the devil likened?

6. When would a celebrity be considered a false prophet?

7. What words are missing? _____ initiates or facilitates all _____ teaching in the world and tempts believers through _____ blocks and pitfalls.

8. Who tempted Joseph and how?

9. What kind of things might have made Joseph particularly susceptible to this temptation?

10. What alerted Joseph to spiritual danger before Potiphar's wife grabbed his cloak?

11. How did Joseph escape from Potiphar's wife?

12. After the Last Supper, what did Jesus say his disciples soon would do?

13. Which disciple(s) committed never to leave Jesus?

14. Which disciple seemed to protest the most that he would never forsake Jesus?

15. What did Jesus say Peter would do very soon?

16. How did Jesus want the eleven disciples to remain watchful?

17. What words are missing from this verse? "_____ and ____ that you may not enter into temptation. The _____ indeed is willing, but the ____ is weak" (Mark 14:38).

God's Work in Believers

Whether from false prophets or Satan himself, temptations are normal, regular, and frequent in every Christian's life. "No temptation has overtaken you that is not common to man" (1 Cor 10:13). Understand that being tempted, without yielding, is not sin. Indeed, Satan tempted Jesus, yet he resisted the attacks and never sinned (Matt 4:1–11; 1 Pet 2:22). But since you will be tempted like other Christians, how can you watch for spiritual danger in a way that safeguards your soul, pleasing and glorifying God?

Through the Holy Spirit's guidance and power, be alert to mistaken notions about temptation that result in either despair or pride. Never assume your temptations are more difficult to resist than those other believers face, which can lead to despair and surrender. Many others undergo the same or similar temptations. "Resist [the devil], firm in your faith, knowing that the same kinds of suffering are being experienced by your brotherhood throughout the world" (1 Pet 5:9). At the other extreme, never assume your spiritual maturity places you beyond Satan's reach. "Though you become greatly sanctified by the Holy Spirit, expect that the great dog of hell [Satan] will bark at [tempt] you still."[1] The sad reality is that believers are tempted and, at times, do yield. Foolishly thinking you have somehow become righteous or holy enough to avoid or resist all temptation is mere spiritual pride, and "pride goes before destruction" (Prov 16:18). Remember Peter's declaration that he would never deny Jesus and take heed. But when you do yield to Satan's temptation, God's grace, once more, provides the solution. Godly sorrow and the Lord's promised forgiveness lead Christians back to a right relationship and close communion with him.

Watch for things that may tempt you. For instance, prayerfully consider the impact of videos you view, music you hear, smartphone usage, and the internet, including social media, on your spiritual walk. Over time, exposing yourself to messages or experiences that tempt you to think or act sinfully dulls your alertness to spiritual danger. As a prime example, viewing pornography, in addition to its inherent sinfulness, diminishes or even deadens your watchfulness in many areas of your life. With good reason, the Bible often warns against all forms of sexual sins. "This is the will of God, your sanctification: that you abstain from sexual immorality" (1 Thess 4:3). Ungodly worldviews promoted in movies and

---

1. Spurgeon, "Tempted of the Devil," 6.

music also can numb your spiritual awareness to God's will. Further, too many hours spent on electronic devices can shortchange the time you devote to God, family, and friends. Developing spiritual alertness may require radical changes to viewing and listening habits as well as social interactions. To make changes in these areas, consider asking a mature Christian friend for advice and help. Among other things, consider placing strict content filters and time restrictions on your internet usage and carefully reading video and music reviews before consuming their full content. Ask the Spirit to counsel you about any changes you should make.

Look for early warnings and possible escape routes. Though temptations will come, God always provides his people with sufficient grace to resist and a way of escape. "God is faithful, and he will not let you be tempted beyond your ability, but with the temptation he will also provide the way of escape, that you may be able to endure it" (1 Cor 10:13). Recall how the ring-necked pheasant stays watchful for predators through its acute hearing and eyesight and then runs away through dense underbrush, occasionally resorting to flight. Remember also how Joseph ran from the spiritual danger threatening him. Yet fleeing is not always the godly response; sometimes, God desires his people to stand firm. Jesus' disciples should have stood with Jesus through his arrest and trial but, instead, played the cowards and ran away. Jesus alerted them beforehand to their spiritual danger—namely, abandoning him when he needed them most—but they failed to pray, yielded to temptation, and fled. So, stay watchful, protecting your most valuable possession—your eternal soul. Seek God's mercy and wisdom in this watchfulness.

Watch for spiritual dangers through all the means of grace God provides. "Be strong in the Lord and in the strength of his might. Put on the whole armor of God, that you may be able to stand against the schemes of the devil. . . . Take up the shield of faith, with which you can extinguish all the flaming darts of the evil one; and take the helmet of salvation, and the sword of the Spirit, which is the Word of God, praying at all times in the Spirit, with all prayer and supplication. To that end keep alert with all perseverance, making supplication for all the saints" (Eph 6:10–11, 16–18). In addition to studying the Bible and praying earnestly, worship regularly, fellowship with other believers, worthily partake of the Lord's Supper, and obey God's commands. These things will develop spiritual alertness within you.

God's Grace for Change

Before examining your heart, considering how you might improve, and seeking divine help, ponder an earlier point one last point—In the darkness of Gethsemane, Jesus warned his disciples against the lurking spiritual danger. "Watch and pray that you may not enter into temptation. The spirit indeed is willing, but the flesh is weak" (Matt 26:41). Let this brief reminder about and appreciation for God's undeserved grace prepare and motivate you to develop more of this lesson's character trait in yourself.

Then, complete the "Heart Assessment, Reflection, and Petition" (HARP) chart, assessing your own watchfulness. Reflect on times the Holy Spirit enabled or empowered you to be watchful as well as times Jesus showed watchfulness during his earthly life. Consider whether the Spirit might be revealing a need for you to become more watchful for spiritual dangers. If you want God to increase your watchfulness, put that desire in writing. This is a very important exercise that can help you respond to God's direction for your life. Pray over your completed chart once or twice this next week.

Finally, talk to the Lord, using the words that follow or incorporating the thoughts into your own prayer: "Dear Father, the only true and living God, I praise your great name. Through your grace, forgive my sins, particularly when I've failed to stay watchful amid so many spiritual dangers or when I've yielded to Satan's shiny but deadly allurements. As Jesus taught, I plead, 'Lead [me] not into temptation, but deliver [me] from evil.' Thank you for all the benefits you have bestowed through Christ's redemption. Now, give me the desire and a plan to develop spiritual watchfulness in my life so I can resist the devil, his false prophets, and his many and varied temptations. Holy Spirit, bring about this work for my eternal good and your eternal glory. Help me to be like Jesus in whose name I pray. Amen."

Remember, the Lord's help is vital to cultivating Christian character. Only his power can enable you to change. When you fail to show the character trait of watchfulness, confess it before God and ask for his forgiveness and help.

HARP Chart for Watchfulness

Definition: Watchfulness is alertness to and wariness of spiritual dangers.

Key verses: "Beware of false prophets, who come to you in sheep's clothing but inwardly are ravenous wolves" (Matt 7:15). "Be sober-minded; be watchful. Your adversary the devil prowls around like a roaring lion, seeking someone to devour" (1 Pet 5:8).

Bible characters: Joseph, the heedful Hebrew, fled from the temptress, obeying God. In contrast, the drowsy disciples did not watch and pray; when tempted, they abandoned Jesus.

How often do you show watchfulness in your life: 5 = nearly always, 4 = most of the time, 3 = about half the time, 2 = less than half the time, or 1 = hardly ever? Your response is ____.
In what ways, if any, has the Holy Spirit enabled you to show watchfulness?
How did Jesus model watchfulness during his earthly life in ways benefiting you?
In what ways, if any, has the Holy Spirit revealed to you a need to be more watchful?
What petition related to watchfulness, if any, would you like to bring before the throne of grace?

Appendix A

Definitions of Christian Character Traits

Attentiveness entails listening and observing to learn truth or show concern and respect.

Availability means reserving time to serve God and others while keeping plans, schedules, and priorities reasonably flexible to meet unexpected needs as they arise.

Caution involves due care in dealing with new or dangerous situations, trusting people of uncertain character or motives, and drawing conclusions from incomplete or unverified facts.

Compassion is pity, sympathy, or concern for those who suffer combined with a strong desire to relieve their hurt.

Contentment entails being satisfied with God's provision.

Courage is the strength of mind or heart that allows people to face threats, pains, dangers, or other difficulties without fear overwhelming them.

Decisiveness involves timely choices that wisely consider future consequences.

Deference is the volitional yielding to another person's opinion, judgment, need, wish, preference, or will.

Diligence means the persistent, steadfast pursuit of a worthwhile objective or purpose.

Discernment is the keen ability to distinguish between right and wrong, truth and error, and good and evil.

Endurance is the capacity to withstand or accept prolonged or intense pain, hardship, misfortune, persecution, affliction, testing, discipline, or other adversity without quitting or losing heart.

Fairness occurs when people apply the same rules and standards in the same way to everyone and treat others as they would themselves like to be treated.

Faith is belief and trust in God and his Word, especially regarding the finished work of Christ for salvation.

Forgiveness is an attitude that waives or surrenders feelings of bitterness, anger, or vengeance for wrongs suffered.

Generosity reflects an altruistic willingness to give time, money, or other resources to people or causes without expecting something in return.

Gentleness involves a mild temperament, soft speech, and tender acts.

Humility entails a lowliness of mind freed from vain thoughts of self-importance.

Joyfulness is an inward sense of divine blessing that encourages the soul regardless of outward circumstances.

Patience requires calm waiting or restraint when dealing with painful suffering, trying people, agonizing losses, daily irritants, or unfulfilled dreams.

Purity is freedom from sexual immorality whether in attitudes, thoughts, speech, or actions.

Repentance involves sorrowing for sin and turning from it to God.

Respectfulness is a gracious regard for the feelings, opinions, rights, accomplishments, or authority of others.

Responsibility requires conscientious performance of duties, principled decision-making, and full acceptance of any negative consequences from performance or decisions.

Thankfulness is gratitude to God for the multitude of his blessings.

Truthfulness means honesty in word and deed, taking care not to deceive or mislead.

Watchfulness is alertness to and wariness of spiritual dangers.

Appendix B

Review Answers

This appendix contains suggested answers to review questions for the twenty-six Christian character lessons. In the free PowerPoint slides (at elark4.wixsite.com/character with password "allgrace"), each answer appears after its related question.

Attentiveness

1. Attentiveness entails listening and observing to learn truth or show concern and respect.

2. hearing / eye / LORD

3. attention / heard / drift

4. His words of truth

5. Parents and guardians wanted Jesus to touch and bless their children. However, for reasons not fully known, the disciples tried to prevent the children from reaching Jesus.

6. Jesus paid attention to the children, taking them into his arms and blessing them.

7. Martha prepared food and drink for the visitors, but Mary sat down and listened to Jesus.

8. Martha complained to Jesus that she had to do all the work while Mary just sat and listened.

9. Mary immediately sat down and paid attention to Jesus' words. Also, unknown before she complained, Jesus paid careful attention

to Martha's busyness and worry. His gentle instruction to her was full of loving concern.

10. Martha paid attention to her preparations, but she did not pay attention to the more important thing—Jesus' words.

Availability

1. Availability means reserving time to serve God and others while keeping plans, schedules, and priorities reasonably flexible to meet unexpected needs as they arise.

2. appeal / mercies / living sacrifice / acceptable / worship

3. not only / interests / others

4. Isaiah prophesied during the reign of several Judean kings, one of whom was King Uzziah (Isa 1:1). The vision occurred during the year King Uzziah died (Isa 6:1).

5. The sight of God in all his glory

   The seraph praising God as holy and glorious

   The vibration of the temple from the seraph voices

   The smoke filling the temple similar to events in the days of Moses and Aaron (Exod 40:34–35) and the last days (Rev 15:8)

   The thought of his own sinfulness in the presence of the perfectly holy God, which caused him to wonder if he might die

6. The seraph assured Isaiah that God had forgiven his guilt and paid for his sin.

7. When God asked with whom to send a message, Isaiah promptly volunteered: "Here am I. Send me!"

8. On his second missionary journey, Paul first met Timothy in the city of Lystra, which was in modern-day Turkey.

9. He left home to accompany the great apostle on his second and third missionary journeys, went where Paul sent him and came when Paul beckoned, ministered to Paul in prison, and pastored the church at Ephesus.

10. Timothy was "genuinely concerned for [that church's] welfare."

Caution

1. Caution involves due care in dealing with new or dangerous situations, trusting people of uncertain character or motives, and drawing conclusions from incomplete or unverified facts.

2. Desire / knowledge / haste

3. disguises / lips / deceit / speaks / abominations

4. This verse does not apply to everyone who speaks well. Rather, it applies only to those whose outward words are pleasant and alluring but whose hearts are evil and full of malice. Unfortunately, it's not always easy to inspect people's hearts, especially if you've just met them or have known them only a short time. That's why it's important to proceed cautiously around strangers or, indeed, anyone of uncertain character or motives. Just because people speak soothingly with words like smooth butter, their hearts might be filled with evil intent like drawn swords brandished in war.

5. evidence / witnesses

6. Christians should be careful in drawing conclusions from incomplete or unverified facts. Like the "trickling tidbits" activity, many people draw conclusions too quickly, sometimes after hearing only one side of an argument. But it's important to hear all sides. Though the first to speak might seem believable, those who speak later might introduce contrary facts or might press the first person to address aspects intentionally or unintentionally omitted before.

7. He chose the well-watered plains of the Jordan River.

8. The biblical text suggests Lot's decision-making process involved nothing more than looking at the land and choosing the best for himself. If so, he was incautious on two counts. First, he failed to pray about this important decision of moving to a new and potentially dangerous area, nor did he consult with his wise uncle. Second, he failed to consider the spiritual risk of moving his family near so many people of sinful character and wrong motives.

9. The Bible mentions three consequences, though Lot might have experienced others that Scripture does not record. First, marauders captured him and almost succeeded in carrying him far away to Mesopotamia. Second, Lot and his daughters barely escaped

from Sodom before God destroyed it. His wife, on the other hand, disobeyed God and died while leaving Sodom. All Lot's property, including his livestock, was presumably destroyed. Ironically, Lot moved to Sodom to become more prosperous, but he left with only his two daughters and little else than the clothes on his back. Third, Lot's family engaged in sexual immorality, perhaps partially due to Sodom's influence on them and partially due to living in total isolation from other people. Query why Lot didn't return to his godly uncle after God destroyed Sodom?

10. An Old Testament judge, Samson led Israel for 20 years. From birth, he was a Nazirite, set apart for God's service and, as such, forbidden to cut his hair (Judg 13:5).

11. Generally, Samson did not exhibit caution but its opposite. Against his parents' wise advice and contrary to God's law, Samson sought to marry a pagan. He tried aligning himself with a woman who, presumably, did not fear or worship the only living and true God. On at least two occasions, he carelessly trusted women around whom he should have been wary. Failing to understand the character and motives of the women he loved, Samson proved to be anything but cautious. God gave Samson great physical strength. Unfortunately, Samson proved impulsive and morally weak.

Compassion

1. Compassion is pity, sympathy, or concern for those who suffer combined with a strong desire to relieve their hurt.

2. teaching / gospel / healing / compassion / helpless / sheep

3. Spiritual, emotional, mental, and physical

4. goods / need / closes / love / word / deed

5. Loving God is correlated with loving others. Loving others includes having compassion for those in need and, to the extent possible, using material possessions to relieve their suffering. Thus, those with no compassion provide little evidence of truly loving God.

6. Priests and Levites were religious leaders in Israel. For historical context, recall that Jacob (aka Israel) had twelve sons, one of whom was Levi. The descendants of these twelve sons became the twelve

tribes of Israel. After enslavement in Egypt, Moses and his brother Aaron (both Levites) led Israel out of bondage to the promised land. God divided the land among the twelve tribes. But the tribe of Levi did not receive land like the others. Instead, God placed the Levites in charge of the nation's religious matters. Within the tribe of Levi, descendants of Aaron became priests. Thus, all priests were Levites, but not all Levites were priests. Priests could offer sacrifices within the tabernacle and, later, the temple. Other Levites could not offer sacrifices but were assigned various duties within the tabernacle or temple.

7. Samaritans were half-breeds, part Israeli and part pagan. In Jesus' time, Samaria was the large central part of Israel between Galilee to its north and Judea to its south. Samaria and Galilee once had been part of Israel's Northern Kingdom. But in 722 BC, Assyria defeated the Northern Kingdom, carrying many into captivity and leaving only the poorest within the land (2 Kgs 17:6). Then, Assyria brought captives from pagan nations to Israel and settled them in what became known as Samaria (2 Kgs 17:24). Over time, Israelis left in the land intermarried with these pagans, becoming a mixed-race, and lapsed further into syncretism, corrupting the worship of the only true and living God with other religious beliefs and practices (2 Kgs 17:33). So, in Jesus' time, those in Galilee and Judah despised Samaritans since their blood lines and religious practices had been, in their view, polluted. As one evidence of this negative view, Galileans traveling to and from Judah often took a circuitous route around Samaria even though it required them to cross the Jordan River twice each way, adding many miles to their journey. Tellingly, Jesus did not go around Samaria (John 4:1–42).

8. Unlike the priest and Levite, the Samaritan sympathized with the beaten and robbed man, binding up his neighbor's wounds, taking the man to an inn for recuperation, and paying for his care. Today, anyone following this example is known as a good Samaritan.

9. First, he disrespectfully demanded his father give him an inheritance in advance. Second, he wasted his inheritance (or family resources) on his own sinful pleasures.

10. No, the younger son did nothing to deserve pity. Thus, the sufferer's merit is not a prerequisite for compassion. Stated differently, God

desires his people to show compassion to others even when it's not deserved.

11. The father ran to meet his younger son, ministering to his mental doubts about returning home. The father immediately forgave his younger son, ministering to the latter's emotional and spiritual needs. Then, the father clothed and fed his younger son, ministering to his immediate physical needs. Jesus' parable about the prodigal son (or pitying patriarch) paints a beautiful picture of compassion.

12. He didn't show compassion. Though just a parable, it's hard not to wonder about the older son. Did he change his tune later and learn compassion? If not, what became of him spiritually? Based on 1 John 4:20, if he never showed compassion to his younger brother whom he could see, then he likely did not love God whom he could not see. Those who love God will love others. Presumably, Jesus included this older son in the parable as a distinct warning to the uncompassionate.

13. Those suffering continue to hurt since relief does not come. Sufferers also might feel disdained or rejected, adding to their existing burdens. But in addition to the sufferer, those without compassion hurt themselves. The spiritual declivity from indifference is real and dangerous.

14. God is full of merciful compassion towards his people. In like manner, believers should show much compassion to others. The Christian's compassion should be like that a father bestows on his child or a mother shows to her baby. It should be always gracious, always righteous, always attentive, never neglectful.

Contentment

1. Contentment entails being satisfied with God's provision.

2. whatever / low / abound / any / every / secret / abundance / need

3. knows / need / seek / all / given

4. Godliness / nothing / anything / food / clothing / content

5. First, he demanded an inheritance from his father. Second, he left home.

6. He wasted his inheritance on riotous living. Then, with no money, he took a job slopping hogs. And yet, he still hungered.

7. In demanding his inheritance, the younger son disrespected his father. In leaving home, he deprived his family of his services and support. In wasting his inheritance, he angered his older brother. Discontent, like other sins, often hurts others.

8. They were unjustly accused, severely flogged in public, unlawfully jailed without trial, and fastened in an inner cell's stocks.

9. They prayed and sang hymns to God.

10. The other prisoners heard Paul and Silas praying and singing and, thereby, learned of Jesus. Also, the jailer observed Paul and Silas' contentment and then God's great power through the earthquake. These things prepared the jailer, with his family, to experience God's saving grace.

11. Though financially rich, the disgruntled descendant (aka the prodigal son) was discontent and became spiritually as well as financially poor. Though financially poor, the tranquil twosome (i.e., Paul and Silas) were content in their difficult circumstances, which made them spiritually rich since "godliness with contentment is great gain" (1 Tim 6:6).

Courage

1. Courage is the strength of mind or heart that allows people to face threats, pains, dangers, or other difficulties without fear overwhelming them.

2. strong / courageous / afraid / dismayed / with / leave / forsake / all / finished

3. King David spoke them to his son, Solomon, who would succeed him as king.

4. Constructing and furnishing the temple in Jerusalem

5. First, God would be with Solomon during this great task. Second, God would never fail nor forsake him.

6. flee / pursues / bold / lion

7. God told Joshua to lead Israel into the promised land and conquer the wicked people living there.

8. First, Joshua always had followed Moses, so he was untried as the first in command. Second, Israel had little combat experience vis-à-vis the military campaign on which they were about to embark. Third, the seven nations occupying the promised land outnumbered Israel, they had better weapons, and they lived in fortified cities.

9. Notably, God did not expect him simply to call up the courage from within him. Instead, God asked Joshua to trust his promises and obey his law. Doing that, God gave him strength and courage as a leader (as well as military success).

10. Jesus told the apostles, "You will be my witnesses in Jerusalem and in all Judea and Samaria, and to the end of the earth."

11. They witnessed to the curious crowd that had gathered to see the crippled beggar, who had been miraculously healed. The next day, they witnessed before the Sanhedrin.

12. The Holy Spirit (Acts 1:8, 2:1–4)

13. "Whether it is right in the sight of God to listen to you rather than to God, you must judge, for we cannot but speak what we have seen and heard" (Acts 4:19).

Decisiveness

1. Decisiveness involves timely choices that wisely consider future consequences.

2. Choose / serve / serve

3. God had shown himself faithful over the centuries, fulfilling all he had ever promised Israel. Joshua wisely based his current decision on what transpired in the past and trusted it would lead to continued steadfast love, abundant mercy, and great faithfulness in the future.

4. Israel would occupy the land of Canaan (aka the promised land). Israel would become a great and numerous people.

5. eye / sin / hand / sin

6. Yielding to temptation and allowing sin to reign leads to much hardship in life. In contrast, making the hard decision to deal sharply with temptation and sin leads to eternal rewards that dwarf any fleeting pleasures from disobedience.

7. He lived in Judah (aka the Southern Kingdom) until Nebuchadnezzar carried him captive to Babylon where he spent most or all his remaining life and, presumably, died in his eighties, though he may have been older. The Bible doesn't specifically mention where he died or when.

8. They decided against eating the choice food and drinking the choice wine the king ordered.

9. The choice food and wine were not allowed under the dietary laws God gave the Jews. Wanting to honor God, Daniel and his friends decided they couldn't consume them.

10. They didn't rudely proclaim their resolve to obey God nor insult those eating the royal fare. Instead, they respectfully requested an alternative food plan for themselves and then trusted God to honor their request and reveal his will.

11. After they consumed vegetables and water for ten days, God made them healthier than those eating the king's food and drinking the king's wine. Their resolve strengthened them for future conflicts in which they brought much glory to God (e.g., Daniel in the lions' den and Shadrach, Meshach, and Abednego in the fiery furnace).

12. He decided to "divorce" her (i.e., break off the engagement) and do so quietly rather than publicly humiliate her.

13. An angel appeared to him in a dream, explained the Holy Spirit placed the child inside Mary, and told him to proceed with the marriage. Joseph then wed Mary in obedience to God's directive.

Deference

1. Deference is the volitional yielding to another person's opinion, judgment, need, wish, preference, or will.

2. another / Honor / above

3. food / stumble / never / brother

4. Eating meat sacrificed to idols is not sinful unless it causes a fellow Christian to fall into sin.

5. Based on knowledge, Paul would have eaten meat sacrificed to idols. But, acting out of love for his weaker brothers and sisters in Christ, he would forgo eating such meat. Thus, Paul advocated acting out of love.

6. When the land proved too small for both their herds, Abraham gave Lot first choice of where to live.

7. "Count others more significant than yourselves."

8. "Look . . . to the interests of others."

9. He "emptied himself, by taking the form of a servant . . . . He humbled himself by becoming obedient to the point of death, even death on a cross." That is, he surrendered his own will and placed the needs of others above his own.

Diligence

1. Diligence means the persistent, steadfast pursuit of a worthwhile objective or purpose.

2. sluggard / sleep / slumber / poverty / want

3. Lazy, indolent, dilatory, indifferent, slothful, lethargic, sluggish, inattentive, careless, and idle

4. Whatever / heartily / Lord / men

5. "Work heartily"

6. Every day, she went into the fields to gather grain the harvesters left behind. In this way, she provided food for herself and her mother-in-law, Naomi.

7. He inspected what little remained of the wall within three days after arriving in Jerusalem. He formed a plan and implemented it. Also, though many difficulties arose, he persisted until the wall stood finished.

8. Under Nehemiah's leadership, they wholeheartedly and immediately committed themselves to rebuilding the wall. Amazingly, they finished the entire wall in only fifty-two days.

Discernment

1. Discernment is the keen ability to distinguish between right and wrong, truth and error, and good and evil.

2. understanding / govern / discern

3. Though young and inexperienced, King Solomon had to administer justice when disputes arose among God's people. He desired the ability to distinguish right from wrong so he could govern equitably and righteously.

4. prophecies / test / good / evil

5. On his second missionary journey (around 51 AD), the apostle Paul preached in Thessalonica's synagogue. Some Jews believed in Jesus, but the non-believing Jews formed a mob and rioted. Paul escaped to nearby Berea where he preached in the Berean synagogue. Unlike most Jews in Thessalonica, those in Berea showed discerning hearts, eagerly hearing Paul preach and comparing his words to those of Scripture. Testing what they heard against God's Word distinguished the Berean Jews from the bulk of the Thessalonian Jews, who spurned Paul's words. But soon, Jews from Thessalonica came to Berea and stirred up trouble for Paul again. So, Paul departed for Athens and then Corinth. From Corinth, Paul wrote the first epistle to the Thessalonian church in which he admonished believers to "test everything" (1 Thess 5:21). That is, he adjured them to be discerning like the Bereans, examining the truthfulness of his preaching in the light of Scripture.

6. Both men lacked discernment. According to his servants and wife, Nabal often acted wickedly and foolishly, scorning the right, true, and good. On this occasion, he ignored the needs of others, greedily refused to share, and unnecessarily insulted David. His motives and actions were wrong and evil. But David bore fault also. He could have turned the other cheek and walked away, depending on God to supply his needs. Instead, he reacted in anger, failing to discern the right, true, and good thing to do.

7. She immediately discerned her husband's wrong and how she might set things right. Loading the donkeys with food and wine, she intercepted David. Acknowledging her husband's wrong, she then expressed concern about what David planned to do. Her gentle,

tactful approach with David calmed him. Abigail's discernment showed David the right, true, and good path, saving him from a grave, regrettable mistake.

8. Presumably, no independent witnesses could corroborate either woman's story. So, the only evidence before Solomon consisted of the women's own testimonies. He needed to discern which woman was telling the truth and which was lying.

9. Realizing it was one mother's word against the other, Solomon elicited the truth through a radical, unexpected approach. He said to divide the baby with a sword and give half to each mother. His shocking pronouncement caused each woman to blurt out their real feelings for the baby. Solomon showed a keen ability to distinguish between right and wrong, truth and error, good and evil.

Endurance

1. Endurance is the capacity to withstand or accept prolonged or intense pain, hardship, misfortune, persecution, affliction, testing, discipline, or other adversity without quitting or losing heart.

2. discipline / endure / sons / father

3. Sometimes, God sends hardship to chastise believers for unrepentant sins. At other times, God sends hardship as a trial to strengthen and improve his people's character.

4. (a) Discipline is not the same as God's wrath. (b) God administers discipline as a loving Father. (c) God's perfect wisdom sends discipline. (d) God works all things out for good in his people's lives.

5. God instructs his people to endure hardship as discipline, and one type of discipline is chastisement for unrepentant sin. When God sends hardship as correction for sin, believers can react appropriately or inappropriately; they can either rebel or repent. Rebellion involves things like complaining and grumbling, whether the actual words are spoken aloud or only within the heart. Repentance, on the other hands, involves godly sorrow and a turning away from sin to God. Thus, true repentance involves a lack of rebellion; repentance silently acknowledges that God is just in sending chastisement.

6. gracious / God / endures / unjustly / sin / endure / suffer / endure / gracious

7. (a) The pain must be undeserved, (b) the believer must endure the pain submissively without rebelling, and (c) the endurance must be due to the believer's "mindful[ness] of God." God-sent hardship as discipline might be either chastisement for unrepentant sin or a trial to strengthen or improve character. Pain of unjust suffering (1 Pet 2:19) seems to be of the latter variety.

8. Both passages are making a similar point, namely, that suffering for doing good or "as a Christian" is commendable, resulting in blessing and "the Spirit of glory and of God [resting] upon you."

9. (a) In the three years before his death, Jesus experienced privation, conflict, derision, persecution, and rejection. (b) After Jesus' arrest, religious leaders made a mockery of justice in pronouncing his guilt, and soldiers ridiculed and beat him. (c) Roman soldiers crucified Jesus. As he hung on the cross, the soldiers and religious leaders taunted him.

10. He remained silent to the false accusations and whenever he might have said something in his own defense.

11. oppressed / afflicted / mouth / slaughter / silent / opened

12. (a) He endured to atone for sin and, thus, save the elect. (b) He endured as the Christian's example of how not to grow weary or lose heart.

13. Soldiers, athletes, and farmers

14. Soldiers endure the constant hardships of sacrifice, strict discipline, fatigue, deprivation, and peril. Athletes endure great stress to their bodies through long hours of training over extended periods. For several months each year, farmers endure the hard labor of tilling soil, planting seeds, and tending crops.

15. Soldiers train for battle, athletes prepare to win competitive events, and farmers seek bountiful harvests.

16. Just as soldiers, athletes, and farmers endure hardship without giving up, so Timothy should endure the hardships of gospel ministry without quitting or losing heart.

Fairness

1. Fairness occurs when people apply the same rules and standards in the same way to everyone and treat others as they would themselves like to be treated.

2. partial / great / righteousness

3. Whatever / others / Law / Prophets

4. The Golden Rule

5. The Golden Rule is, "Whatever you wish that others would do to you, do also to them" (Matt 7:12). The second greatest commandment is, "Love your neighbor as yourself" (Matt 22:39). Jesus characterized both as summing up the Old Testament law and prophets. Both provide simple expressions about how to treat other people in all circumstances. Both identify yourself as the proper touchstone to regulate social relationships and interactions.

6. The citizenry's celebration of David's military victories stoked Saul's fierce jealousy. As a result, Saul sought to kill David on several occasions.

7. In every matter, Jonathan treated David justly, following what would later become known as the Golden Rule. Whether consciously or unconsciously, Jonathan dealt with his friend as he would have desired to be treated if their situations had been reversed.

8. Arguably, the reference highlights the difficulty of reconciling the glory due Jesus with the glory sometimes given to people for paltry, frivolous reasons. Believers properly extol Christ for his glorious attributes and work of redemption. How can believers glorify a mere human based on earthly standards like wealth?

9. Their evil thoughts might be (a) the rich are good people, but the poor are not, and (b) currying favor with the rich can benefit me, while doing so with the poor cannot.

Faith

1. Faith is belief and trust in God and his Word, especially regarding the finished work of Christ for salvation.

2. faith / sight

3. live / faith

4. justified / law / faith

5. grace / faith / gift / works

6. walked / not / took

7. It refers to a godly or righteous way of life, including faith, obedience, service, and worship.

8. God justified Enoch through faith. Faith enabled Enoch to walk, and persisted as he daily walked, with God.

9. Though Scripture is silent on this point, God might have been rewarding Enoch for his strong faith and, its outgrowth, his close walk with God. Moreover, sparing him physical death might have been a means to draw attention to Enoch's solid faith and faithful walk as an example for others to follow.

10. God promised Abraham his descendants would (a) be numerous and (b) possess Canaan.

11. God promised his descendants would be numerous, yet Isaac was his only offspring. Since God commanded him to sacrifice Isaac, Abraham thought God must be planning to bring Isaac back to life. In that way, God would fulfill his promise. Abraham believed and trusted God.

12. Both promises involved his descendants, so Abraham never saw the promises fulfilled during his earthly life. It was centuries afterwards when Moses led a great multitude (Abraham's descendants) out of Egyptian bondage and decades later when Joshua led them into Canaan, conquering the wicked inhabitants and possessing the land.

13. No, God justified Abraham through faith, not obedience, deeds, or morality. Once justified, Abraham obeyed and served God, not vice versa.

Forgiveness

1. Forgiveness is an attitude that waives or surrenders feelings of bitterness, anger, or vengeance for wrongs suffered.

2. forgive / trespasses / Father / not / neither

3. mercy / mercy

4. kind / forgiving / Christ / forgave

5. Kindness and tenderheartedness

6. Some of his brothers wanted to murder Joseph. Instead, they took his robe, threw him into a pit, and then sold him into bondage. Due to his powerlessness in Egypt as a slave, he also spent several years in prison.

7. Joseph's words to his brothers indicate what had transpired in his heart. While stating the wrong they had done, he also reassured them. He did not want them distressed about their situation nor angry at themselves for their past actions. He observed God used their wrong intents to bring about good in all their lives. When Jacob, their father, died years later, Joseph reassured his brothers again with similar words.

8. The Jewish leaders brought Stephen before the great ruling council or Sanhedrin, falsely accusing him about the temple and law. After Stephen, in turn, accused them of rebelling against God like their forefathers and killing the Messiah, they stoned him to death.

9. In his last recorded words, Stephen prayed, "Lord, do not hold this sin against them." These words evidence the forgiveness that, no doubt, had taken place within his heart. He appeared to have no bitterness nor anger about his martyrdom. Instead, he desired God's mercy for those wronging him.

Generosity

1. Generosity reflects an altruistic willingness to give time, money, or other resources to people or causes without expecting something in return.

2. gives / gains / withholds / poverty / generous / refreshes

3. The Macedonians, which included the churches at Philippi, Thessalonica, and Berea

4. They sent gifts to Jewish believers in Jerusalem. The need is not completely clear, but many speculate these Christians suffered persecution or hungered from famine.

5. test / poverty / generosity / gave / means / favor / relief

6. Someone might argue that David could not demand provisions, but, on three counts, he wasn't wrong in approaching Nabal. First, it was customary to share one's bounty with others after sheepshearing. David's overture was not that unusual. Second, David's armed band had resided next to Nabal's shepherds for some time and never taken any sheep, so they probably didn't intend to start now. In other words, the request was just that; it was not a veiled demand. Third, David's men had protected Nabal's sheep from loss, which might merit some token of appreciation in return.

7. He didn't. Instead, he showed just the opposite. Nabal was a mean, stingy, foolish man. Surly stinginess characterized his empty life.

8. Jonathan promised to warn David of any danger arising from his father, King Saul. David, in turn, promised to show kindness to Jonathan's family.

9. After becoming king, David searched for and found Mephibosheth, the only surviving son of Jonathan. In kingly kindness, David restored Saul's land to Mephibosheth, instructed Ziba and his sons to care for Mephibosheth and the land, and gave Mephibosheth a permanent seat at the king's meal table. The last kindness reflected David's generosity to Mephibosheth.

Gentleness

1. Gentleness involves a mild temperament, soft speech, and tender acts.

2. gentle / wrath / harsh / anger

3. gentle / mother / children

4. First, a person should always speak gently to others, friends or not, even when difficult things must be said. Second, Job had lost his children, livestock, and health; presumably, he had little or nothing left to comfort him or enjoy in life. His wife still lived but seemed

discouraged herself; she gave Job bad advice, which plunged him further towards despair. Considering Job's heavy losses as well as his sadness and confusion, the three friends should have been especially gentle with Job.

5. Eliphaz insinuated Job would be "impatient" with his not-yet-spoken monologue and admonished him to listen without interruption or agitation. Bildad referred to Job's articulation of his distress and misery as a "great wind," implying that Job made more noise than his situation merited. Zophar sarcastically referred to his friend as "a man full of talk" and suggested Job should not be allowed to vindicate himself.

6. He called them "worthless physicians" and "miserable comforters," adding that their words tormented and crushed him. Job perceived no gentleness from his so-called friends.

7. Jesus chose not to debate the Jewish leaders as he had done on other occasions. This time, a woman's physical and spiritual life hung in the balance. So, Jesus took a gentler route, calculated to calm the crowd and avoid escalation. He began with quietness as he stooped to write on the ground. Even when pressed, he did not denounce the woman's accusers as hypocrites, nor did he comment on her guilt. Instead, Jesus turned the tables on the woman's accusers, so the clamor died down and everyone slowly, one by one, drifted away.

8. After the crowd dispersed, Jesus did not condemn but, rather, urged the woman gently towards repentance: "Go, and from now on sin no more." Such tenderness of speech and the kindness of his unexpected deliverance exhibited Jesus' gentleness to someone in great need.

Humility

1. Humility entails a lowliness of mind freed from vain thoughts of self-importance.

2. Diotrephes, who "likes to put himself first"

3. ambition / conceit / humility / significant / own interests

4. Clothe / humility / opposes / grace / Humble / exalt

5. Paul urged humility as a means of preserving unity among the saints or within the church. Peter urged humility as a means of avoiding God's opposition and receiving grace.

6. Herod perceived that he became more popular after executing the apostle James. So, his prideful desire for popularity motivated him to imprison Peter, whom he likely would have executed.

7. Through his angel, God killed Herod because of the latter's sinful pride; he did not give God glory for his position or skill.

8. Jesus washed his disciples' feet.

9. Jesus left heaven's glory to be born in a lowly manger. On earth, Jesus lived as a humble servant and died as a despised criminal.

10. Nebuchadnezzar credited himself with Babylon's greatness, claiming the glory as his own. As a result, God banished him from the kingdom, causing him to live like a wild animal.

Joyfulness

1. Joyfulness is an inward sense of divine blessing that encourages the soul regardless of outward circumstances.

2. cares / cheer / soul

3. The "wicked" distressed the psalmist through their boasting and oppression.

4. "Your consolations cheer my soul" (Ps 94:19). That is, God comforted the psalmist amid great anxiety, and this comfort produced joyfulness.

5. Rejoice / always / again

6. In prison

7. Wicked Judean leaders distressed Habakkuk because they oppressed the poor.

8. Habakkuk fretted that the Lord would use Babylon, a nation more wicked than Judah, to punish his people.

9. Habakkuk resolved to "rejoice in the LORD" and "take joy in the God of [his] salvation."

Patience

1. Patience requires calm waiting or restraint when dealing with painful suffering, trying people, agonizing losses, daily irritants, or unfulfilled dreams.

2. tempered / dissension / patient / quarrel

3. patient / bear / love

4. Love / patient

5. God promised to make his offspring into a great nation whose members would be numerous like the dust of the earth and stars in the heavens.

6. Isaac per Gal 4:22–23

7. God promised Abram when he was seventy-five, and Isaac was born when Abraham was one hundred. So, the couple waited twenty-five years.

8. Abraham waited patiently according to Heb 6:15 during most of the twenty-five years between God's promise and Isaac's birth. However, he showed impatience when he agreed with his wife to bear a child through Hagar.

9. Initially, Job showed patience from losing so much. Instead of fretting or complaining, he acknowledged the Lord's right to take back whatever he had given. Later, however, Job grieved aloud that he had been born since he presently suffered so greatly, revealing impatience. As the book of Job progressed, Job became impatient at other times as well.

10. Certainly, saints please and glorify God when they show patience. However, Scripture does not guarantee an earthly reward for being patient. Though God rewarded Job in this life, that does not mean he deals with every saint the same way.

Purity

1. Purity is freedom from sexual immorality whether in attitudes, thoughts, speech, or actions.

2. Flee / immorality / outside / sexually / body

3. Members of Christ and temples of the Holy Spirit (1 Cor 6:15, 19)

4. sexual immorality

5. Believers are united to Christ. To commit sexual immorality involves a union that defiles the body, using it in a way God never intended (1 Cor 6:13). Defiling the body pollutes a member of Christ and a temple of the Holy Spirit (1 Cor 6:15, 19). Further, sexual immorality can lead to physical disease.

6. will / sanctification / immorality / body / lust / impurity / holiness

7. First, he told Ruth to remain at his feet, avoiding sexual temptation and immorality. Second, he respected and preserved her good reputation, instructing her not to let anyone know she stayed overnight on the threshing floor. Third, he married Ruth before having sexual relations with her.

8. Some say David should have been involved with the military campaign rather than at ease back in the palace; thus, neglecting his duty to be with his troops led to his temptation and fall. Of course, the king could have immediately turned away from the sight of Bathsheba bathing and sought the Lord's help in resisting the temptation. Certainly, after lusting, committing sexual immorality in his mind, David should not have inquired about the woman's identity nor brought her to the palace. Lustful thoughts are sinful, but lustful actions are worse because they cause more damage to everyone involved.

9. As a direct result of David's impurity, he deceived and murdered Uriah. Thus, the man after God's own heart broke, at a minimum, the Sixth, Seventh, and Ninth Commandments. And it all began with an unchecked, lustful thought one spring evening.

Repentance

1. Repentance involves sorrowing for sin and turning from it to God.

2. my / name / humble / seek / turn / hear / forgive

3. grieved / repenting / godly / repentance / worldly

4. Worldly grief starts with sadness over an earthly loss and generally seeks to reverse the loss, if possible, through earthly means. In

contrast, godly sorrow begins with a broken and contrite spirit at having broken God's moral law and seeks reconciliation through turning from sin to the Lord. Godly grief leads to genuine repentance, whereas worldly sorrow does not.

5. Repentance is not a "once and done" experience. True repentance not only occurs when saints first unite with Christ through regeneration and justification but also throughout their earthly lives as an essential part of sanctification. Thus, this curriculum presents repentance as a Christian character trait the Holy Spirit gives and develops within believers during their time on earth.

6. David (a) lusted after Bathsheba, committing mental adultery, (b) committed actual adultery with Bathsheba, (c) attempted to deceive Bathsheba's husband, Uriah, (d) effectively murdered Uriah, and (e) dishonored God in all these things.

7. Scripture doesn't explicitly state why David failed to repent sooner, but here are some possibilities: (a) Like many people, David may have assumed time would heal all wounds. But time does not extinguish sin; only true repentance can remedy sin. (b) Again, like many people, David may have thought his good deeds could offset his bad ones. Maybe he thought caring for Bathsheba, being a good husband to her, perhaps combined with other good deeds, would offset his prior sins. (c) Perhaps David began to think too much of himself and the privileges of his high office as king. Thus, he may have presumed on God's goodness, assuming the Lord would overlook his sins, considering David's prior accomplishments and God's past blessing.

8. The prophet, Nathan, delivered a difficult message to David through a parable. Often, God uses other people to rebuke those who sin and need repentance.

9. God forgave David for his sins involving Bathsheba and Uriah. As Nathan said at the time, "The LORD also has put away your sin" (2 Sam 12:13). However, though repentance took away David's guilt and restored his fellowship with the Lord, his sins had far-reaching consequences. The son born to David and Bathsheba died (2 Sam 12:14–18). Also, David's household experienced one calamity after another for many years, each attributable to David's lust after Bathsheba and the subsequent sins his immoral thoughts set in motion (2

Sam 12:11–12). For instance, Amnon (David's eldest son) raped his half-sister Tamar, Absalom (David's third son and Tamar's brother) murdered Amnon in revenge, David and Absalom were estranged for several years after the murder, Absalom sought David's life and kingdom, Absalom died in battle against David's forces, and Adonijah (David's fourth son) tried to usurp David's throne when the king grew old and feeble.

10. He practiced sorcery, which involves the use of black magic to summon evil powers for ignoble ends. Scripture condemns all such dark arts. For example, God commanded the Israelites before they entered the promised land, "There shall not be found among you . . . anyone who practices divination or . . . a sorcerer . . . . These nations, which you are about to dispossess, listen to fortune-tellers and to diviners. But as for you, the LORD your God has not allowed you to do this" (Deut 18:10, 14). Simon also boasted about his greatness, but "haughty eyes and a proud heart, the lamp of the wicked, are sin" (Prov 21:4).

11. He tried to buy the ability to give the Holy Spirit through laying on hands. In response, the apostle Peter characterized him as full of "bitterness and in the bond of iniquity." Perhaps Simon felt bitter about losing power over the masses and continued captive to such thoughts and desires. If so, pride persisted in his heart.

12. Repentance

Respectfulness

1. Respectfulness is a gracious regard for the feelings, opinions, rights, accomplishments, or authority of others.

2. respect / labor / over / admonish / esteem / love

3. Several phrases point to religious leaders as the recipients of respect, especially godly pastors and elders, though the verses also may apply to teachers within the church as well as deacons. As to pastors and elders, they "labor among" the "brothers" (or believers) and, among other duties, "admonish" them.

4. respect / everyone

5. God made all mankind in his own image with eternal souls. Thus, every person should be respected, if for no other reason, because of their creation in God's image.

6. Yes, the Bible singles out certain individuals who should receive more respect. As 1 Thess 5:12–13 shows, pastors and elders should be "esteem[ed] very highly in love." Other passages indicate wives should submit to husbands, children should obey parents, employees should submit to employers, and citizens should submit to government authorities, identifying these relationships as ones calling for greater than common respect. At the same time, Scripture says those who recklessly scorn sound wisdom and instruction (aka fools) deserve less respect.

7. God made Saul in his own image, and God established Saul as king over Israel.

8. Even though Saul repeatedly tried to kill David for no valid reason, David spared his life twice. As David said, "Who can put out his hand against the LORD's anointed and be guiltless?"

9. They showed no gracious regard for Job's twofold opinion (a) he had not sinned in a way to merit so much affliction and (b) bad (good) things sometimes happen to good (bad) people. Though they had several opportunities to address these points, they never did. To show respect, they should have responded directly to both arguments. If they could not, they should have respected Job's opinion, withdrawing their assertions and apologizing to Job for assuming things they did not know or understand.

10. Elihu remained silent until the three older friends spoke even though his counsel was best.

Responsibility

1. Responsibility requires conscientious performance of duties, principled decision-making, and full acceptance of any negative consequences from performance or decisions.

2. responsible / tabernacle / Testimony

3. The Levites were one of the original twelve tribes of Israel. Particularly notable among Levites were Moses and his brother, Aaron, who

led Israel out of Egyptian bondage. After the exodus, God assigned Levites responsibility to care for the tabernacle. However, only Levites from Aaron's family could serve as the tabernacle's priests and offer sacrifices.

4. The tabernacle was a portable tent where God dwelt with Israel during their forty wilderness years as well as their early history in the promised land of Canaan. After King Solomon built the Jerusalem temple for worship, Israel no longer needed the tabernacle.

5. The Testimony is another term for the moral law God spoke to Israel at Mt. Sinai. It appeared on two stone tablets and became known as the Ten Commandments. In the tabernacle, the stone tablets rested inside the Ark of the Covenant, which itself resided in the small enclosure known as the Holy of Holies or Most Holy Place.

6. seven / Spirit / wisdom / duty

7. Deacons

8. They should be "full of the Spirit and of wisdom."

9. The early church chose these men to oversee a fair distribution of food (or perhaps alms) to the poor within the church. Presumably, most recipients were widows.

10. Eve had duties to her Creator as well as her husband; eating the forbidden fruit and then offering it to Adam shirked both responsibilities. She failed in her duties to trust and obey God, and she failed to let her husband lead. Her decision to eat was an unprincipled one, not grounded in truth; it was based on what she desired without due concern for others or the decision's consequences. When God confronted her, Eve did not take full responsibility for her sin but attempted to shift blame to the serpent.

11. Adam had a duty to trust and obey God, which he neglected in eating the forbidden fruit. He might have eaten for the same reasons Eve ate or, instead, because he preferred following Eve into sin rather than obeying God; perhaps, he had other reasons. Regardless, Adam's decision to eat was unprincipled. Then, when God confronted him, Adam offered a flimsy excuse for his sin, laying part or all the blame on God and Eve.

12. When Eve thought about how good the fruit might taste and how nutritious it might be, her flesh craved it. When Eve gazed on the

fruit's beauty, she experienced desires of the eyes. When Eve believed Satan's lie that eating would give her par excellence wisdom with God, she experienced the ambitious, boastful pride of life.

13. Pilate did not conscientiously perform his duty to administer justice fairly. He capitulated to the Jewish leaders' demands for crucifixion when he believed Jesus to be innocent. Then, he tried to shift blame to the Jews for his own failure to do right.

Thankfulness

1. Thankfulness is gratitude to God for the multitude of his blessings.

2. thanks / all / will

3. The command calls for thanksgiving *in* all circumstances, not *for* all circumstances. When Christians receive diagnoses of terminal cancer, for example, the verse does not urge them to thank God *for* the disease and its attendant hardships. But they should thank the Lord while going through the ordeal for his blessings *in* the difficult circumstances. Thus, they can thank God for things like his presence, provision, people, and promises.

4. grateful / kingdom / shaken

5. Israel had been shaken many times, but here are a few of the more prominent occurrences: (a) civil strife split the nation around 932 BC between the Northern Kingdom of Israel with Jeroboam as king and the Southern Kingdom of Judah with Rehoboam as king, (b) the brutal, warlike Assyrians defeated and exiled the Northern Kingdom in 722 BC, (c) the Babylonians captured Jerusalem in 586 BC and completed its third and final exile of the Southern Kingdom, and (d) the Romans subjugated and occupied Judea in 63 BC. The occupation continued throughout Jesus' earthly life and the completion of the Hebrew epistle.

6. The reference likely is to the kingdom of grace, which saints enter through faith in Christ. However, the reference also might be to the kingdom of glory, which resurrected believers enter after Jesus' second coming. Neither the kingdom of grace nor the kingdom of glory can be shaken in the same sense that the earthly nation of Israel often found itself shaken. The kingdom of grace cannot be

shaken because true saints of God are secure in Christ during this life and the next. The kingdom of glory cannot be shaken because God will not permit anything evil to enter heaven.

7. "One of them, when he saw that he was healed, turned back, praising God with a loud voice; and he fell on his face at Jesus' feet, giving him thanks. Now he was a Samaritan" (Luke 17:15–16). First, he returned to Jesus rather than heading home, though it's not clear whether he returned before seeing the priest or afterwards. Second, he praised God loudly when, only a short time before, he might have been unable to speak above a hoarse whisper due to the ravages of leprosy. Third, he didn't just offer a formal, obligatory word of thanks, but he fell at Jesus' feet out of a heart bursting with gratitude. Maybe the other nine lepers appreciated their change in circumstances. But, even if they did, they failed to express that thankfulness to the one who healed them.

Truthfulness

1. Truthfulness means honesty in word and deed, taking care not to deceive or mislead.

2. false / neighbor / sword / arrow

3. False testimony can harm someone mentally or emotionally just as much as weapons of war can hurt someone physically. Sometimes, in fact, false testimony causes more damage than physical assault.

4. Many parents and teachers have used this expression for decades to dissuade youngsters from responding physically or emotionally to mere words, encouraging them, instead, to ignore childish taunts. Though this purpose might be noble, the idiom itself is not entirely true. Prov 25:18 says a "false witness" can inflict great harm.

5. falsehood / truth / members

6. Paul mentions the put-off, put-on principle. As to false testimonies, the principle instructs saints to stop deceiving others and, instead, practice honesty.

7. Believers are "members one of another" since the Father adopted them, made them Jesus' brothers and sisters, and united them as one church. Dishonesty towards those outside the church reflects

negatively on the entire body. Also, when believers deceive each other, it fosters distrust and disunity within the body.

8. Peter promised Jesus, "Even though they all fall away, I will not. . . . If I must die with you, I will not deny you."

9. After promising not to disown his Lord, Peter pretended not to know Jesus three times.

10. Peter lied three times to those questioning him. On two of those occasions, Peter said, "I neither know nor understand what you mean" and "I do not know this man [Jesus] of whom you speak." Thus, Peter proved untruthful in two respects—he promised to stand by Jesus but didn't, and he knew Jesus but lied about it.

11. He might have said, "Yes, I know Jesus. He's the Christ, the Son of the living God." Such a declaration would have been consistent with his earlier great confession.

12. Giving the church only part of the sale proceeds was not wrong. However, lying about it, possibly for prestige, was untruthful.

13. They lied to the apostle Peter who questioned them, church members whom they wished to impress, and the Holy Spirit whom they dishonored.

Watchfulness

1. Watchfulness is alertness to and wariness of spiritual dangers.

2. false prophets / sheep's / wolves

3. watchful / devil / lion

4. "False prophets," which include leaders and anyone else teaching spiritual error and leading people astray

   "The devil" or Satan, who is the ultimate source of all false prophecy and temptations

5. Ravenous wolves and a roaring lion

6. Any celebrity with influence or authority who leads others astray through promoting or endorsing ungodly views or sinful behaviors would be a false prophet.

7. Satan / false / stumbling

8. Potiphar's wife tried seducing Joseph to sleep with her.

9. First, Joseph had been sold into slavery by his own brothers, who hated him, so he might have felt entitled to something that temporarily helped him forget some of his trouble and attracted to someone who seemed to admire him. Second, Joseph was alone with Potiphar's wife and might have reasoned that no one would ever find out about this sin. Third, the master's wife had some power over Joseph, who was a mere slave or household servant.

10. Sometimes, it's hard to see temptation coming. But, in this case, Potiphar's wife had tried seducing him on other occasions. So, Joseph had time to prepare. He was aware of this temptation already and, thus, to some extent, could plan for it. Likely, he asked God to remove the temptation or, if not, cause him to withstand it or escape from it. In short, Joseph probably stayed on high spiritual alert whenever Potiphar's wife was nearby. He may have already purposed what he would do if the spiritual danger became too great.

11. He fled even though it meant leaving his cloak behind and allowing Potiphar's wife to accuse him falsely. Staying right with God was more important to Joseph than committing sin.

12. Jesus said they would scatter from him like sheep without a shepherd.

13. All eleven disciples said they would never leave nor disown Jesus. (Judas was away conspiring with the chief priests to betray Jesus.)

14. Peter

15. Deny him three times

16. He wanted them to pray for spiritual strength so they might withstand their upcoming temptation to forsake him and flee.

17. Watch / pray / spirit / flesh

Appendix C

Similar Traits

When the "Table of Contents" doesn't show a lesson for the character trait you wish to teach or study, trace that trait from the left column to a lesson covering a similar trait in the right column.

For these Traits	See these Lessons
Accessibility	Availability
Accountability	Responsibility
Acumen	Discernment
Admiration	Respectfulness
Alertness	Caution and Watchfulness
Altruism	Generosity
Amenability	Deference
Amiableness	Gentleness
Answerability	Responsibility
Appreciation	Thankfulness
Assertiveness	Decisiveness
Attrition	Repentance
Belief	Faith
Beneficence	Compassion and Generosity
Benevolence	Compassion and Generosity
Bigheartedness	Compassion and Generosity
Bliss	Joyfulness
Boldness	Courage
Bravery	Courage

Calmness .... Contentment, Gentleness, and Patience
Candidness .... Truthfulness
Candor .... Truthfulness
Carefulness .... Caution and Watchfulness
Charitableness .... Compassion and Generosity
Chastity .... Purity
Circumspection .... Caution and Watchfulness
Civility .... Deference
Cleanliness .... Purity
Commitment .... Diligence and Responsibility
Compliance .... Deference
Composure .... Patience
Concentration .... Attentiveness
Concern .... Compassion
Confidence .... Faith
Conformity .... Deference
Congeniality .... Deference
Conscientiousness .... Diligence and Responsibility
Consideration .... Gentleness
Contriteness .... Repentance
Contrition .... Repentance
Cordiality .... Gentleness
Correctness .... Truthfulness
Credibility .... Truthfulness
Decency .... Purity
Decorum .... Purity
Dedication .... Responsibility
Delight .... Joyfulness
Dependability .... Responsibility and Truthfulness
Determination .... Courage, Decisiveness, Diligence, and Endurance
Directness .... Truthfulness
Discretion .... Gentleness
Drive .... Diligence and Endurance
Dutifulness .... Responsibility
Earnestness .... Decisiveness and Diligence
Encouragement .... Compassion

Energy...Diligence and Endurance
Enjoyment .... Joyfulness
Equanimity .... Patience
Equitableness...Fairness
Esteem .... Respectfulness
Evenhandedness ....Fairness
Exactitude...Truthfulness
Faithfulness ....Truthfulness
Fearlessness .... Courage
Focus ....Attentiveness
Forbearance.. Patience
Forthrightness...Truthfulness
Fortitude .... Courage and Endurance
Frankness..Truthfulness
Fulfillment ....Contentment
Genuineness..Truthfulness
Giving... Deference and Generosity
Gladness.. Joyfulness
Goodness........................... Compassion, Gentleness, and Generosity
Goodwill... Compassion
Graciousness .... Compassion, Deference, Forgiveness, and Gentleness
Gratefulness..Thankfulness
Gratitude...Thankfulness
Grief ....Repentance
Grit .... Courage and Endurance
Guardedness..Caution and Watchfulness
Happiness .... Contentment and Joyfulness
Hard Work...Diligence and Endurance
Heedfulness..Caution and Watchfulness
Holiness .... Purity
Honesty...Truthfulness
Honor................................... Respectfulness and Truthfulness
Hospitality ....Generosity
Humbleness... Humility
Impartiality..Fairness
Industriousness....................................Diligence and Endurance

Initiative.. Decisiveness and Responsibility

Insight ....Discernment

Integrity ....Truthfulness

Intellect .... Discernment

Interest ....Attentiveness

Jubilance .... Joyfulness

Judgment .... Discernment

Justice ....Fairness

Kindness ....Compassion, Generosity, and Gentleness

Largesse...Generosity

Leadership .... Responsibility

Leniency...Gentleness

Liberality..Generosity

Long-Suffering .... Patience

Love .... Compassion

Lowliness .... Humility

Magnanimity... Compassion and Generosity

Maturity .... Responsibility

Meekness .... Deference, Gentleness, and Humility

Mercifulness .... Compassion

Mettle .... Courage and Endurance

Moderation...Gentleness

Modesty ....Purity

Munificence...Generosity

Obedience...Deference and Respectfulness

Obligingness.. Deference

Observance..Attentiveness

Openhandedness.. Compassion and Generosity

Openness ....Truthfulness

Passion ....Diligence and Endurance

Peacefulness ....Contentment

Penance..Repentance

Penitence...Repentance

Perception.. Discernment

Perseverance..Diligence and Endurance

Persistence ....Diligence and Endurance

Pity .... Compassion

Plainspokenness... Truthfulness

Politeness .... Deference

Productiveness .... Diligence and Endurance

Propriety .... Purity

Prudence .... Caution and Watchfulness

Punctuality .... Responsibility

Purpose .... Decisiveness

Quietness .... Contentment, Gentleness, and Patience

Readiness .... Availability

Regard .... Respectfulness

Regret .... Repentance

Rejoicing .... Joyfulness

Reliability .... Responsibility and Truthfulness

Remorse .... Repentance

Reserve .... Humility

Resilience .... Endurance

Resolve .... Decisiveness

Restfulness .... Contentment

Restraint .... Gentleness and Patience

Reverence .... Deference and Respectfulness

Sacrifice .... Availability

Sagacity .... Discernment

Satisfaction .... Contentment

Self-Control .... Patience

Selflessness .... Availability and Deference

Sensitivity .... Gentleness

Serenity .... Patience

Servanthood .... Availability and Deference

Shame .... Repentance

Sincerity .... Truthfulness

Sorrow .... Repentance

Spirit .... Diligence and Endurance

Steadfastness .... Diligence and Endurance

Steadiness .... Diligence and Endurance

Stewardship .... Availability, Generosity, and Responsibility

Straightforwardness ....Truthfulness
Strength.. Courage
Studiousness.....................................Diligence and Endurance
Submission ....Deference and Respectfulness
Sweetness..Gentleness
Sympathy .... Compassion
Tenacity...Diligence and Endurance
Tenderness..Gentleness
Tirelessness.......................................Diligence and Endurance
Tolerance .... Patience
Tranquility.. Patience
Trust .... Faith and Truthfulness
Trustworthiness .... Responsibility and Truthfulness
Unbiasedness...Fairness
Understanding .... Discernment
Unpretentiousness.. Humility
Unselfishness..Generosity
Valor .... Courage
Veneration .... Respectfulness
Veracity...Truthfulness
Verity..Truthfulness
Vigilance ....Caution and Watchfulness
Vigor..Diligence and Endurance
Virginity.. Purity
Vitality..Diligence and Endurance
Wariness..Caution and Watchfulness
Warmness ....Gentleness
Wholesomeness .... Purity
Wisdom.. Discernment
Work Ethic...............................Diligence, Endurance, and Responsibility
Yieldingness .... Deference
Zeal..Diligence and Endurance
Zest..Diligence and Endurance

Appendix D

Teaching and Learning Guide

Appropriate for teens and adults, *Christian Character: Why It Matters, What It Looks Like, and How to Improve It* (*CC*) functions as a traditional textbook, daily devotional, or self-study program. Teachers can use *CC* in a variety of settings, including Sunday school, Bible study, home school, and private school. *CC* is even suitable for children and tweens if the parent, guardian, or teacher chooses age-appropriate language to present the materials. Biblical counselors also might discover helpful information in these pages.

Many teens and adults will find the text easy to read. The Flesch-Kincaid Grade Level scores for the lessons range between 8.4 and 11.1 and average 9.4, corresponding to the reading ability of ninth graders. The Flesch Reading Ease score ranges between 50.8 and 61.4, averaging 55.2 and suggesting an average eleventh grader can comprehend the text. Of course, prior familiarity with biblical narratives (e.g., Abraham's life) and doctrine (e.g., salvation through faith) facilitates understanding.

This guide organizes topics under eight headings: (a) Focus and Desired Impact, (b) Initial Considerations, (c) Introductory Activities and Definition, (d) God's Word to Mankind, (e) God's Work in Believers, (f) God's Grace for Change, (g) PowerPoint Slides, and (h) Special Request. Whether adopting *CC* as a teacher, using it as a student, or just perusing the text, read through the first six sections of this guide. If using PowerPoint as a presentation or self-study aid, read that section as well.

Focus and Desired Impact

CC stresses two things: (a) God expects believers to follow his moral law; ignoring the law involves disobedience. (b) Only God can enable believers to follow his moral law; disregarding the Holy Spirit's power and pursuing morality on your own terms can devolve into rank legalism. Understanding these two truths lays a solid foundation for all who desire to cultivate Christian character. Though the "Introduction" covers both points in some depth, each of the twenty-six lessons bears explicit and repeated witness to them as well.

Starting from this perspective, for whom was CC intended? What impact should be desired or can be expected, through God's grace, from studying the book's contents? Consider four overlapping groups of believers that CC might benefit, those desiring to glorify and enjoy God, see the church strengthened, improve relationships, and overcome persistent sin.

Saints wishing to fulfill their chief purpose of glorifying God and enjoying him forever should find this book helpful. To improve character is to love the Lord and neighbors according to the moral law, which glorifies God. Loving God and others also kindles appreciation for and enjoyment of God's person, wondrous works, and Word. Thus, this study can lead believers to exalt God and enjoy him, experiencing redemption's blessings more fully.

CC seeks to strengthen and aid God's people (i.e., the church), clarifying the biblical perspective about morality and how to cultivate Christian character through divine power. As the "Introduction" explains, the entire moral law is grounded in love, which is why love does not appear as a separate character trait in the book. Indeed, all twenty-six traits are deeply rooted in the preeminent Christian character trait of love. Perhaps you have seen much evidence of great love among God's people. And yet, you also may have witnessed long-simmering conflicts and unloving undercurrents that weakened and hurt the church and its essential work. Consider the effect on the church if the Holy Spirit used CC to change individual members, making them more and more attentive, more and more available, more and more content, more and more forgiving, more and more gentle, more and more humble, more and more patient, more and more pure, more and more repentant, more and more respectful, and more and more thankful. In short, what would be the impact if church members became more and more loving through the Spirit molding and forming their Christian character? How much richer would be the public worship, how much deeper the communion, how much closer the bond of unity, and how much more effectual the outreach.

Relying fully on the Holy Spirit's power can strengthen and restore relationships. Given the ongoing fragmentation within families, churches, and societies, individual Christians who improve character through increased attention to God's moral law can become part of the solution. Indeed, many conflicts that arise are not political or cultural so much as they are moral. The right perspective about God's law for Christian conduct can enlighten the mind, comfort the soul, and heal damaged or broken relationships. The cultivated Christian character seasons attitudes, thoughts, words, and deeds with gospel salt and shines gospel light into darkened recesses of the heart.

Lastly, readers who struggle with recurring or besetting sins but fail repeatedly to obtain any lasting victory can find hope in a biblical study of Christian morality. Even in churches, some think conquering sin depends primarily on how hard they struggle against it. When they continue sinning, in their minds, it's because they didn't try hard enough, meaning they should try harder still. However, the only real power to overcome sin comes from God alone. Regularly petitioning the Lord while completely trusting him prepares saints for divine deliverance. Christians who have struggled long and hard against sin can find rest and hope in depending on the Holy Spirit, bringing about what they cannot achieve on their own through mere self-effort. Just as God's power enabled Zerubbabel to restore the Jerusalem temple, the great God of glory works in and through his people "not by [human] might, nor by [earthly] power, but by [the Holy] Spirit" (Zech 4:6).

Initial Considerations

Don't skip the "Introduction" nor hesitate to revisit it as necessary. It contains important information about the moral law and its relationship to Christian character traits, the danger of dismissing the moral law, and the danger of moralism without the gospel. The introduction provides a rationale for teaching or learning good Christian character and warns against urging or seeking morality through self-effort. It supplies the proper touchstone for each lesson. If you ever lose focus while teaching or studying this curriculum, reread the introduction.

Seeking to encompass much of Scripture's moral law, CC contains twenty-six lessons corresponding to separate character traits. Through precise definitions of each trait, the selection reflects an attempt to leave few gaps in areas essential to good character while avoiding significant overlaps.[1] At times, you might desire information about traits not found among these twenty-six. When that occurs, consult "Similar Traits" in Appendix C. This resource directs someone looking for information about the attribute of calmness, for instance, to the lessons on contentment, gentleness, and patience.

Though organized alphabetically, the twenty-six lessons can be approached in any order, which necessitates repeating some language in each lesson. Of course, many will choose to teach or study the lessons as they appear, starting with "attentiveness" and proceeding straight through "watchfulness." But, to accommodate any narrower study, here are groupings of related traits that can be taught or studied one after the other:

1. Regeneration (faith and repentance)

2. Ten Commandments' second tablet about duties to others (contentment, generosity, gentleness, purity, respectfulness, and truthfulness, relating to the Tenth, Eighth, Sixth, Seventh, Fifth, and Ninth Commandments, respectively)

3. Beatitudes (compassion, deference, gentleness, humility, patience, purity, and repentance, relating to the merciful, meek, peacemakers, poor in spirit, persecuted, pure in heart, and mournful, respectively)

4. Fruit of the Spirit (compassion, contentment, generosity, gentleness, joyfulness, patience, and truthfulness, relating to love, peace, kindness and goodness, gentleness, joy, patience and self-control, and faithfulness, respectively)

5. Core character traits (compassion, fairness, faith, forgiveness, repentance, respectfulness, responsibility, thankfulness, and truthfulness)

6. Family and friends (attentiveness, availability, compassion, deference, fairness, forgiveness, generosity, gentleness, humility, patience, repentance, respectfulness, responsibility, thankfulness, and truthfulness)

7. Romantic relationships (caution, compassion, deference, purity, respectfulness, responsibility, truthfulness, and watchfulness)

8. Work ethics for chores, school, and employment (attentiveness, diligence, respectfulness, responsibility, truthfulness, and watchfulness)

1. Appendix A lists all definitions for quick reference and easy review.

9. Difficulties or struggles in life (caution, contentment, courage, endurance, faith, forgiveness, joyfulness, patience, repentance, responsibility, thankfulness, and watchfulness)

10. Decision-making (caution, decisiveness, discernment, fairness, generosity, responsibility, and watchfulness)

Each lesson begins with one or more activities to stimulate interest and a precise definition of the Christian character trait under study. Three main sections follow. The first, entitled "God's Word to Mankind," explains why character matters, namely, that the Scriptures say so through key verses and the examples of various Bible characters. Consider the best way to teach with the review questions concluding this section. Of course, if part of a self-study program, do your best to complete review questions before checking your answers. The second section, "God's Work in Believers," discusses sundry aspects of the Christian character trait and draws applications. The last section, "God's Grace for Change," provides an opportunity for assessment, reflection, and petition. A fuller discussion of these main sections appears later in this guide under separate headings.

Don't rush through the lessons. It's better to take your time rather than hurry and retain little. When teaching, cover each lesson in two or more class sessions rather than dealing with it too quickly. For example, lessons may contain too much material to cover adequately in one Sunday school hour. With twenty-six lessons, however, spending two (four) Sunday school periods on each lesson should permit the entire curriculum to be covered in about a year (two years), especially if the teacher can host the class one or two weekday evenings per month to introduce new character traits. Here are some sample plans:

Cover Entire Curriculum in One Year

Weekday evening	Lead one or more introductory activities from new lesson and, afterwards, discuss each activity over pizza and dessert or other favorite food.
First Sunday	Review weekday evening activities, define character trait, teach "God's Word to Mankind" with one or more key verses and Bible

characters, and cover related review questions.

Second Sunday   Review character trait and "God's Word to Mankind," teach "God's Work in Believers," instruct everyone to complete the "Heart Assessment, Reflection, and Petition" chart, and lead final prayer for God's grace and power to change.

Cover Entire Curriculum in Two Years

Weekday evening   Lead one or more introductory activities from new lesson and, afterwards, discuss each activity over pizza and dessert or other favorite food.

First Sunday   Review weekday evening activities, define character trait, and teach "God's Word to Mankind" with key verses.

Second Sunday   Review character trait and key verses, teach "God's Word to Mankind" with Bible characters, and cover related review questions.

Third Sunday   Review character trait and "God's Word to Mankind" and begin teaching "God's Work in Believers."

Fourth Sunday   Review character trait and "God's Word to Mankind," finish teaching "God's Work in Believers," instruct everyone to complete the "Heart Assessment, Reflection, and Petition" chart, and lead final prayer for God's grace and power to change.

When teaching, thoroughly prepare before entering the classroom. If stumbling through a presentation, the most likely reason is insufficient preparation. Many talented people with busy lives readily accept teaching assignments but then short-change the advanced preparation necessary to teach smoothly and effectively. The decision often is whether to (a) spend sufficient time before class preparing to teach well or (b) prepare marginally and, as a result, be less effective in the classroom and risk participants learning less and, perhaps, improving their character less. There's no substitute for solid, conscientious, advance preparation. Go over and over every aspect of the lesson until you feel comfortable with the material. The point is not to memorize the presentation but to become familiar enough with it so you can lead the class straight through without struggling about how to say things, reading directly from the book, forgetting what comes next, wandering down rabbit trails, or finding it hard to transition smoothly. Advance preparation involving two or more practice deliveries before presenting the materials in class can enable you to teach more effectively and feel better about your performance. But, more importantly, it can help your audience learn more and increase the likelihood they desire to improve their Christian character.

Introductory Activities and Definition

Each lesson begins with introductory activities that stimulate interest and prepare everyone to learn. These "teaching hooks" use interactive, experiential exercises for grabbing attention. Activities used in multiple lessons include brainstorming sessions, hymn sings, intriguing insights (quotations), movie nights, and nature studies.[2] Dive right into these without necessarily mentioning the character trait up front. That is, let their gradual unfolding and the ensuing dialog reveal the character trait naturally. One caveat: For the "Movie Night" activities, read online reviews beforehand to assure the film's appropriateness for your audience.

If the activity uses photos, videos, or audio recordings from the internet, download and show them directly from your hard drive, if possible, to avoid issues with the off-location server where these items reside. Don't begin your presentation only to discover the distant server is down for maintenance or the webmaster changed the site's organization and web addresses (or URLs). Notwithstanding such issues, if you must use photos, video, or audio directly from the internet, go to the relevant

---

2. Those using CC for self-study might adapt the tasks for their personal benefit or, as appropriate, involve family and friends.

webpages just before class starts and make sure they load properly and the sound works.

If using a computer or the internet, leave no time gaps from the time you mention an activity and the start of the activity. The activity is intended to stimulate interest in the topic, but if you fumble around on the computer trying to find a photo or start a video or audio recording, the delay suppresses or squashes interest. It also can make the audience doubt your ability to teach or reduce your confidence. So, make sure everything works properly at two times: (a) in your advanced preparation to teach each lesson and (b) after you arrive on site just before you begin teaching.

The text offers a smooth transition between the activities and a definition of the character trait. Definitions, which set the scope within each lesson, are precise. Many are multifaceted, leading to a broader coverage and deeper understanding of the specific attributes. For example, the three distinct dimensions of caution are "care in [a] dealing with new or dangerous situations, [b] trusting people of uncertain character or motives, and [c] drawing conclusions from incomplete or unverified facts." Similarly, fairness is evident "when people [a] apply the same rules and standards in the same way to everyone and [b] treat others as they would themselves like to be treated."

God's Word to Mankind

Character matters because the Bible says it does. The moral law permeates the Old and New Testaments, clarifying that God desires his people to be holy. This section presents what Scripture says about the Christian character trait under study. It begins with two key verses or passages (three in the "Caution" lesson), some of which you might assign for memorization or choose to memorize. Short commentaries follow these verses to guide your discussion; they focus on what the verse says and means, leaving most applications until the following section. Always emphasize the portion of each verse involving the character trait. If pressed for time in a classroom setting, you might consider using only one key passage.

Next, the lesson presents Bible characters who act as positive role models exhibiting the good character trait or provide negative examples of those lacking the trait. To begin, read aloud the referenced Scripture passage in full. The book's text explicates the biblical passage; the former does not stand alone and will have much less meaning if you neglect to read the latter beforehand. Use the commentary to guide your discussion and assure you cover the main points; it often provides historical, geographical, cultural, contextual, or other background that enhances understanding. Explain the biblical narrative as you go along, always emphasizing the portions that deal with the character trait. If time is short, you might use only one Bible character.

Concluding this section, the review questions deal with the character trait's definition, key verses, and Bible characters.[3] This assessment shows whether participants have listened carefully and learned salient points. It's an opportunity to reemphasize essential principles, clear up any misconceptions, and assure a reasonable familiarity with the biblical substratum. When done, everyone should understand the teaching of God's Word before proceeding to a discussion of his work in believers' hearts.

God's Work in Believers

Scripture often commands believers to follow God's moral law using the imperative mood. Here are three examples with the relevant verbs italicized: "*Consecrate* yourselves, therefore, and *be* holy" (Lev 20:7), "*Refrain* from anger, and *forsake* wrath! *Fret not* yourself; it tends only to evil" (Ps 37:8), and "*Put away* all filthiness and rampant wickedness and *receive* with meekness the implanted word" (Jas 1:21). These biblical directives presuppose divine grace for obedience and stipulate prescribed changes for which to pray. Saints can never obey these or any other of the Bible's moral imperatives in their actions, thoughts, and hearts without gospel power.

As does Scripture, this middle section presents many applications in the imperative mood. Nonetheless, don't misinterpret this literary approach as an indication Christians can become moral through trying hard or self-exertion. Remember that believers seek to follow the moral law out of thankful hearts for the Father's love, Christ's redemption, and the Spirit's guidance, not because they wish to or can win God's favor. From their overwhelming sense of gratefulness, they depend solely on the Holy Spirit's strength to change. Without such power, they can make

3. Appendix B contains answers to review questions, while PowerPoint slides (discussed in a separate section of this "Guide") present questions and answers together. Introspective queries come later within the "Heart Assessment, Reflection, and Petition" chart.

no progress in their sanctification, they cannot become more like Jesus, they will not succeed in their pursuit for moral living, and they will fail to cultivate Christian character in their lives.

As the first cause, God must work in believers' souls to make them moral. Interestingly, however, this gospel work empowers the saints to work towards the same end. That is, God mysteriously and wonderfully weaves the human will together with his own will to accomplish the divine purpose. The following verses highlight the intertwined efforts: "*Work* out your own salvation with fear and trembling [second cause], for it is God who *works* in you [first cause], both to will and to work for his good pleasure ['good purpose' in NIV]" (Phil 2:12–13). Similarly, the Lord said to his chosen people, "I will put my Spirit within you, and *cause* you [first cause] to *walk* in my statutes and be careful to *obey* my rules [second cause]" (Ezek 36:26). Only as the Holy Spirit enables and empowers believers can they obtain or develop Christian character (and then, only in a secondary capacity). It's vital to recognize from whence comes the ability to change and to seek that power diligently and regularly through prayer. "For the grace of God has *appeared* [first cause], . . . training us to *renounce* ungodliness and worldly passions, and to *live* self-controlled, upright, and godly lives in the present age [second cause]" (Titus 2:11–12). Consistent with these passages, the imperative mood in this book should never be viewed as a call to mere human works but, rather, as a call to petition God. Pray earnestly for the Lord's undeserved, powerful grace to change. Any appearance of virtue or morality attained apart from God's grace is a mere facade; it's only skin deep and does not lodge within the heart nor endure. Sowing seeds of character obtained from earthly stores never produces wholesome or lasting fruit.

In summary, maintain a gospel focus on the Holy Spirit's power as the first cause. Throughout the suggested applications appearing in the imperative mood (as well as any applications from your personal experience and wisdom), remember to pray for divine strength to progress in holiness. Only then will character develop and lives conform to the moral law. "May the God of peace himself sanctify you completely, and may your whole spirit and soul and body be kept blameless at the coming of our Lord Jesus Christ. He who calls you is faithful; he will surely do it" (1 Thess 5:23–24).

God's Grace for Change

Certainly, believers should understand God's moral law and its application to their lives. But how do they develop good character? As a strategy, self-effort falls far short and often leads to bad places. Only the Holy Spirit's power can enable anyone to follow the moral law and, thus, cultivate Christian character. Therefore, saints must earnestly petition the Spirit for true holiness in attitude, thought, speech, and behavior. In each lesson, the first two sections—"God's Word to Mankind" and "God's Work in Believers"—often allude to God's undeserved favor as the only way to improve. However, this last section concentrates more intently on the Holy Spirit's power, emphasizing the importance of daily divine grace for lasting, godly change.

For most lessons, this final section begins with a brief statement and Bible verse about how God epitomizes and embodies the specific trait under study, often sharing it with his people. Sometimes the statement and verse explain how Jesus displayed the trait during his earthly ministry in ways benefiting the saints. This opening can motivate change, magnifying and highlighting God's wonderful grace, preparing each person to desire more of the character trait in their own lives and pray for it. Stated differently, it shows how God's traits or attributes (e.g., perfect compassion) bless his people, who, experiencing the benefit, are encouraged to seek the same trait's development within themselves.

Even if engaging in self-study, allow sufficient time to complete the "Heart Assessment, Reflection, and Petition" (HARP) chart.[4] This is a vital exercise that helps individuals respond to God's purpose for their lives, facilitating and promoting positive spiritual growth. Atop the chart appears the character trait's definition, key verses, and sentence summaries about the Bible characters. Review this information before beginning. It reminds everyone what they have learned, focusing their attention during this important activity.

The chart's top box urges participants to assess how often the lesson's trait characterizes them. The middle two or three boxes involve reflection. The last box asks whether they'd like to bring a specific petition before God. During this exercise, be careful not to pressure anyone unduly to commit in writing since any such desire should arise from

---

4. If you need larger, full-page versions of the HARP charts for personal or classroom use consistent with the book's copyright, download them from https://elark4.wixsite.com/character (password is allgrace).

within individual hearts. Tell everyone their written responses will not be seen by others unless they choose to share. Offering such assurance encourages forthrightness. Urge the class to take completed charts home and pray over them once or twice this next week.

After allowing reasonable time for completing the HARP charts, end with the suggested prayer, which is tailored closely to each lesson's theme, or incorporate portions of that prayer into your own. Alternatively, pray aloud the words in unison with the class.[5] Always remind everyone, before praying or as part of the prayer, why they are studying the character trait—to be like Jesus, become more and more holy, grow in grace, conform to Christ's image, or make progress in sanctification. Ask explicitly for the Holy Spirit's help in developing the specific character trait. The closing prayer often alludes to the Lord's full and perfect possession of the same attribute under study and the blessing it bestows on his people. For example, the "Decisiveness" prayer reminds suppliants the Father decided to save them, and Christ chose to pay sin's penalty. Such reminders encourage petitions from thankful hearts, beseeching God for grace and power to change. The prayer provides one more opportunity to reflect on God's will and seek his power and direction in cultivating Christian character.

Finally, as appropriate, reemphasize how vital God's help is in this process, reminding everybody that only the Spirit's power enables them to change. Trying to become good without God's help is the wrong approach, which is an essential point in this book's "Introduction." When failing to show the character trait, encourage each person to confess the failure before God and ask for his forgiveness and future help to change.

PowerPoint Slides

Everyone purchasing the book or receiving it as a gift can use the free PowerPoint slides that coordinate with the text. Pre-configured presentations for the "Introduction" and twenty-six lessons are downloadable from elark4.wixsite.com/character, using "allgrace" as the password. Of course, you'll need PowerPoint, presentation software within Microsoft Office. If you don't have the most recent version of Office, consider upgrading before using PowerPoint to teach these materials. Also, keep original PowerPoint files in a safe place. Make copies to edit and present.

5. The sample prayer appears in the first-person singular to make it more personal, but groups might prefer praying in the first-person plural.

If you delete something in error or your copies become corrupt, you can always return to the original files.

When teaching, open PowerPoint presentations from your hard drive rather than a removable storage device (e.g., CD or memory stick). If using someone else's computer, temporarily copy your slideshow to their hard drive and open it from there. Trying to run PowerPoint from an external device can cause delays between your command and the program's response, complicating your delivery.

With small groups, personal computers with small screens are fine. For instance, two or three individuals might be seated close enough to a single monitor, so they see everything clearly. For large groups, however, you will need multiple displays or a sizeable screen.

If unfamiliar with the room in which you will be presenting, arrive early for a quick trial run. A PowerPoint presentation that looks terrific in one location might appear washed out in another room where the lighting differs. Know beforehand which lights need dimming or which shades lowering. Similarly, if you will be using another person's computer for the presentation, try the PowerPoint slides on that machine ahead of time. Not only might different system software or PowerPoint versions result in presentation differences, but even settings like the amount of "play" in the mouse can affect your presentation. Make sure outlets where you plan to plug in your computer actually work. Also, if you will be using projection equipment, check cables to assure they function properly and connect with your laptop.

Many things affect the way a PowerPoint presentation looks. Differences in platforms (Windows vs. Mac), versions of system software, versions of PowerPoint, amount of memory, type of monitor and its viewing angle or tilt relative to the audience, available fonts, option (or preference) settings, and room lighting can alter the way a PowerPoint slideshow appears. Upgrades or improvements in any of these areas can increase the overall quality of your slideshow.

Learn enough about PowerPoint so you can make a smooth presentation, even if the unexpected happens. For example, suppose someone asks a question about a prior slide. Can you easily navigate to that slide and then back to the current one? Though PowerPoint allows multiple ways to navigate, which is easier for you, or, perhaps more importantly, which provides a smoother transition for your audience? Did you know, for instance, that typing a slide's number and hitting return will take you to that slide quicker than most other methods? For those with general knowledge of and experience with computers, acquiring basic Power-Point presentation skills is not too difficult. Just a few hours or days of study and practice can increase your knowledge and confidence and may be time well spent. The pull-down "Help" menu within PowerPoint explains basic presentation skills, and the internet contains many online tutorials.

Just as you would not walk in cold with no advance preparation to deliver a lecture, you should practice a PowerPoint presentation ahead of time. Certainly, you should feel comfortable with the textbook content and its layout in PowerPoint. But also, you should practice the presentation using PowerPoint. Become familiar, for instance, with how many times you must click the mouse (or tap return, enter, or the spacebar) on each slide to animate the next text or visual. The required clicks are coordinated with the flow of the textbook material. Use PowerPoint's "Coach" as you rehearse to obtain feedback about your pace, pitch, use of euphemisms, cultural sensitivity, wordiness, and other verbal matters. Also, add your own speaker notes that only you see when using "Presenter View" in class.

If unfamiliar with PowerPoint or otherwise lacking confidence to teach with it, you might enlist someone's help who knows it well. Have them practice the presentation with you and, later, operate the slideshow while you teach. Similarly, if you do not have the know-how to address unexpected problems, like program crashes, keep a computer techie nearby, if possible, during your presentation.

A better solution, however, is to invest a few hours or days to learn PowerPoint so you can present slideshows yourself. Many online tutorials teach the basics. At a minimum, you should learn to:

1. Open a PowerPoint file or document. It typically opens in edit mode where slides can be modified to customize your presentation. To enter edit mode, select "Normal" from the "View" pull-down menu.

2. Enter teaching mode by starting the slideshow within an open PowerPoint file or document. From the "View" pull-down menu, select "Slide Show" or "Presenter View." Alternatively, select from the "Slide Show" pull-down menu choices or select the "Slide Show" icon at the bottom of the open window.

3. Make text and other objects appear throughout the slideshow by clicking the mouse (or, instead, tapping return, enter, or the spacebar).

4. Navigate among slides. All slides within a presentation appear in a predetermined order, and you may wish to follow that order. If you simply click straight through a presentation to the end, all the slides will appear in that sequence. But what if someone asks a question and you wish to show a slide out of order? Or, what if you inadvertently do something that takes you to the wrong slide? You should know how to navigate to a slide other than the next sequenced one.

CC consists of the "Introduction" followed by twenty-six lessons or character traits. Each PowerPoint presentation or slideshow corresponds to a single lesson. The opening title slide displays scenic beauty from God's creation, which signals the beginning of class and might assist in quieting everyone. The second slide lists all character traits the curriculum covers and highlights the trait for the current lesson. After that, the centered, large font headings atop slides correspond with main headings in the text, and centered, smaller font headings (if any) correspond with subheadings in the text. Following its initial disclosure, the trait's definition appears at the bottom of each slide to maintain focus.

For self-study, you might have little reason to customize the PowerPoint slides. Indeed, the slides are ready for use "as is" with the related text. However, if teaching a Sunday school class, vacation Bible school, home school group, Bible study, family devotional, or Christian school course, you might wish to alter the slides before teaching with them, though doing so is not an absolute necessity.

Customizing your presentation allows you to follow your own teaching style and emphasize things you deem more important. Indeed, you might want to delete some slides, shorten answers to some questions, or alter slides in other ways. The increased control over content and the way it presents justifies the extra time for many teachers.

You might find some slides behave unusual on different computers. To minimize the chances of such things happening unexpectedly during a slideshow presentation, it's preferable to use the same computer for your teaching preparation and your actual teaching. Alternatively, you might quickly click through all slides on the computer you'll use for teaching just before class begins and, if necessary, make needed adjustments before starting.

Editing PowerPoint slides requires more knowledge than teaching with already-prepared slides. Consider an online tutorial to learn about PowerPoint's edit tools and special features. Once you acquire some editing skills and can customize your presentations, you still might need technical advice occasionally. The "Help" menu within PowerPoint addresses many questions that commonly arise. For specific guidance with a wide range of more difficult issues, see sites like "The PowerPoint FAQ—PowerPoint Help" at rdpslides.com/pptfaq.

Special Request

If you find this book helpful, would you consider leaving an online review so others might benefit too? If uncertain how to proceed, use this search request to find easy-to-follow instructions: "How do I write a book review on amazon.com and goodreads.com?" Thank you for supporting this work.

Bibliography

Answers in Genesis. "Noah's Ark." April 5, 2022. https://answersingenesis.org/noahs-ark.

Augustine (Saint). *The Confessions of Saint Augustine*. Edited by Temple Scott. New York: E.P. Dutton & Co., 1900. https://archive.org/details/confessionssainooscotgoog.

Austen, Jane. *Pride and Prejudice*. London: J.M. Dent & Sons, 1906. https://archive.org/details/in.ernet.dli.2015.46179.

Bierce, Ambrose. *The Devil's Dictionary*. Cleveland: World Publishing Company, 1911. https://archive.org/details/cu31924014323772.

Brady, James Boyd. *Beacon Search-Lights on Pioneers and Millionaires*. Boston: Cushman, 1905. https://archive.org/details/beaconsearchligoobradgoog.

Bunyan, John. *The Entire Works of John Bunyan* II. London: James S. Virtue, 1863. https://archive.org/details/entireworksofjoho2buny.

Calvin, John. *The Institutes of the Christian Religion*. Translated by Henry Beveridge. Grand Rapids: Christian Classics Ethereal Library, 1845. https://www.ccel.org/ccel/c/calvin/institutes/cache/institutes.pdf.

Carden, Jim, and Jeanie Carden. *Christian Character Curriculum*. Edited by Brad Winsted and Tom Waldecker. 3 vols. Tucker, Georgia: Children's Ministry International, 2006.

Chambers, Oswald. *Studies in the Sermon on the Mount*. Cincinnati: God's Revivalist, 1915. https://archive.org/details/studiesinsermonoocham.

Chesterton, G.K. *A Short History of England*. London: Chatto and Windus, 1917. https://archive.org/details/shorthistoryofeooches.

Congressional Record; Proceedings and Debates of the 98th Congress, First Session 129—part 4, March 9, 1983. Washington: U.S. Government Printing Office, 1983. https://archive.org/details/sim_congressional-record-proceedings-and-debates_march-7-1983-march-15-1983_129.

Congressional Record; Proceedings and Debates of the 108th Congress 150—part 5. Washington: U.S. Government Printing Office, 2004. https://archive.org/details/sim_congressional-record-proceedings-and-debates_march-30-april-19-2004_150.

Cooksey, N.B. *Doctrine and Duty Made Plain and Attractive*. Olney, Illinois: Cooksey, 1916. https://archive.org/details/doctrinedutymadeoocook.

Dickens, Charles. *A Christmas Carol and Other Christmas Books*. London: J.M. Dent & Sons, 1907. https://archive.org/details/in.ernet.dli.2015.174279.

Dostoevsky, Fyodor. *Crime and Punishment*. Translated by Constance Garnett. London: William Heinemann, 1914. https://archive.org/details/dli.ministry.11628.

Dryden, John. *Poems*. London: Cassell & Company, 1898. https://archive.org/details/poemsoodryd_o.

Edwards, Tryon. *A Dictionary of Thoughts*. Detroit: F.B. Dickerson, 1908. https://archive.org/details/adictionarythouoounkngoog.

———. *Light for the Day; or, Heavenly Thoughts for Earthly Guidance*. Philadelphia: Presbyterian Board of Publication, 1877. https://archive.org/details/lightfordayooedwa.

Emerson, Ralph Waldo. *Works of Ralph Waldo Emerson*. Edited by A.C. Hearn. Edinburgh: W.P. Nimmo, Hay, & Mitchell, 1907. https://archive.org/details/in.ernet.dli.2015.24906.

Felltham, Owen. *Resolves, Divine, Moral, and Political, of Owen Felltham*. Edited by James Cumming. 2nd ed. London: John Hatchard and Son, 1820. https://archive.org/details/resolvesdivinemo5fellgoog.

Franklin, Benjamin. *Poor Richard's Almanack*. Waterloo, Iowa: U.S.C. Publishing Co., 1914. https://archive.org/details/poorrichardsalmaoofranrich.

Fuller, Thomas. *Aphorisms of Wisdom; or, A Complete Collection of the Most Celebrated Proverbs*. Glasgow: R. & D. Malcolm, 1814. https://archive.org/details/aphorismsofwisdooofull.

Hall, Joseph. *A Selection from the Writings of Joseph Hall*. Edited by A. Huntington Clapp. New York: Robert Carter and Brothers, 1850. https://archive.org/details/selectionfromwrioohall_1.

Henry, Matthew. *Exposition of the Old and New Testaments: with Practical Remarks and Observations*. Joshua to 1 Kings II. London: Nisbet, n.d. https://archive.org/details/expositionofoldno2henruoft.

———. *Matthew Henry's Concise Bible Commentary*. Brattleboro: Fessenden and Company, 1834. https://archive.org/details/matthew-henrys-concise-bible-commentary-ellen-g-white-estate.

Hodge, Bodie. "How Long Did It Take for Noah to Build the Ark?" Answers in Genesis. April 5, 2022. https://answersingenesis.org/bible-timeline/how-long-did-it-take-for-noah-to-build-the-ark.

The Holy Bible (English Standard Version). Wheaton: Crossway, 2011.

The Holy Bible (New International Version). Colorado Springs: International Bible Society, 1984.

Hubbard, Kin. *Abe Martin: Hoss Sense and Nonsense*. Indianapolis: Bobbs-Merrill Company, 1926. https://archive.org/details/abemartinhosssenoohubb.

Johnson, Samuel. *The Life and Writings of Samuel Johnson* II. Selected and arranged by William P. Page. New York: Harper & Brothers, 1840. https://archive.org/details/lifeandwritingso1johngoog.

Jones, Jr., Bob. "Broken Things." Greenville, South Carolina: Bob Jones University Press, n.d.

Keller, Helen. *Practice of Optimism*. London: Hodder and Stoughton, 1909. https://archive.org/details/practiceofoptimioohele.

Lincoln, Abraham. *The Lincoln Year Book: Axioms and Aphorisms from the Great Emancipator*. Compiled by Wallace Rice. Chicago: A.C. McClurg & Co., 1907. https://archive.org/details/lincolnyearbookoolincrich.

Luther, Martin. *The Table Talk of Doctor Martin Luther*. New York: Frederick A. Stokes Company, 1893. https://archive.org/details/tabletalkofdoctoooluth.

Maclaren, Alexander. *Music for the Soul: Daily Readings for a Year.* Selected and arranged by George Coates. New York: A.C. Armstrong and Son, 1897. https://archive.org/details/musicforsouldailoomacl.

Moore, Thomas. *The Poetical Works of Thomas Moore.* Philadelphia: J. Crissy and Thomas, Cowperthwait & Co., 1845. https://archive.org/details/poeticalworksoft01mooreth.

O'Malley, Austin. *Keystones of Thought.* New York: Devin-Adair Company, 1915. https://archive.org/details/KeystonesOfThought.

Osgood, Charles Grosvenor. *Boswell's Life of Johnson.* New York: Charles Scribner's Sons, 1917. https://archive.org/details/boswellslifeofjoooboswiala.

Owen, John. *The Works of John Owen* V. Edited by Thomas Russell. London: Richard Baynes, 1826. https://archive.org/details/worksofjohnoweo5owen.

Paine, Albert Bigelow. *Moments with Mark Twain.* New York: Harper & Brothers, 1920. https://archive.org/details/momentswithmarktoopainuoft.

Pliny the Younger. *The Letters of the Younger Pliny.* Translated by Betty Radice. London: Penguin, 1969. https://archive.org/details/lettersofyoungerooplin.

Plumer, William S. *Vital Godliness: A Treatise on Experimental and Practical Piety.* New York: American Tract Society, 1867. https://archive.org/details/vitalgodlinesstrwsooplum.

"Question Drawer." *Gospel Herald* II (June 3, 1909) 49. https://archive.org/details/gospelherald190902kauf.

"Reviews of Recent Literature." *The Princeton Theological Review* 15 (July 1917) 451–500. https://archive.org/details/princetontheolog1531arms.

Ryle, J.C. *Expository Thoughts on the Gospels.* New York: Robert Carter & Brothers, 1860. https://archive.org/details/expositorythougooryle.

Sammis, John H. *"Trust and Obey" and Other Songs.* Los Angeles: T.C. Horton, 1918. https://archive.org/details/truthersooosamm.

Scarry, Richard. *Richard Scarry's Lowly Worm Storybook.* New York: Random House, 1977.

Sibbes, Richard. *The Complete Works of Richard Sibbes, D.D.* I. Edinburgh: James Nichol, 1862. https://archive.org/details/completeworks001sibb.

Simmons, Charles. *A Laconic Manual and Brief Remarker.* North Wrentham, Massachusetts: Charles Simmons, 1852. https://archive.org/details/alaconicmanualaoosimmgoog.

Smith, Christian, and Melinda Lundquist Denton. *Soul Searching: The Religious and Spiritual Lives of American Teenagers.* New York: Oxford University Press, 2005.

Southey, Robert. "The Devil's Walk." In *The Book of Familiar Quotations,* 207. London: Whittaker & Co., 1860. https://archive.org/details/bookoffamiliarquoogent.

Spurgeon, Charles H. "The Bed and Its Covering." *Spurgeon Gems* 5 (January 9, 1859) 1–8. https://www.spurgeongems.org/sermon/chs244.pdf.

———. "Christ's First and Last Subject." *Spurgeon Gems* 6 (Aug 19, 1860) 1–9. https://www.spurgeongems.org/sermon/chs329.pdf.

———. "The Ear Bored with an Awl." *Spurgeon Gems* 20 (May 3, 1874) 1–8. https://www.spurgeongems.org/sermon/chs1174.pdf.

———. "Faith and Repentance Inseparable." *Spurgeon Gems* 8 (July 13, 1862) 1–9. https://www.spurgeongems.org/sermon/chs460.pdf.

———. "Forgiveness and Fear." *Spurgeon Gems* 50 (March 26, 1876) 1–9. https://www.spurgeongems.org/sermon/chs2882.pdf.

———. "Joseph Attacked by the Archers." *Spurgeon Gems* 1 (April 1, 1855) 1–8. https://www.spurgeongems.org/sermon/chs17.pdf.

———. "The Pierced One Pierces the Heart." *Spurgeon Gems* 10 (June 19, 1864) 1–8. https://www.spurgeongems.org/sermon/chs575.pdf.

———. "Repentance Must Go with Forgiveness." *All of Grace: An Earnest Word with Those Who Are Seeking Salvation by the Lord Jesus Christ.* https://www.spurgeongems.org/chs_all-of-grace.pdf.

———. "Tempted of the Devil." *Spurgeon Gems* 52 (1864) 1–8. https://www.spurgeongems.org/sermon/chs2997.pdf.

Thoreau, Henry D. *Walden; or, Life in the Woods.* Boston: Ticknor and Fields, 1854. https://archive.org/details/waldenorlifeinwo1854thor.

Trapp, John. *Commentary on the New Testament.* Edited by (Richard D. Dickinson) W. Webster. Reprint, Grand Rapids: Baker Book House, (1865) 1981. https://archive.org/details/commentaryonnewtoojohn.

Warfield, Ethelbert D. "John Knox, Reformer of a Kingdom." *Princeton Theological Review* 3 (July 1905) 376–98. https://archive.org/details/princetontheolo10semigoog.

Watson, Thomas. *A Body of Practical Divinity.* Philadelphia: John Wiley, 1833. https://archive.org/details/bodyofpracticaldoowats_0.

———. *Discourses on Important and Interesting Subjects,* 1. Reprint, Ligonier, PA: Soli Deo Gloria Publications, (1829) 1990. https://archive.org/details/discoursesonimpooooowats.

Webster, Daniel. *The Writings and Speeches of Daniel Webster* 11. Boston: Little, Brown, & Company, 1903. https://archive.org/details/cu31924092894967.

Weniger, Francis Xavier. *The Perfect Religious According to the Rule of St. Augustine.* Dublin: M. H. Gill and Son, 1888. https://archive.org/details/theperfectreligiooweniuoft.

Westminster Assembly. *Westminster Confession of Faith,* 1646. https://westminsterstandards.org/westminster-confession-of-faith.

———. *Westminster Shorter Catechism,* 1646. https://westminsterstandards.org/westminster-shorter-catechism.

Wharton, Anne Hollingsworth. *Martha Washington.* New York: Charles Scribner's Sons, 1897. https://archive.org/details/marthawashingtonoowharrich.

Wood, James. *Dictionary of Quotations from Ancient and Modern, English and Foreign Sources.* London: Frederick Warne and Co, 1893. https://archive.org/details/DictionaryOfQuotationsFromAncientAndModern.

Young, Edward. *The Complaint; or Night Thoughts on Life, Death, & Immortality.* London: Thomas Teeg, 1812. https://archive.org/details/complaintornighto1younuoft.

Name Index

Aaron
    departure from Egypt under,
        57, 200
    grandson of, 165
    priesthood under, xvi
Abednego, 49, 58
Abigail, 81–82, 133
Abraham or Abram
    counsel to, from Sarai, 22, 160
    impatience of, about
        childlessness, 159–60, 162
    nephew of, 18–19, 66, 68
    promises to, from God, 106–7,
        159
    submission to, by Sarah, 192
    travels of, in Canaan, 57, 106
Abrahams, Harold, 104
Absalom, 157
Adam, 22, 53, 141, 201–2, 205
Aesop, 71
Agabus, 125
Agrippa, *see* Herod Agrippa
Ahab, 96
Ananias, 222, 224
Asaph, 210
Asherah or Ashtoreth, 169

Balaam, 54
Balak, 54
Barnabas, 222
Bathsheba, 165, 168, 170, 179
Bildad, 134
Boaz, 73, 167
Buttercup, 64

Caesar, Claudius, 143, 202
Calvin, John, xvii

Chitwood, Jimmy, 55
Claudius, 143, 202
Clemens, Orion, 199
Clemens, Samuel, 199
Colburn, Hoke, 65

Daisy (Miss), 64–65
Dale, Norman, 55
Daniel
    decision of, to pray, 49
    food and drink of, 58–59
    refusal of glory by, 141
David
    adultery of, with Bathsheba, 165,
        168, 170, 173, 179
    battle of, with Goliath, 49
    conflict of, with Nabal, 81–82,
        83, 125–26, 133
    danger to, from Saul, 189
    failure of, to repent, 179, 181–82
    friendship of, with Jonathan,
        97–98, 126
    hospitality of, towards
        Mephibosheth, 129
    instructions of, to Solomon, 45
    insults to, from Shimei, 157
    refusal of glory by, 141
    thankfulness of, to God, 208,
        210
Delilah, 19
Devil, *see* Satan
Dickens, Charles, 25, 127
Dinah, 165
Diotrephes, 67, 141

Edison, Thomas, 37
Einstein, Albert, 37

Elihu, 190, 193
Eliphaz, 134, 160
Enoch, 106
Esau, 159
Eve, 22, 53, 141, 201–2, 205
Ezra, 73

Finch, Atticus, 96
Fischer, Bobby, 187
Flatch, Wilbur "Shooter," 55
Fleener, Myra, 55

Geshem, 74
Gideon, 49, 133
Goliath, 49
Graber, Ida, 113

Habakkuk, 151–52, 153
Hagar, 22, 160
Haydn, Pop, 1
Henry VIII, 44
Herod Agrippa, 143–44, 147
Hezekiah, 21
Hickam, Homer, 71
Hoke, 65

Isaac
    birth of, as God promised,
        159–60
    sacrifice of, to God, 106
    travels of, in Canaan, 57
Isaiah, 11, 13
Iscariot, see Judas Iscariot
Ishmael, 160

Jacob
    family of, 159, 165, 200
    marriages of, 96, 157
    travels of, in Canaan, 57
James, 138, 143, 157
Jezebel, 96
Job
    covenant of, with eyes, 165
    harshness towards, from friends,
        134, 136–37, 190
    patience of, while suffering, 160,
        162

John
    brother of, 143
    courage of, before Sanhedrin,
        46–47, 48–49, 55
    hands of, laid on converts, 180
    impatience of, with Samaritans,
        138, 157
Jonathan, 97–98, 126
Joseph, husband of Mary, 59
Joseph, son of Jacob
    forgiveness of, for brothers'
        hatred, 115
    refusal of glory by, 141
    response of, to seduction, 165,
        172–73, 235, 238
Joshua
    carelessness of, about
        Gibeonites, 22–23
    decision of, to serve God, 57–58
    leadership of, in Canaan, 46,
        49, 106
Judah, 165
Judas Iscariot
    betrayal of Jesus by, 54–55, 221,
        235
    faith of, 108

Kappler, Herbert, 43
Knox, John, 43

Laban, 96, 157
Leah, 96
LeVar, Kevin, 113
Levi, 200
Liddell, Eric, 104
Lincoln, Abraham, 205
Livermore, Vinnie, 187
Lloyd, 132
Lot
    choice of land by, 18–19, 21,
        66, 68
    daughters of, 19, 165
    visitors to, 165

Martha, 3, 5
Mary, mother of Jesus, 59
Mary, sister of Martha, 3, 5
Mary, Queen of Scots, 43

Mephibosheth, 126, 129
Meshach, 49, 58
Miss Daisy, 64–65
Monsignor O'Flaherty, 43–44
More, (Sir) Thomas, 44
Moses
    accusations concerning law of,
        116
    choice of, to suffer, 53–54
    death of, 46
    departure from Egypt under, 57,
        106, 200
    judgments of, involving
        disputes, 96
Mozart, Wolfgang, 37

Nabal, 81–82, 125–26, 128
Naboth, 96
Naomi, 73, 167
Nathan, 179
Nebuchadnezzar, 49, 58, 145
Nehemiah, 73–74, 75
Nickleby, Nicholas, 25
Noah, 71–72, 76, 157

O'Flaherty, (Monsignor) Hugh,
    43–44
Ohr, Michael, 25

Pandolfini, Bruce, 187
Paul
    admonition of, about giving, 125
    advice of, about meat offered to
        idols, 66
    afflictions of, 93, 152
    care of, like a nursing mother,
        133–34, 136
    contentment of, in every
        circumstance, 34, 35, 36,
        39–40
    encouragement from, to be
        humble, 143, 144
    examples, gave about endurance,
        90
    gospel message of, 108, 181
    imprisonment of, 35, 151
    perspective of, regarding the
        moral law, xvii

regard of, for Timothy, 11–12,
    67–68
Peter
    confession and disloyalty of,
        221–22, 224, 235, 237
    courage of, before Sanhedrin,
        46–47, 48–49, 55
    deliverance of, from Herod, 143
    encouragement from, to be
        humble, 143
    perspective of, regarding the
        moral law, xvii
    rebuke of, to Simon the sorcerer,
        180
Pharaoh, 57, 115, 229
Philip, 179–80
Phinehas, 165
Pilate, 89, 202, 205
Potiphar (and his wife), 165, 172,
    235

Rachel, 96, 157
Radley, Arthur "Boo," 96
Rahab, 229
Raskolnikov, 45
Rehoboam, 22, 133
Rickey, Branch, 158
Robinson, Jackie, 158
Robinson, Tom, 96
Rogers, (Mr.) Fred, 132
Ruth, 73, 75, 167

Samson, 19–20
Samuel, 5, 157
Sanballat, 74
Sapphira, 222, 224
Sarah or Sarai
    counsel of, to Abram, 22
    impatience of, 159–60, 162
    submission of, to Abraham, 192
Satan or the Devil
    danger from, 17, 49, 134, 160,
        174, 190, 234
    deceitfulness of, 201, 230, 234
    defeat of, 209
    schemes of, 171, 235, 238
    temptations from, 54–55, 172,
        201, 237

Saul, the missionary, *see* Paul
Saul, king of Israel
  death of, on Mount Gilboa, 126
  descendants of, 126
  faith of, 108
  hatred of, towards David, 81,
    97–98, 125, 189
  meeting of, with medium, 22
  offering by, contrary to the law,
    157
Scarry, Richard, 141
Scrooge, Ebenezer, 127
Shadrach, 49, 58
Shechem, 165
Shimei, 157
Silas, 35, 40, 108, 133
Simon, 108, 179–80
Smike, 25
Smith, (Mr.) Jefferson, 43–44
Solomon
  temple built by, in Jerusalem, 45,
    49, 116, 178, 200
  wisdom of, from God, 80–81,
    82, 83
Squeers, Wackford, 25
Stephen, 116, 121

Stoneman, Will, 87

Tamar, 165
Taylor, Hudson, 64
Timothy
  examples given to, about
    endurance, 90
  service of, 11–12, 13, 67–68, 133
Tobiah, 74
Twain, Mark, 199

Uriah, 165, 168
Uzzah, 210
Uzziah, 11

Vinnie, 187
Vogel, Lloyd, 132

Waitzkin, Josh, 187
Werthan, (Miss) Daisy, 64–65
Westley, 64

Zamperini, Louis, 113
Zerubbabel, 73, 280
Ziba, 126
Zophar, 134

Scripture Index

Genesis

2:24	170
3:1–19	53
3:1–13	201
3:5	141
3:17	22
5:21–24	106
6:9–22	157
12:1–9	106
12:1–7	159
13:1–13	18
13:5–13	66
13:14–17	159
14:1–24	19
15:1–6	159
15:6	107
16:1–5	159
16:2	22
17:1–8, 15–19	159
19:1–38	66
19:1–5, 30–36	165
19:1, 15–26, 30–38	19
21:1–7	159
22:1–19	106
29:15–28	96
29:20	157
34:1–2	165
37:1–36	115
38:12–18	165
39:1–23	115
39:1–12	235
39:6–12	165
39:12	173
40—41	115
41:16	141
42—44	115
45:4–5	115
50:15–21	115

Exodus

1:15–22	229
2:11–15	53
18:1–27	96
20:3–17	xiii
20:12	192
40:34–35	244

Leviticus

13:2, 45–46	211
19:15	97, 100, 191
19:32	193
20:7	286

Numbers

1:50–53	200
3:25–31	201
5:2–4	211
22:1–31	54
24:10	54
25:6–13	165

Deuteronomy

7:1	46
15:10	128
18:10, 14	265
22:10	xvi
30:1–20	54
32:48–52	106

Deuteronomy (*continued*)

33:27	154
34:1–4	106

Joshua

1—12	107
1:1–11	46
2:1–24	229
6:17–25	229
9:14	23
13:22	54
24:12, 15	57
24:20	58

Judges

2:13	169
7:10–12	50
8:1–3	133
13:5	246
14:1–20	19
16:1–31	19
19:16–28	165

Ruth

1:16	73
2:1–23	73
3:7–14	167
4:13	167

1 Samuel

3:10	5
4—6	210
10:8	157
13:14	168
13:5–14	157
16:14–23	189
17:1–58	189
17:37	49
18:1–4, 15–16, 30	97
18:5–11, 17–27	189
18:10—19:15	98
19:1–2, 9–24	189
20:1–42	97
20:14–17	126
22:11–19	189

23:7–13, 19	189
24:1–22	189
25:1–35	81
25:1–11	125
25:23–35	133
25:38	126
26:1–25	189
31:1–6	126

2 Samuel

6:1–15	210
7:18	141
9:1–13	126
11:1–27	179
11:1–17	168
11:2–5	165
11:6—18:33	173
11:17	170
12:1–14	179
12:11–12	265
12:11	168
12:13–18	264
16:5–13	157

1 Kings

3:9	80, 82
3:16–28	82
11:5	169
12:1–33	22
17:7–16	129
18:19	169
21:1–29	96

2 Kings

6:8–18	104
17:6, 24, 33	247
23:4–7	169

1 Chronicles

10:13–14	22
11:41	168
15:1–3	210
16:1–36	210
28:20	45

2 Chronicles

7:1, 13–14	178
7:15	6
10:1–19	22
10:13–14	133

Nehemiah

4:1–23	73
4:6	74
6:1–16	73
6:3, 9, 11, 15	74
8:10	152

Job

1:1—4:6	160
1:1—2:13	134
1:21	160
2:10	160
2:12–13	137
3:1–26	160
4:2, 5	160
4:2	134
8:2	134
11:2	134
13:4	134
16:2	134
19:2	134
31:1	165
32:1–12	190
42:10–17	160

Psalm

16:6	154
18:35	139
19:12	84
20:7	109
23:1	38
23:6	154
27:1	39, 50
29:2	xx
31:23	143
32:2	230
34:10	40
34:12–13	230
37:7	162
37:8	286

46:1	39
51:1–17	179
55:21	20
62:5	109
84:11	214
94:3–6, 18–19, 22	151
97:12	153
100:1–2	153
100:4–5	213
103:1	xx
103:12	121
103:13	29
106:3	99
107:21	212
116:5	29
118:6	39
118:24	153
119:14	154
126:2–3	153
131:1	146
141:5	146

Proverbs

3:5	108
5:8	172
6:6–8	71
6:9–11	72
6:25–27	173
11:14	22
11:24–25	124
12:22	227
13:10	83, 146
14:29	162
15:1	133, 134, 138
15:18	158
15:22	22
16:5	143
16:18	237
17:5	191
17:10	83
17:27	162
18:17	20
18:24	38
19:2	17
19:11	117
20:3	146
20:12	2

Proverbs (*continued*)

21:4	145, 265
25:17	195
25:18	221, 225
26:1, 8	192
26:17	146
26:24–25	17
27:2	146
28:1	45
28:13	147, 182
28:21	191
30:25	71

Ecclesiastes

5:1	xiii
7:14	92
7:26	173
11:1–2	123
12:13–14	xviii

Isaiah

1:1	244
2:11	143
6:1–8	11
6:1	244
6:9	5
30:15	162
39:1–7	21
49:15	29
53:5–6	214
53:7	89

Jeremiah

9:23–24	146

Lamentations

3:22–23	30

Ezekiel

34:12	76
36:26	287

Daniel

1:1–20	58

2:27–28	141
3:16–18	49
4:29–33	145
6:10	49

Habakkuk

1:1—2:20	151
2:4	105
3:16–19	151

Zechariah

4:6	280
9:9	148

Malachi

3:7	182

Matthew

1:18–26	59
3:8	183
4:1–11	237
5:17–19	xvii
5:21–22	xiii
5:29–30	58
6:1	146
6:13	171, 234
6:14–15	114
6:19–21	124
6:32–33	34
7:12	97
7:15	234
8:2–3	100
9:10–11	100
9:35–36	26, 29
10:42	129
11:15	2
11:28–29	109
11:29	136
16:16	222
18:35	118
20:26–28	13
22:37–39	xiii, 148
22:39–40	97
23:27	100
25:35–36	29

Matthew (*continued*)

26:39 — 50
26:41 — 171, 239
26:53 — 89, 93
26:57–67 — 89
27:11–14, 27–50 — 89
27:24 — 202
28:20 — 39

Mark

3:17 — 138
4:39 — 135
8:37 — 171
10:13–16 — 2
10:44 — 67
14:27–72 — 235
14:27–31, 66–72 — 221
14:38 — 236

Luke

6:31 — 195
6:38 — 129
9:52–55 — 157
9:54 — 138
9:58 — 40
10:25–37 — 27, 221
10:38–42 — 3
11:7–8 — 13
15:11–32 — 27, 34
16:10 — 204
17:3 — 118, 119
17:11–19 — 210
17:15–16 — 269
21:1–4 — 124
22:1–6, 47–53 — 54
22:27 — 144

John

1:14 — 230
3:16 — 108
3:30 — 147
3:36 — 108, 213
4:1–42 — 247
4:9 — 27
6:38 — 206
8:3–11 — 134
8:19 — 108
8:44 — 100, 230
10:30 — 108
11:41 — 215
13:4–17 — 144
13:34–35 — 65
14:6 — 230
15:11 — 154
18:28—19:16 — 202
19:30 — 93

Acts

1:8 — 47
1:18–19 — 55
2:1–4 — 47
2:41, 45, 47 — 222
3:1—4:31 — 46
4:4, 32–37 — 222
4:13–31 — 55
4:19 — 250
5:1–11 — 222
6:1–6 — 222
6:3 — 201
6:5—7:60 — 116
6:5 — 180
8:1–24 — 179
11:28 — 125
12:2–3, 6–11, 19–23 — 143
16:1 — 11
16:16–34 — 35
16:31 — 108
17:11 — 81
20:4 — 11
20:21 — 181

Romans

2:4 — 163
3:20, 24 — xvii
3:22, 24 — xx
5:3–4 — 93
6:12–14 — xv
6:12–13, 19 — 173
7:12, 22 — xvii
8:28 — 39, 92, 109, 162, 213
10:9 — 108
10:17 — 110

Romans (*continued*)

12:1	10
12:10	65, 68, 92, 191
12:12	153
12:13	129
12:15	145, 153
12:16	146
13:1–2	193
13:14	171

1 Corinthians

4:7	146
5:1–5	165
6:13, 15–19	166
6:15–20	173
7:19	xvii
8:13	66
9:22	64
10:13	170, 171, 237, 238
10:31	147
13:4	159
15:3–4	108

2 Corinthians

1:20	230
4:7–9	152
4:16–18	93
5:1, 5, 7	105
6:4–10	152
7:4–7	152
7:9–10	178
7:9	179
8:1–4, 9	125
8:2–4	129
9:6, 11, 13	129
9:7	128
10:1	136
10:4	170
11:23–29	152
12:10	93
13:1	18

Galatians

1:6–7	xx
2:16	105
3:3, 10	xvi

3:25	xv, xvi
4:4–5	61
4:22–23	160
5:16	171
5:22–23	136
5:22	153
6:1	138
6:9	93
6:10	128

Ephesians

1:3–5	55
2:8–9	xx, 105
2:10	13, 147
2:19	226
4:2–3	121
4:2	159
4:25	221
4:32	114, 117
5:20	211
5:21	191
5:22–24	192
5:25–26, 28–30	193
5:33	192, 193
6:1, 4	192
6:5–9	194
6:10–11, 16–18	238
6:10	170
6:11	171
6:12	234
6:16	109

Philippians

1:13, 29–30	151
2:1–4	142, 143
2:3–8	66
2:4	10
2:5–8	144
2:7–8	68
2:12–13	xxii, 287
2:19–23	11
2:20–21	68
4:4	151, 153
4:5	136
4:11–12	34
4:11	36

Philippians (*continued*)

4:12	35, 39
4:19	32, 214

Colossians

2:18–23	147
3:12	136, 163
3:13	118
3:14	xiv
3:19	193
3:21	192
3:22	194
3:23	72, 75, 204
4:1	195

1 Thessalonians

2:6	133
2:7	133, 136
2:12	134
4:3–7	167
4:3	237
5:12–13	188
5:13	193
5:16	153
5:18	209, 212
5:20–22	81
5:23–24	287

1 Timothy

1:3	11
1:6–7	147
4:8	171
5:1–2, 17	193
6:1–2	194
6:4	146
6:6–8	34
6:8	39

2 Timothy

2:3–12	90
2:22	173
2:25	138

Titus

2:11–12	287
3:1	193
3:2–3	146

Hebrews

1:1–2	2
2:1	2
2:3	2
5:14	84
6:15	159
6:18	230
7:18–19	xvi
9:12, 28	xvi
10:36	93
11:1	109
11:3	213
11:5–6, 8–12, 17–19	106
11:24–27	53
11:31	229
12:2–3	90
12:7, 9	92
12:7, 11	88
12:28	209, 214
13:4	170
13:5	14, 38, 39
13:6	50
13:16	129
13:17	193

James

1:4	93
1:5	130
1:15	174
1:19	137, 146, 162
1:21	286
1:27	128
2:1–9	98
2:1, 9	191
2:13	114
2:15	128
2:19	108
3:9–10	191
5:11	160
5:16	147

1 Peter

1:8	154
1:14–16	xvii
2:13–14, 18	194
2:17	188, 191
2:19–20	89
2:19	92
2:22	237
2:23	89
3:4	136
3:5, 7	192
3:15	138
4:14–16	91
5:5–6	143
5:8	234
5:9	237
5:10	93

2 Peter

2:15–16	54

1 John

1:9	173
2:3–6	xviii
2:16	203
3:17–18	27
3:17	129
4:1	83
4:20	27
5:5	109

3 John

9	67, 141

Jude

4	xv

Revelation

15:8	244

Subject Index

abortion, 170

adoption, xxii, 25, 55, 61, 88, 154, 214, 221, 226, *see also* child(ren)

adultery, *see also* fornication
    David committed, 165, 168, 173, 179
    definition of, 170
    God forbids, xiii
    harm from, 170, 173
    woman caught in, 134–35, 136

afflictions, 162, *see also* chastisements and hardships
    Christ endured, 90
    churches experience, 125, 151
    God sends, for good, 93, 162
    Jesus healed, 26, 29
    life involves, 92
    orphans and widows have, 128
    Paul experienced, 152
    test of, 125

"Amish Grace," 113

Ammonites, 168

angels, 54, 59, 89, 93, 143, 144, 154, 234, *see also* seraphs

animals, 1, 49, 66, 76, 233
    ants, 71
    camels, 87
    earthworms, 141–42
    hummingbirds, rufous, 79–80
    lambs, 89, 179
    lions, 19, 26, 45, 49, 234
    meerkats, 123
    opossums, 9
    peacocks, 165–66
    pheasants, ring-necked, 233
    sheep, 26, 76, 82, 89, 125, 214, 234
    wolverines, 44
    wolves, 234
    zebras, African, 25–26

antinomianism, xv, xvii

ants, 71

Aphek, battle of, 210

apologies, 118–19, 138, 183–84, 191, 223

apostles
    James, 138, 143, 157
    John, 46–47, 48–49, 55, 138, 143, 157, 180
    Judas Iscariot, 54–55, 108, 221, 235
    Peter, 46–47, 48–49, 55, 143, 180, 221–22, 224, 235, 237
    Paul, xvii, 11–12, 34, 35, 66, 90, 125, 133–34, 136, 143, 151, 152

ark of the covenant, 45, 200, 210

ark of Noah, 71–72, 76, 157

armor of God, 171, 238

Asherah, 169

Ashtoreth, 169

Assyrians, 54, 209

athletes, 90, 234, *see also* sports

authority, *see also* submission
    church leader as, 133, 193
    elder as, 193
    employer as, 194
    gentleness and, 135–36
    God as ultimate, 43
    government official as, 193–94
    husband as, 193–94

authority (*continued*)
  Joseph in position of, 115
  king as, 189
  parent or guardian as, 192, 225, 227
  people in, 68, 119, 161, 187
  respect for, xiii, 5, 6, 189
  struggle against, 229, 234

Babylon
  envoy from, to visit Hezekiah, 21
  exile to, 54, 73, 105, 151–52, 153, 209, *see also* captives or captivity
  king of, 58
  Nehemiah and, 74
Baptism, 180
baseball, 158, 228
"Beautiful Day in the Neighborhood, A," 132
Berea, 125
bias, *see* prejudice
black magic, 179
blame-shifting, 35, 183, 202, 205
"Blind Side, The," 25
"Brainstorm," 32, 96, 141, 157, 165

Caesarea, 143–44
Calvary, xxii, 114, 214, *see also* crucifixion
camels, 87
Canaan(ites), 18, 57, 106, 115, 169, 210
captives or captivity, 54, 58, 73, 105, 153, 174, 209, *see also* Babylon, exile to
Carmel, 125
cell phone, 4, 6, 233, 237
ceremonial law, xvi–xvii, 107
charades, 16
chariots, 104, 109
chastisements, 55, 88, 170, 214, *see also* afflictions and hardships
chess, 187, 228
child(ren), *see also* adoption
  birth of, to Hagar, 160

  care of nursing mother for, 133–34, 136
  desire of, to see Jesus, 3, 5
  dispute about, before Solomon, 82
  harm to, from sexual immorality, 170
  holiness of God's, xvii
  honesty of and to, 225, 227
  instruction to, about love, 26–27
  loss of Job's, 134, 160
  prayer for, by Abram and Sarai, 159, 162
  protection of, 196, 229
  repentance of, 181
  respect of and to, 192
choices, *see* "Critical Choices" and decision(s)
chore, 12, 72, 75, 204, 281
church(es)
  Berean, 125
  Corinth, 165
  Ephesus, 11
  false prophets in, xxi, 81, 83, 234, 237
  Jerusalem, 125, 180, 201, 204, 222
  local, xxi, 127–28, 143, 193, 226, 279
  Macedonia, 125
  Philippi, 151
  Thessalonica, 133
  universal, 192–93, 221, 280
civil law, xvi
clergy, *see* elder
conclusions, 16–17, 18, 22, 61, 79
consequences
  arguments and, 146
  carelessness and, 23
  decisions and, 53–55, 56–57, 60–61, 204, 205
  falsehood and, 2, 224, 230
  fear and, 128
  foolishness and, 19, 28
  harshness and, 132
  immorality and, 168, 170
  neglect and, 199–200
  pardon from, 118–20

consequences (*continued*)
    pride and, 145
    remorse and, 182
core beliefs, xix
core traits, 281
core values, xv
counsel, 188, 190, 238, 278
    Abram received, from Sarai, 22
    Adam received, from Eve, 22
    Elihu delayed, 190
    failure to seek or benefit from,
        23, 83
    Holy Spirit provides, 238
    pastors and elders give, 188, 278
    reconciliation through, 183
    recovery through, 172
    safety through, 23
    wisdom through, 22, 61, 84
Crime and Punishment, 45
"Critical Choices," 53, *see also*
    decision(s)
criticism, 79, 100, 136, 146, 169
crucifixion, 47, 55, 89, 202, 222, *see*
    also Calvary

danger
    courage to face, 45, 46
    dismissal of moral law and its,
        xiv–xix
    enemies and, 74, 189
    faith overcomes, 105
    haste can be a, 17, 21
    lies and, 225–26
    Lot ignored, 18–19
    morality without gospel
        involves, xiv, xix–xxii
    sexual immorality and, 170, 172
    situations involving, 16, 21, 44,
        49, 135, 233
    watchfulness for spiritual, 235,
        237–38
deacons, 116, 180, 193, 201, 204,
    222
Dead Sea, 73, 210
death
    Abigail prevents, 133
    adulteress threatened with, 135
    bitterness worse than, 173

    Enoch avoided, 106
    fear of, 49
    grief of the world produces, 178
    hour of, 182
    Isaiah feared, 11
    Jesus', 67, 89, 92, 144, 214, 221
    Nazi, camps, 229
    one, bed repentance, 176
    pain of, by crucifixion, 202
    Pilate sentenced Jesus to, 205
    Samson's, 20
    Saul's, 126
    sin brings forth, 174
    Solomon rules about child's, 82
    souls brought from, to life, 173
    Stephen's, 116
decision(s), 55–57, 58, 229, *see also*
    "Critical Choices"
    Adam and Eve's, 53, 201–2
    Balaam's, 54
    bias in, 97
    control over, 224
    Daniel's, 58–59
    David's, 189
    distortion of purchase, 220
    food and related, 66
    foolish, 199–200
    God's, 55
    Holy Spirit and, 84
    Israel's, 54
    Joseph's, 59
    Joshua's, 57–58
    Judas Iscariot's, 54–55
    Lot's, 18–19, 66
    Mary's, 3
    Moses', 53–54
    motives for, 205
    Naomi's, 73
    parents', 227
    Peter and John's, 55
    Pilate's, 202
    righteousness and, 203, 205
    Solomon's, 82
    support for, 68
    timeliness of, 60, 61
    vocation and, 225
    wisdom for, 61, 83
deism, xix, xx–xxi

Depression, Great, 128
discrimination, *see* prejudice
dogs, 87, 146, 150, 196, 237
"Driving Miss Daisy," 64

earthworms, 141–42
education(al)
    choices about, 56
    dedication to, 72, 204, 224
    differences in, 193
    discontent with, 38
    ethics related to, 281
    exchanges within, system, 225
    messages from, system, xv
    perspective on, 37, 79
    thankfulness for, 214
elder, 11, 81, 180, 188, 190, 193, *see
    also* pastor
electronic devices, 4, 32, 127, 172,
    238, *see also* social media
employment
    authority and, 6, 68, 194
    ethics for, 281
    heartiness in, 72
    honesty in, 225
    mutual respect in, 194, 204
    thankfulness for, 214
Ephraimites, 133
evidence
    accusation or condemnation
        without, 190, 202
    assertion of knowledge without,
        147
    faith and its, xviii, 104
    gentleness and its, 136
    God's promises when,
        unobservable, 109
    impatience as, of distrust, 162
    wrongdoing and its, 18
ex nihilo, 213
execution, *see* murder
exile, *see under* Babylon, *see* captives
    or captivity
Exodus, 57, 106, 200

false prophet, 81, 83, 234, 237
family
    conversation with, members,
        137

discontent with, 37–38, 160, 161
endangerment to, 18–19, 21,
    168, 182
God's, 214, 221
honesty within, 225, 226
loss of Job's, 160, 190
ministry of, 25, 127
neglect of, 5, 13, 128, 238
prodigals within, 35–36
protection of, 76, 87, 126, 224,
    229
thankfulness for, 212, 214
farmers, 90
favoritism, *see* prejudice
fear
    courage mitigates, 48, 49
    David had, of Saul's wrath, 98
    generosity impeded by, 128
    God warrants reverential, xviii
    Jesus did not, religious leaders,
        100
    Job had, of God, 134
    Joseph's brothers had, of
        revenge, 115
    Lot had, of cities, 66
    Mephibosheth had, of David,
        126
    Peter and John had more, of
        God, 55
    Peter had, for safety, 222
    Philistines had, of Samson, 19
    Pilate had, of crowd, 202
    salvation "worked out" in, xxii,
        287
    Saul had, of David's exploits, 97
    things causing, 11, 45, 49, 210
    trust in God overcomes, of man,
        38–39, 43, 50, 55, 109, 151,
        194, 213
federal head, 201
first and second causes, xxii, 171,
    287
foot washing, 144
football, 25
fornication, 165, 170, *see also*
    adultery
"42," 158
France, 229

fruit
    forbidden, 22, 53, 141, 201–2
    gospel, 177, 183
    Spirit's, 136, 153, 281

Galilee, 143, 179, 210–11
"Game Night," 218–19
games, *see also* sports
    chess, 187, 228
    Jenga, 132
    Operation, 132
    public, at Caesarea, 143
    "Tell the Truth, To," 218–19
    thimblerig aka shell, 1
German, *see* Nazi
Gethsemane, Garden of, 47, 235,
        239
Gibeonites, 22
Gilboa, Mount, 126
Golden Rule, 97, 100–1, 195
good confession, 222
good Samaritan, 27
gossip, 152, 161, 167, 183, 221, 224,
        226
Great Depression, 128
Great Physician, 2, 26, 29, 144, 177,
        178, 180, 211, 214, 269
grief
    David's, if he had killed, 82
    David's, over adultery, 179
    endurance of, over unjust
        suffering, 88–89
    godly, 173, 178, 179, 181, 183,
        184, 237
    Habakkuk's, over wickedness,
        151
    Job's, over suffering, 134
    Paul's, while rejoicing, 152
    remorse differs from godly, 182
    Simon's need for, 180
    worldly, 178, 184

hand washing, 202
hardships, *see also* afflictions and
        chastisements
    content amid, 93
    discipline through, 88
    focus hindered by, 39
    importance of enduring, 90

Jesus endured, 90
Job bore, 160
life involves, 92, 105, 162, 209
Paul experienced, 152
sin leads to, 58
"Heart that Forgives, A," 113
"Hearth and Home," 150
hell, 237
Holocaust, 229
"Hoosiers," 55
hospitality, 128, 129, 130
"Hudson Taylor," 64
Huguenot, 229
human trafficking, 194
hummingbirds, rufous, 79–80
hymns, *see also* music
    faith, 104
    forgiveness, 113
    joyfulness, 150, 154
    Paul and Silas sang, 35
    repentance, 176
    thankfulness, 208
hypocrisy, xv, 84, 100, 190, 202

"Intriguing Insights"
    contentment, 32–33
    discernment, 79
    humility, 141
    patience, 157
    repentance, 176–77
    respectfulness, 187
    thankfulness, 208–9
    truthfulness, 219–20
"Iron Will," 87

Jerusalem
    accusations regarding, temple,
        116
    ark arrives in, 210
    David fled, to escape Absalom,
        157
    David lusted after Bathsheba
        in, 168
    David summoned
        Mephibosheth to, 126
    defeat of, by Babylon, 58, 73
    Herod Agrippa executed James
        in, 143

Jerusalem (*continued*)
  holy feasts held in, 210
  Nehemiah rebuilt wall around,
    73–74
  Passover in, 202
  Philip left, for Samaria, 179–80
  saints in, 125
  temple in, 45, 200
job, *see* chore or employment
"John Knox," 43
jokes, practical, 228
Jordan River, 18, 46, 66, 168, 210
Judah (or Judea)
  church in, 129
  exiles return to, 73, 153
  Isaiah sent to, 11
  Naomi lived in, 73, 167
  Pilate was governor over, 202
  Romans subjugated, 209
  southern province of, 210–11
  Uzziah was king of, 11
  vassal state of, 58
  wickedness and doom of, 105,
    151
judges
  Gideon, 49, 133
  Samson, 19–20
  Samuel, 5, 157
justification, xv–xvi, xvii–xviii, xx,
    105, 107, 109, 214

Keilah, 189
"Kill a Mockingbird, To," 96
kingdom
  Babylonian, 58
  God's, of glory, xvii, 209–10, 214
  God's, of grace, 34, 209–10, 214
  gospel of the, 26
  northern, of Israel, 54, 209, 247
  southern, of Judah, 54, 209
kings
  Ahab, 96
  Balak, 54
  Caesar, Claudius, 143, 202
  David, 45, 126, 129, 141, 165,
    170, 173, 179, 181–82, 210
  Henry VIII, 44
  Herod Agrippa, 143–44, 147
  Hezekiah, 21
  Jesus, 11, 109, 148, 209–10, 214
  Nebuchadnezzar, 49, 58
  Pharaoh, 57, 115, 229
  Rehoboam, 22, 133
  Saul, 81, 97, 108, 125, 126, 157,
    189
  Solomon, 82, 83, 178, 195, 200
  Uzziah, 11
Kiriath Jearim, 210

labor, *see* employment
Lamb of God, 89, 92, 110, 214
lambs, 89, 179
Last Supper, 144, 235, *see also* Lord's
    Supper
law, *see also* Ten Commandments
  ceremonial, xvi–xvii, 107
  civil, xvi
  moral, xiii–xix, xxi–xxii, 105,
    107, 181, 200, 203, 278–80,
    285, 286–88
  secular, xviii
Le Chambon-sur-Lignon, 229
legalism, xiv, xix, 279
leprosy, 211
Levites, xvi, 27, 29, 165, 200–1, 204,
    210
libel, *see* gossip
"Lion King, The," 123
lions, 19, 26, 45, 49, 234
Lord's Prayer, 171, 234, 239
Lord's Supper, 238, *see also* Last
    Supper

Macedonians, 125, 128, 129
magic, black, 179
"Man for All Seasons, A," 43
"Marketing Malarkey," 220
marriage, 59, 167, 168, 169–70, 195
means of grace, 171, 214, 238
meerkats, 123
Midianite, 49, 115, 165
midwives, 229
military
  David's, victories, 97
  discipline of, life, 90
  Gideon fought, of Midianites, 49

military (*continued*)
    Joshua, leader of Israel, 23, 46,
        106
    Roman, 55, 89, 202
    Saul sent David on, mission, 189
    Uriah fought in, campaign, 168
Mimosa pudica, 132
minister, *see* elder
missionary
    Paul, 11, 35, 108, 133
    Silas, 35, 108, 133
    Taylor, Hudson, 64
    Timothy, 11, 133
    visit of, 129
Moab(ite), 54, 73, 167
mobile phone, 4, 6, 233, 237
moral law, *see under* law
moralism, xix, xxi
moralistic therapeutic deism, xix–
    xxi
Mount Gilboa, 126
"Movie Night"
    "Amish Grace," 113
    "Beautiful Day in the
        Neighborhood, A," 132
    "Blind Side, The," 25
    "Chariots of Fire," 104
    "Driving Miss Daisy," 64
    "42," 158
    "Hoosiers," 55
    "Iron Will," 87
    "Kill a Mockingbird, To," 96
    "Man for All Seasons, A," 43–44
    "Mr. Smith Goes to
        Washington," 43–44
    "Nicholas Nickleby," 25
    "October Sky," 71
    "Princess Bride, The," 64
    "Roughing It," 199
    "Scarlet and the Black, The,"
        43–44
    "Searching for Bobby Fischer,"
        187
    "Unbroken: Path to
        Redemption," 113
"Mr. Smith Goes to Washington,"
    43–44

murder
    Ahab and Jezebel committed, 96
    brothers wanted to, Joseph, 115
    commandment not to, xiii
    David ordered, of Uriah, 168
    guilty of first-degree, 101
    Saul attempted to, David, 98
    Stephen forgave his, 116
    wicked, the fatherless, 151
music, 113, 153, 172, 210, 237–38,
    see also hymns

"Name that Danger," 233
"Name that Person," 187–88
"Nature Study," *see* animals
Nazareth, 47
Nazi, 43, 229
Nazirite, 19–20
"Neglect and Consequences,"
    199–200
neighbor
    "Boo" Radley as, 96
    commandment to love your, xiii,
        97, 98
    false witness against, 221, 225
    foot seldom in house of, 195
    Mr. Rogers as, 132
    treatment of, should be
        impartial, 97, 100, 191
    truth spoken with, 221
"Nicholas Nickleby," 25
"Noah's Ark," 71–72, 76, 157
Nob, 189
Northern Kingdom of Israel, 54, 209

Obed-Edom, 210
"October Sky," 71
Olympics, 104
opossums, 9
original sin, 201

pantomimes, 16
partiality, *see* prejudice
Passover, 202, 221
pastor, 188, 193, *see also* elder
    Calvin, John, xvii
    Knox, John, 43
    Timothy, 11

patriarchs, 57
    Abraham, 18–19, 22, 66, 106–7,
        159–60, 192
    Isaac, 106, 159–60
    Jacob, 96, 157, 159, 165, 200
    Joseph, 115, 141, 165, 172–73,
        235, 238
peacocks, 165–66
Pentecost, 222
Perea, 210
"Perilous Pantomime," 16
person of God, 212
Peter's good confession, 222
pheasants, 165, 233, 238
Philistines, 19, 126, 210
"Physical Challenge," 87–88
Physician, Great, 2, 26, 29, 144, 177,
        178, 180, 211, 214, 269
physician, worthless, 134
poison, 117
politicians, 44, 226, 234
pornography, 237
practical jokes, 228
preacher, see elder and pastor
prejudice
    lack of, 100, 191, 194
    placements involving, 98
    race and, 96, 158
    self-discernment and, 79
    wealth and, 97
priests
    Aaron, xvi, 57, 165, 200
    Ezra, 73
    Phinehas, 165
    Samuel, 5, 157
"Princess Bride, The," 64
procrastination, 71, 75, 76, 137, 205
prodigal, 28, 34–35
prophets
    Agabus, 125
    Balaam, 54
    Daniel, 49, 58–59, 141
    Habakkuk, 151–52, 153
    Isaiah, 11, 13
    Moses, 46, 53–54, 57, 96, 106,
        116, 200
    Nathan, 179
    Samuel, 5, 157

prostitution, 82, 165, 166, 169
providence, 34, 115, 212, 214
punctuality, 204–5
put-off, put-on principle, 221

quarrels, 18, 66, 143, 146, 158–59,
    219
queen, 43
quiet, see silence

reconciliation
    David delayed, 173
    goal is, 118, 182
    guidelines for, 183–84
    repentance and forgiveness lead
        to, 114, 118, 178, 182
ring-necked pheasants, 233, 238
rockets, 71
Rome, 11, 162
"Roughing It," 199
rufous hummingbirds, 79–80
running, 87, 104

sacrifice(s)
    Abraham's willingness to, Isaac,
        106
    Christ as, for sin, xvi
    faith's role in, 109
    fools offer evil, xiii
    meat, to false gods, 66
    Old Testament, xvi
    own life as living, 10, 11, 13, 65,
        90, 129
    Solomon's, when dedicating
        temple, 178
Samaria or Samaritan, 27, 157,
    179–80, 210–11
sanctification
    expressions for, xviii, xxii, 287,
        289
    Holy Spirit empowers, 36, 182,
        237, 286–87
    means of, 38
    moral law and, xvi
    repentance and, 179
    salvation includes, 55, 154, 214
    sexual purity and, 166–67, 173,
        237

Sanhedrin
    Jesus before, 55, 89, 202, 221–22
    Peter and John before, 46–47,
        48, 55
    Stephen before, 116
"Scarlet and the Black, The," 43
school, *see* education(al)
schoolmaster, xvii
"Searching for Bobby Fischer," 187
second cause, *see* first and second
    causes
selfishness, 127–28, 142–43
sensitive briar, 132
seraphs, 11, *see also* angels
servant
    debtor in parable, 117–18
    employees, 194–95
    Jesus, 13, 66–67, 68, 144
    Joshua, 23
    Paul, 152
    Peter and John, 47
    preachers, 81
    prodigal son, 28, 35
    Samuel, 5
    slaves, 194
    Smike, 25
    Solomon, 80
    Timothy, 11–12, 67–68
"Shapes and Sequences," 80
sheep 26, 76, 82, 89, 125, 214, 234
shell game, 1
silence
    calm, deep in soul, 136
    deference may require, 68
    gentleness may require, 137
    insults borne in, 138
    Jesus bore injustice in, 89, 92
    Job's friends maintained, 137,
        190
    patience may require, 162
slander, *see* gossip
slavery, *see* servant
sledding, 87
slippery slope, 227
smartphone, 4, 6, 233, 237
social distancing, 211
social justice, 100, 193

social media, xv, 4, 21, 237, *see also*
    electronic devices
Sodom(ites), 18–19, 66, 165
soldiers, *see* military
songs, *see* hymns and music
Sons of Thunder, 138
sorcerer, 108, 179–80
sorrow, *see* grief
Southern Kingdom of Israel, 54, 209
sovereignty, 68, 134, 152, 162, 179,
    214
sports, *see also* athletes and games
    baseball, 158, 228
    football, 25
    hiking, 21, 87, 119
    running, 87, 104
    sledding, 87
submission, *see also* authority
    believers show, 191, 193
    children give, 192
    citizens yield, 193–94
    David gave, to Saul, 189
    employees show, 194
    Jesus modeled, 89, 144
    patience as, to God, 162
    wives give, 192, 195
Switzerland, 229
syncretism, 210

tabernacle, 200, *see also* temple
"Talking and Walking," 233
"Task Ask," 9
"Tell the Truth, To," 218, 228
temple, *see also* tabernacle
    Herod the Great rebuilt, 46, 116,
        135
    Holy Spirit's, within believers,
        166
    Solomon built original, 11, 45,
        49, 178, 200
    Zerubbabel rebuilt, 73
"Temporal Treasure," 123–24
temptation(s)
    blame-shifting as a, 205
    cheating as, 225
    common to experience, 237
    David yielded to, 168
    deceit as, 224, 227

temptation(s) (*continued*)
  earthly things as, 98
  Eve yielded to, 201
  focus on self as, 143
  food offered to idols as, 66
  impatience as, 162
  Jesus experienced, 237
  Judas succumbed to, 55
  prayer about, 234, 238
  resistance to, 58, 171–73, 235,
      237–38
  Satan initiates every, 234, 237
  sexual impurities as, 166–67,
      168, 170–74, 235, 237
Ten Commandments, xiii, xix, 200,
    203, 281, *see also* law
Thessalonian church, 81, 125,
    133–34
"Thimblerig," 1
trafficking, human 194
Transjordan, 126
"Trickling Tidbits," 16, 22
"Trust and Obey," 154
Tyre and Sidon, 143–44

"Unbroken: Path to Redemption,"
    113
unity
  church involves, 221, 226

dishonors, if sexually immoral,
    166, 173
Holy Spirit provides, with
    Christ, 121, 142–43, 166,
    173, 214, 221
humility for sake of, 143

values, secular core, xv
Vichy, 229

white lies, 202, 228–29
wizard, 108, 179–80
wolverines, 44
wolves, 234
work, *see* employment
works of God, 212, 213–14
World War II, 43, 229
worms, 141–42
worship
  Canaanite, of Asherah, 169
  laws forbidding, 194
  meat associated with idol, 66
  proper, of God, xiii, xx, 10, 13,
      106, 238
  seraphs engaged in, 11
"Would You Rather?" 55–57

zebras, African, 25–26
Ziphites, 189

Made in the USA
Middletown, DE
05 November 2022

14186626R00195